FEDERAL SOLUTIONS TO EUROPEAN ISSUES

FEDERAL SOLUTIONS TO EUROPEAN ISSUES

Edited by

BERNARD BURROWS, GEOFFREY DENTON
and GEOFFREY EDWARDS

Contributions by
Bernard Burrows, Geoffrey Denton, Douglas Dosser, Geoffrey Edwards, Tom Ellis,
MP, Michael Fogarty, Neville March Hunnings, Ghita Ionescu, Tim Josling, Giovanni
Magnifico, Roderick MacFarquhar, MP, John Marsh, John Pinder, Michael Shanks,
Helen Wallace, William Wallace and Ernest Wistrich

St. Martin's Press   New York

Library of Congress Cataloging in Publication Data

Main entry under title:

Federal solutions to European issues.

　Includes index.
　1. European federation—Addresses, essays, lectures.　2.　Federal government—
Addresses, essays, lectures.　I.　Burrows, Bernard, Sir, 1910-　　　II.　Denton,
Geoffrey R.　III.　Edwards, Geoffrey.　　*78- 9138*
JN15.F38　　　　341.24'2　　　78-8066
ISBN 0-312-28546-9

Contents

Notes on the Contributors   vii

INTRODUCTION   The New Federalism   1

PART A   POLITICAL NEEDS AND INSTITUTIONS   15
1   The Community, the Nation State and the Regions   *Roderick*   17
    MacFarquhar
2   Institutions in a Decentralised Community   *Helen Wallace*   25
3   Why a Federal Britain?   *Tom Ellis*   37
4   The Future of Community Law   *Neville March Hunnings*   51
5   Promoting a European Identity   *Ernest Wistrich*   62
6   The European Social Partners *Ghiţa Ionescu*   71

PART B   ECONOMIC AND SOCIAL POLICIES   85
7   European Monetary Unification: Problems and Perspectives   87
    Giovanni Magnifico
8   A Federal Budget for the Community?   *Douglas Dosser*   98
9   Industrial Policy for a Federal Europe   *Geoffrey Denton* 108
10 The New European Enterprise   *Michael Fogarty*   122
11 European Social Policy: the Next Stage   *Michael Shanks*   136
12 European Agricultural Policy: A Federalist Solution   *John* 147
    Marsh

PART C   EUROPE IN THE WORLD   161
13 How Large a Community?   *Geoffrey Edwards*   163
14 A Common European Foreign Policy: Mirage or Reality?   174
    William Wallace
15 European Defence   *Bernard Burrows*   187
16 Buying Europe's Raw Materials   *Tim Josling*   198
17 A Federal Community in an Ungoverned World Economy   *John* 211
    Pinder

Postscript   The Value of Federalism   *Geoffrey Denton*   221

Notes on the Contributors

SIR BERNARD BURROWS served in the British Diplomatic Service from 1934 to 1970 and was Ambassador to Turkey from 1958 to 1962. Between 1966 and 1970 he was Permanent Representative on the NATO Council. In 1973 he was appointed Director-General of the Federal Trust for Education and Research, and he held this post until 1976 when he became Consultant. He is the co-author, with Christopher Irwin, of *The Security of Western Europe*.

GEOFFREY DENTON has been Director of the Federal Trust since 1976. He is Reader in Economics at the University of Reading and Specialist Adviser to the House of Lords European Communities Committee. His publications include *Economic Planning and Policies in Britain, France and Germany* (joint author), *Economic Integration in Europe, Economic and Monetary Union in Europe, The Economics of Renegotiation*, and *Beyond Bullock: Economic Implications of Worker Participation in Control and Ownership of Industry*.

DOUGLAS DOSSER is Professor and Head of the Department of Economics at the University of York, and has held visiting professorships at Columbia and other US universities. A specialist on EEC taxation and budgetary questions, he is a member and rapporteur of the Commission's Study Group on Economic and Monetary Union. His publications include: *Fiscal Harmonisation in Common Markets, British Taxation and the Common Market*, and *European Economic Integration and Monetary Unification*.

GEOFFREY EDWARDS has been Assistant Director of the Federal Trust since 1975. He is the co-author, with William Wallace, of *A Wider European Community: Issues and Problems of Further Enlargement*, and, with Helen Wallace, of *The Council of Ministers of the European Communities and the President in Office*. He was joint rapporteur of the Helsinki Review Group, under the chairmanship of Lord Thomson of Monifieth, which published *From Helsinki to Belgrade*.

TOM ELLIS was born in 1924 at Rhosllanerchrugog, North Wales. He was a coal miner in North Wales from 1947 to 1951, gained a degree in mining engineering in 1952, and was a colliery manager for the National Coal Board from 1958 until 1970, when he became Member of Parliament for Wrexham. Since July 1975 he has been a Member of the European Parliament. He is the author of *Mines and Men*.

MICHAEL FOGARTY is Senior Fellow and Deputy Director of the Centre for Studies in Social Policy. He was previously Director of the Economic and Social Research Institute, Dublin, and Professor of Industrial Relations at University College, Cardiff. His publications include *Company and Corporation—One Law?* (on the history of German co-determination), and a number of other books and PEP broadsheets on industrial participation and company law reform.

NEVILLE MARCH HUNNINGS is the Editor of *Common Market Law Reports* and *European Law Digest*, and Assistant Editor of the Index to *Foreign Legal Periodicals*. He is also a visiting lecturer in European Law at Queen Mary College, London, and a member of the Law and Technology Committee of the *Union Internationale des Avocats*. His publications include *Film Censors and the Law* and *Legal Problems of an Enlarged European Community* (joint editor).

GHIŢA IONESCU is Professor of Government at the University of Manchester, and the Editor of *Government and Opposition*, a quarterly journal of comparative politics. He is the author of *Comparative Communist Politics* and the editor of *The New Politics of European Integration*.

TIM JOSLING is Professor of Agricultural Economics at the University of Reading. He was previously Reader in Economics at the London School of Economics. He is an expert adviser to the Consumers' Consultative Committee of the European Commission in Brussels and adviser to the World Food Council (WFC) Secretariat and to the UN Food and Agriculture Organisation (FAO). He is the author of many publications on the problems of European agriculture, of world trade in temperate zone commodities, and in the economics of commodity markets.

RODERICK MACFARQUHAR has spent most of his professional life writing on the problems of China, Asia and the communist world, but he has been committed to and worked for the cause of European unity since his student days. He has been Member of Parliament for Belper since February 1974 and is Parliamentary Private Secretary to the Secretary of State for Social Services.

GIOVANNI MAGNIFICO is Chief Economic Adviser to the Banca d'Italia. He has previously been Financial Adviser to the Italian Embassies in London and Bonn, Professor at the University of Rome and at Johns Hopkins University in Bologna, and a member of several working groups sponsored by European and international economic and financial organisations. His publications include *European Monetary Unification* and numerous articles on economic theory and policy.

JOHN MARSH is Professor of Agricultural Economics in the University of Aberdeen and Head of the Economics Division of the North of Scotland College of Agriculture. He was formerly Reader in Agricultural Economics in the University of Reading. His publications include *Agricultural Policy in the Common Market*, *Farmers and Foreigners*, *European Agriculture in an Uncertain World*, and many articles in journals.

JOHN PINDER is Director of PEP, a Trustee of the Federal Trust and Professor at the College of Europe in Bruges. He is Vice-Chairman of the European Movement and is active in a number of other European organisations. Publications on Europe include *Britain and the Common Market*, *Europe after De Gaulle* (with Roy Pryce), *The European Community and Eastern Europe* (with Pauline Pinder), and many articles and contributions to books.

MICHAEL SHANKS was Director-General for Social Affairs in the European Commission from 1973 to 1976. He is currently a director of a number of multinational and UK-based companies, and a Visiting Professor at Brunel University. An economist, his previous career has included periods in journalism, business management, and as Chief Industrial Adviser to the UK Government. He is the author of a number of books, including *The Stagnant Society*, *The Innovators*, *The Quest for Growth*, *Planning and Politics*, *Britain and the New Europe*, and *European Social Policy Today and Tomorrow*.

HELEN WALLACE is Lecturer in European Studies at the University of Manchester Institute of Science and Technology, and Chairman of the University Association for Contemporary European Studies. Her publications include *National Governments and the European Communities* and *Policy-Making in the European Communities* (joint editor).

WILLIAM WALLACE is Lecturer in Government at Manchester University and Research Fellow at Chatham House, studying the management of foreign policy in Britain, France and Germany. His publications include *The Foreign Policy Process in Britain* and *Policy-Making in the European Communities* (joint editor).

ERNEST WISTRICH is Director of the European Movement in Britain, and was responsible for organising the Movement's campaign between 1970 and 1972 for British entry into the European Community, and its referendum campaign in 1975. He was an elected member of his local authority from 1969 to 1974, and a Parliamentary candidate in the 1964 and 1966 General Elections. He is the editor of a number of journals and the author of many articles on European issues.

Introduction
The New Federalism

As the economic, industrial and social climate becomes seemingly more
adverse, governments attempt to keep up with events by more interventions and innovations. Not least, they pursue radical proposals to alter
the structures of government and of society. Yet the more governments intervene the more complex and costly they become, and the more remote from,
and unacceptable to, the people. As the new structures of government proliferate, and their interventions multiply, there is a pressing need to com-
prehend in its totality what is going on; to conceptualise it in a framework
of thought which will enable us to understand, and therefore to control,
what is happening. We have given the name 'The New Federalism' to the
framework which we describe.

'Federalism' is a much misused word, feared by some as being no more
than a concentration of power at the centre of a system, an attempt to impose
autocratic decision-making over a wide area in opposition to local rights, and
by others as meaning the dissolution of all government. More accurately it
means the distribution of powers and responsibilities to appropriate political
levels and types of institution, both up and down the scale, so as to combine
representation and authority, union and diversity, organisation and freedom.
This is the subject we have chosen to study in this series of papers.

Many of the more important decisions affecting the lives of individuals
are taken at the level of the nation state, which still commands much
loyalty in Western Europe. But there is no inherent reason why this should
continue to be so. The very existence of the European Community is
evidence that the majority of people within its borders no longer believe the
nation state to be a unit large enough for the efficient management of the
economy. At the same time, the pressures for regional autonomy or independence demonstrate that smaller areas now claim the loyalty of their
inhabitants as well as, if not instead of, the nation. The nation state in fact
is a comparatively short-lived phenomenon in world history, and both city
states and empires have been common and of at least as great duration.
There need be no surprise if the nation state is found of less value in an age
when it can no longer meet the needs of its people for security, which was
the main reason for its creation.

The revival of interest groups as centres of allegiance and of power may
require changes in political forms but may respond more closely to the needs

of significant numbers of the population. The relative impotence of present political institutions was demonstrated in the UK when industrial legislation, approved by a majority in Parliament, became impossible to apply. Sufficient electors in their alternative capacity as trade unionists refused to allow it to work because it did not secure their agreement. The trade union obtained more effective loyalty than the traditional authorities of the state.

Changes are not necessarily for the worse if they weaken the nation state and its political institutions. Analysis should start with clarifying the tasks of government and administration in the modern world, the size of unit in which these tasks can most efficiently be done, and the size and type of organisation in which people can have a sense of belonging and participation. These two criteria are not likely to give the same answer, and compromise will be required. The administrator will tend to favour a high degree of centralisation and hierarchy, but in modern society this will not work, because government is now largely by consent, and consent will not readily be given to a too remote central parliament or bureaucracy. The choice will be between a centralised overall plan, potentially efficient, but which will be inadequately applied because of local resistance or indifference, and a series of less efficient local plans, which will be more fully implemented because they have been drawn up at a level which has allowed of participation, and therefore of consent.

Examples of such dilemmas are numerous, for demands are not necessarily consistent with each other, nor are the innovations in government and society which reflect them. The same individual who relies on his trade union to assert his sectoral interest against other sectors in the economy also asserts his own personal independence when his freedom to work or to associate is affected by decisions of that trade union. Those who demand more regional representation should be aware, if they are not already, that more levels of government must mean more complex inter-relations between different levels of government, and probably an increase in the financial costs of government and in their interference in the life of individuals.

During the brief ascendancy of the centralised parliamentary nation state citizens have been regarded almost exclusively as voters. The disproportion between the numbers who vote in the national and in local elections suggests that even the function of voting is effectively limited to choosing the national government, possibly because the local authorities are the wrong size, and have the wrong powers. Now people are becoming more aware of their other classifications: as consumers, producers, middlemen, regionalists, environmentalists, as members of pro- or anti-groups on a variety of subjects. Some of these groupings are more developed and effective than others; but they all reflect, at least in part, dissatisfaction with the existing distribution of power and wealth in conditions of continuous change. Thus, demands for regional devolution are an expression of restiveness in some areas with the remoteness of national government. A new world economic order may be the outcome of dissatisfaction of people in less developed countries with the existing world-wide distribution of economic activity, income and wealth. Industrial democracy is an attempt to reduce the alienation of individual

2

workers from an industrial society in which they find the ownership and control of industry too far removed from the work-place.

There is therefore a need to define the scope and nature of the changes under way. It should not be imagined that they will lead to a uniform system. An entity like the European Community, with limited powers at the centre, may be a better safeguard for diversity than the nation state. More options will be open in a wider system, but there will be limits, set by the need to compete in the outside world, and to ensure security from outside pressure. The aims of analysis should be twofold: to see how far a wider dissemination of power, both to the European Community and down to the local community of the work-place or the super-market, can encourage more constructive participation; and secondly, to find a way that is not too complex or top-heavy of relating the various levels and aspects to each other to form a reasonably coherent system. To define the changes, to adopt progressive but cautious attitudes towards the many contradictory and risky aspects of the new federalism, to find a sensible blend of positive welcome for innovations that can offer solutions to the problems of nationalism, selfishness and alienation, while avoiding the evils of excessive dirigism, bureaucracy, and loss of individual liberties, is the purpose of these New Federalist Papers.

Integration in the European Community

The European Community has reached a stage in its development when debate is needed on the appropriateness and adequacy of present political structures and levels of government. As common policies are accepted by the member states the traditional political and economic structures are modified, however subtly or imperceptibly. These common policies reflect the inadequacies of the nation state. But they have been introduced piecemeal and their effects are not always predictable or consistent either with each other or with popular expectations or aspirations. The Community is being presented with options to adopt a number of inter-related advances which would transform it, if they were carried through, from a customs union and common agricultural policy into a new form of federal state.

The recent enlargement by the incorporation of Britain, Denmark and Ireland has already increased the interest in how to build a more effective central decision-making structure. The Council system of ministerial meetings has been given more political leadership by means of more frequent 'Summit' meetings of heads of state and government. But these essentially inter-governmental arrangements cannot provide an effective solution in the longer term to the problem of effective political management. The prospective further enlargement of the Community to include Greece and Spain and possibly later Turkey and Portugal, and others, would make it imperative to find new political structures to enable decisions to be taken effectively and rapidly in a Community of 11, 13 or more states.

The present indirect system of election to the relatively powerless European Assembly is inadequate. Democratic control remains solely in the hands of national parliaments to the extent that they can control their executives, who in turn make up the European executive. The principle of direct elections to a European Parliament has now been accepted by all member governments. If direct elections are held in 1978, the new European Parliament could be exercising a growing influence on policy, and could become a growing point towards a federal system in the 1980s.

On the economic front, these administrative (and political) developments are reinforced and indeed made inescapable by the prospect of monetary union. While there is certainly nothing approaching full agreement on early moves to complete monetary unification, there is a wide recognition that the scope for national governments to pursue an independent economic policy with the help of parity adjustments is becoming narrower as the interdependence of the economies continues to increase. Though parity changes are not yet irrelevant, taking a longer view monetary unification appears to be a matter of tactics and timing rather than a substantially controversial strategy. There are also substantial arguments for monetary union in the many benefits it would confer in facilitating economic transactions across the frontiers, common sectoral policy etc. A monetary union, when it eventually comes about, would require administrative developments; a European Central Bank and a European Treasury, for the management of the Community economy. This in turn would make inevitable the simultaneous development of an effective political executive, and of a representative Parliament with substantial powers, to supervise and direct the operation of economic policies by these new administrative organs, if indeed these political developments had not already taken place.

Substantial new powers of economic decision-making transferred to the Community would imply wider responsibilities for economic and social policy. In the context of monetary union the Community would be obliged to accept substantial responsibility for regional problems and unemployment, not only because it would be argued that it was in part responsible for them, but because it would have control over many of the relevant economic policy instruments. Such development would increase the direct political influence of Community institutions, the desire of regions and other interests for direct representation in the European Parliament, and pressure on the European executive in Brussels.

Apart from the need for development of Community economic and social policy over a broad front in order to redistribute the benefits of monetary union, there are direct pressures for the development of social policies at the Community level; indeed it is widely held that without the creation of adequate Community funds to alleviate regional imbalance, unemployment, etc., it will be impossible to obtain political agreement on the creation of a monetary union. If the Community is to develop, there must be carefully synchronised progress in all the major interdependent policy areas: political and administrative institutions, monetary policy, economic and industrial policy, and not least in social policy.

The Community budget has already become an issue in the political development of the Community despite its still very small size. The decision of 1970 to move to a system of own resources, and the British renegotiation in 1974–5 of the budgetary terms of membership, drew attention to the development of a kind of federal financing, and to the problem of equitably sharing the burdens and benefits of membership. As other policies develop, the growth in the size of the budget will increase this concern, and will also widen the discussion to include the normal problems of federal finance, such as the assignment of roles to federal and national budgets.

Development of sectoral policies in the European Community has so far been more a matter of reports and proposals than of any real action. Only the common agricultural policy and the Coal and Steel Community are firmly established. For all the criticism it has encountered, the agricultural policy has the immense advantage of guaranteeing security of supplies though it is widely agreed that major reshaping will be needed. So far as energy, aircraft, transport, and other sectors are concerned, the logic of common policies can only be underlined year after year, and the development of common policies comes closer as advances are made in the creation of the necessary political and monetary infrastructure on which common industrial policies could be effectively based.

The growth in the power of sectoral interest groups (sometimes insistent upon security of employment and pay regardless of economic performance) and the growing involvement of government in the finance and control of industry have far-reaching implications. Can collective bargaining remain as it is at present? Will there remain a role for private risk-taking capitalists? If the market system is being modified, perhaps even abandoned, without solutions being found to the many problems caused by such changes, a system could emerge by default in which there is greater centralised authority, more bureaucracy and still less individual freedom.

This description of the potential lines of development of an incipient European federation could be prolonged, but these remarks are already sufficient to indicate how appropriate it is at this moment in the Community's history to assess the implications of recent and prospective developments for the structures of government at each level.

Regional Devolution in the Nation States

The debate on Community and national responsibilities is made considerably more complex for Britain by its coincidence with the current debate on national and regional responsibilities. Special historical and current economic problems in Northern Ireland, Scotland, and to a lesser extent Wales, have brought about a fluid political position, which, though it may not lead to major devolution of powers to all the regions of the UK, will almost certainly result in some structural changes. In the rather insular way in which these problems are discussed in Britain, it is sometimes forgotten that another member country in the European Community, West Germany, already has a federal system of government. There considerable powers are granted by the 1948 Constitution to the Lander authorities. France, despite a centralising tradition, has periodically attempted to devolve more economic decisions to the regions. Italy has recently reinforced a powerful regional tradition with new regional assemblies. Belgium, though small, has developed a regional structure to alleviate its religious and linguistic divisions. The possible creation of new regional assemblies in Scotland and Wales must therefore be seen in this broader European context.

Relations between the regional assemblies, national governments, and the Community must also take account of other local authorities. The reorganisation of local government in the UK had as its aim the creation of larger and therefore more viable and effective units. They as well as the new regional assemblies may see advantage in being in direct relation with the Community.

Up to now the regional policy of the Community has been largely limited to grants of money to economically backward regions of the member states. These areas, usually designated as development areas by national governments, often evoke little local identity and have few means of representation for other purposes. The views of the regions therefore can affect Community policy only via national governments and the Council of Ministers. Regional movements, particularly those with an ethnic or cultural identity, are increasingly seeking direct access to the Community to express their needs and aspirations and hence lessen their dependence upon the national government. To some extent this has been institutionalised in the West German case with the representation of the Lander at the Council. Although unrecognised by the Community, the Scottish, Welsh and Breton nationalists have formed a Bureau of the Unrepresented Nations in Brussels.

However, larger and possibly more efficient local government units do not necessarily meet the popular wish for more say in what concerns the local community. The centres of larger units are necessarily further away from many of the people. The larger the units the more bureaucratic they become and elected councils will be less able to control them. The way through these dilemmas will only be found by a new look at the functions which have to be performed throughout the range of authorities and representative institutions from those of the European Community to those of the parish.

Regional Representation

The allocation of seats in a directly elected European Parliament could provide for some kind of regional representation in a Community institution, and may materialise in Scotland where the Scottish National Party might win a majority of the Scottish seats in the European Parliament. Elsewhere in Europe, except in Belgium where linguistic parties exist and the major parties are themselves divided into linguistic wings, the national parties dominate elections even to regional assemblies. Within those national parties regional interests may conflict with party interests but the latter tend to predominate. If specific regional representatives did organise, on the basis say of greater powers to the regions, they might provide a greater counter-attraction to existing parties, but the latter are likely to remain of greater significance.

Consideration of the future powers and composition of the European Parliament and its relations with the other institutions raises further possibilities for regional representation. Keen regionalists envisage the long-term future of the Community as 'L'Europe des régions', with the regions, not the national states, represented in an upper chamber. Critics of this view argue that even if there were widespread support for such an idea, its accomplishment must be so remote, bearing in mind the political, social and cultural predominance of the nation state, that it hardly provides a basis for practical politics today. Moreover the differences among the kinds of region existing now are so great that a very long evolution would be required before they were all capable of fulfilling such a role on a reasonably equivalent basis.

On the other hand even a federal constitution for the Community, if it were based on nation-states and not regions, would not necessarily solve the problem. In such a system the powers reserved to the centre would presumably include foreign policy, defence and certain powers of overall financial and economic management. These powers would for the foreseeable future be exercised by a Council of national authorities, possibly with some participation by an embryo European Executive developing out of the Commission. A further wide range of powers would belong to lower authorities, which to an important degree would mean the regions. But some of the regions would not be satisfied with deciding how to use funds allocated to them from above. They will want a say in the central decisions about economic management, fiscal policy and distribution of public spending. This is already apparent in Scottish criticism of the present devolution proposals of the British Government. Would greater national flexibility towards the regions reduce this pressure for a regional voice at the centre?

Interest Groups and Government

The development of new and more complex relations between the different levels of government, local, regional, national, and Community, is complemented by the development of new relationships between interest or pressure groups and governments at all levels. At the national level the TUC and CBI, and the equivalent social partners in other countries, participate in the formulation of overall economic policy. The result is that the form and content of social and economic policy are adapted directly to meet the wishes or to observe the constraints imposed by these interest groups. Not only are macro-economic decisions affected; pressure is brought to bear on government when micro-economic or sectoral decisions have sufficient impact on local or regional communities. More fundamentally, the basic structure of the economic system is beginning to be modified by changes, or proposals for change, in the control and ownership of firms and other economic units.

To the many and considerable changes in the structure of government therefore must be added the development of more powerful associations representing various interest groups. Sectoral groups such as trade unions seek to advance the status and conditions of their members, resist, modify or encourage economic, industrial and technological changes, exercise pressure upon government at all levels and compete with other interest groups. Other groups are concerned with particular problems which cut across sectoral interests and may even be in conflict with them. They include groups for the protection of the environment, for the safeguarding of consumers, for equality of opportunity for coloured people, and for women.

The great majority of these groups operate simply as pressure groups or lobbies, using whatever means they can find to influence decision-makers in parliaments, governments, local authorities and the bureaucracy. It is com-

7

paratively rare for them to have a formal or institutionalised position in government or administration. Exceptions are to be found in the more formalised version of industrial democracy, as in the German *Mitbesttim-mungsrecht*, which guarantees to workers a place in the decision-making processes in industry; in the Economic and Social Councils which have a constitutional role in several west European countries; and in a still more institutionalised sense in the multi-cameral system of Yugoslavia, which provides representation both for the federated regions and for producers in their functional capacity.

Various forms of industrial democracy are now under active discussion in the UK and in the Community generally, and this subject is more fully described below. Other forms of functional representation within the system of government are still widely denounced as corporatism because they were adopted by the fascist regime in Italy and later by Nazi Germany, and because they are held to infringe the sovereignty of parliament. On the other hand the reality of the power of corporations, such as trade unions or professional associations, is there for all to see. The question is not whether they have power to influence society but whether this power should be recognised in *ad hoc* bilateral dealing by the government with particular corporations, or in a more organic relationship providing for representation of the interest concerned, and the place of this representation in the overall framework of government. There would perhaps be less fear of the threat to democracy posed by such representation if the various corporations were themselves organised on more democratic lines providing for further participation by their actual and potential membership.

There are examples within the Community of ways in which such corporate interests can be brought into an organic relationship with government. The Community itself has the Economic and Social Committee, containing representatives of employers, workers and other interests, and having the right to be consulted in certain areas of legislation. Economic and Social Councils in some of the individual countries have a wider and more influential part in the governmental decision-making process. Is this consultative relationship enough? It would be possible to go further either by giving such Councils constitutional power in the initiation or debating of certain classes of legislation, or by delegating authority to them for the execution of laws passed by Parliament. In the former case at least something like a Supreme Court would be required to sort out the respective powers of Parliament and Council.

We have finally to consider how to bring regional and functional devolution together into a comprehensive, and comprehensible, system. Do we need functional Councils corresponding to every geographical level of government, with an obligation for consultation by every regional or local authority? Or would this mean an intolerable proliferation of institutions, and unacceptable delays in getting anything done? Can we afford the time and money to make sure that every possible interest both local and functional, has its say, or must we be more rough and ready, with the safeguard of appeals to an Ombudsman or an Administrative Court? At a Community level perhaps we could think of a Community Chamber or Council representing both regions and corporations together in well defined constitutional relationship both to the Council of Ministers and the European Parliament. It would necessarily have both the right of initiation and the right to be consulted. The extent to which other institutions were obliged to take its advice, and over which areas of business would be a matter for keen debate. But this itself may be no bad introduction to the question of the future organisation of the Community and its responsiveness and accountability, and indeed to similar questions at a national and regional level.

Industrial Democracy

In addition to the incorporation or representation of interest groups in political institutions, functional federalism is also concerned with relationships between the different interests in the various firms and other economic organisations. The key debate in this area is about the relationships between wage earners, owners of capital, and the professional managers who mediate between them. In recent years the term 'industrial democracy' has come to be used to describe a variety of new ways of handling the competitive-cooperative relationship between owners and employees. Although the concept of industrial democracy remains ill-defined it is one of considerable importance both economically and politically, involving demands for employee control through the formal participation in decision-making of a wider group of employees than the existing managers, and direct or indirect employee ownership of capital.

A variety of methods have been adopted or proposed for the introduction of employee participation control. The most common has been to provide for worker representation on company boards, sometimes, as in West Germany, by using a two-tier structure of supervisory and management boards. This type of participation in control raises many difficulties both for owners and managers, and for employees. The former fear the extension of collective bargaining into board meetings, while the latter fear that involvement in decision-making will inhibit their freedom to press for more benefits whether in the form of take-home pay or in other forms. The implications of a high degree of employee control in industry raise awkward questions for the shareholders, and thus for the supply of capital, except to the extent that this can be provided by self-financing. But the extent of ploughing back of profits is itself likely to be constrained by employee representatives seeking shorter-term benefits to the detriment of future development of the firm. Moreover, employee representation on boards leaves untouched the position at the workplace, and is therefore regarded by many employees as irrelevant, though a combination of works councils and employee representation on boards can provide an effective comprehensive structure of participation.

Elements of more 'democratic' ownership are already present in, for example, the diffusion of capital by means of pension funds and insurance companies or by means of public ownership. Neither, however, fulfil sufficiently directly demands for the employees to own the enterprise they work in. Ownership is too far removed from the workplace, there is little identification between individual and corporative objectives and needs, and thus economic incentives to greater efficiency and improved industrial relations at industry and plant level are inadequate.

In Britain and elsewhere more direct forms of employee ownership have been adopted in some firms to reconcile the competing claims of wage demands and investment requirements. Elsewhere in Western Europe other methods have been employed. In West Germany worker ownership of shares has been encouraged by incentives to capital savings out of wages; in Denmark proposals have been made for the creation of capital funds for investment out of a levy on payrolls in both private and public industry and controlled by workers' organisations.

Such solutions however have had limited effects. The linkage between worker ownership of capital and work units small enough to have meaning involves high risks for worker-capitalists. A complete guarantee of workers' capital, provisional in Denmark, would limit the scheme to little more than a redistribution of wealth. Moreover technological and economic forces tend towards larger units and so militate against decentralised ownership.

The involvement of the state in the ownership and control of industry limits the scope for employee participation. It also makes a contribution to the politicisation of the economy. Recognition of the need for the national interest to be taken into account is of course apparent in the nationalisation of particular industries. But it has also been proposed that private industry should submit its investment proposals and other key decisions to a National Enterprise Board for approval. Elsewhere in Western Europe procedures of 'concertation' have been instituted for a similar purpose, and it has been suggested that they should be introduced at a Community level. These various proposals are aimed at the evolution of a socio-economic structure which operates both fairly and efficiently. A comprehensive view as to how industrial democracy ties in with the economic incentives and disciplines of either a market or planned type of system is necessary. It is not sufficient, for example, to propose the introduction of solutions which have been adopted by other countries with very different institutional and behavioural patterns without clearly perceiving the differences.

In nationalised industry the socialisation of ownership has been already achieved, but only in a very remote form which does little to contribute to an effective industrial democracy. Worker directors on the boards of some nationalised industries provides an element of participation, but again in a very remote form. Given the ultimate power of the State to subsidise nationalised industry out of tax revenues, the introduction of industrial democracy without the destruction of financial incentives and disciplines is peculiarly difficult. Demands are made for the modification of the usual commercial objectives by the introduction or extension of social objectives, especially those of interest to the employees. This has frequently resulted in confusion about the whole operation, as between the interests of the State itself, the commercial users, the social users, and the employees.

Europe and the world economic order

Since the energy and related crises began in 1973 world economic relations have become increasingly politicised, and new methods are being sought for regulating trade and other economic relations between different groups of states. These may loosely be characterised as 'federal' in nature. World trade has become increasingly cartelised, and in place of the free exchange of goods between independent firms or at least individual governments, bargains are being negotiated between large groups of producers or consumers. The major decisions on prices and quantities of the major raw materials, energy and foodstuffs and even of capital and skills are being influenced increasingly by these conferences of cartels seeking to exercise combined bargaining power against each other.

Such conferences are so far often unprepossessing, appearing to have more of conflict than of cooperation in their make-up. However they represent a kind of forum for the taking of really important decisions, and not merely a talking shop like the General Assembly of the United Nations. The trade issues are not confined to the resource needs of western Europe, but include the question of access to the rich markets of the EEC for the growing output of manufactured goods in developing countries. Many other economic issues are involved besides trade. It is probably premature to envisage a permanent new federal world government emerging from the confusion of the energy and related crises, though the 'new economic order' is a step in that direction. Recent events in the world at large may certainly be interpreted as forming part of the pattern of changes affecting government at all levels. International crises have encouraged the formation of regional groupings such as the European Community itself in order to allow nation states to exercise combined bargaining power at the international level. Developments in the world economy therefore contribute an important element in discussions on what we have termed the new federalism. In this period of disconcertingly hectic innovation, the gamut is run from local, through regional, to national, to bloc and finally to world levels of decision.

To many if not most sections of opinion in developed industrial countries, the politicisation of world trade is a most unfortunate occurrence, likely to result in the distortion of trade flows, as decisions on what to export or import, and at what prices, to or from whom, are increasingly subject to political interference, rather than based on objective economic needs and resources. The structure of production, and its allocation to different parts of the world is also likely to suffer, with growing inefficiency and loss of economic welfare. There will also be damaging disruptions of the world economy, as the various cartels try to exercise their influence on each other. The risks of such disruptions are of course increased by the inevitable linking of economic relations with broad political and strategic issues, as indicated in the embargo on oil supplies during the Arab-Israeli war in the autumn of 1973, or the linking in the Jackson amendment to the US Trade Bill of most-favoured-nation treatment for the USSR with Soviet concessions on human rights. On the other hand, a stable and secure world economy cannot be envisaged without effective international economic management, and the Lomé agreement between the European Community and 46 African, Caribbean and Pacific under-developed countries, generally regarded as a beneficial development, would not have been made without the pressure of moral and political ideas.

European Foreign Policy?

What other external pressures are there to influence the degree and extent of integration among a group of countries like the European Community? There is a simple question of size. The combined population of the Community countries is about 250 million, which is of the same order as the population of the US and the USSR. In terms of economic strength the Community falls between the two super-powers. In terms of external trade it is superior to both. But there is another element in the make-up of a world power, often thought indeed to be the most distinctive mark of super-power; namely military strength, including nuclear military strength. In this the Community is not in the same class as America or Russia, and shows no evidence of wanting or being able to attain comparability. Does this mean that even a high state of integration of foreign and defence policy among the Community countries will not allow the Community to fulfil the aspirations of many of its inhabitants for independence? Or is it possible to combine an acceptable degree of economic and political independence with continuing dependence on others for the ultimate capability to resist external threat? Here again the way is open for new concept and perhaps new forms of relationship, both internal and external, to be weighed against the continuance of existing systems which many elements in European society are finding increasingly outmoded.

Is federalism the way?

Many who are concerned about the loss of confidence in national governments would prefer to see direct action to restore their authority, rather than allow what remains to be crushed between the millstones of European and regional governments. To opponents and even to many cautious supporters of the European Community, its transformation into a political federation may be regarded as an unnecessary and even harmful surrender of national sovereignty, and the creation of a new unwieldly bureaucracy. The idea of a federal Europe conjures up the model of the USA, with its appearance of a strong and centralising federal government and relatively weak state governments. In view of the unpredictability of future developments there is a genuine fear that Western Europe may evolve a similar system of mechanistic checks and balances which seem to allow only the continuing expansion of the central government at the expense of its component units.

The argument about clinging to the nation state for fear of something worse overlooks the fact that in many respects it has been abandoned already. No country of Western Europe now believes that it can wage war single-handed. Hence most of them have accepted in NATO a large degree of pooling of command, planning and logistics. Even in other organisations which are supposed to remain inter-governmental, such as the IMF, GATT, IEA etc., national governments have accepted significant limitations on their freedom to decide on a national basis how they should manage their economies. The European Community already acts like a government in foreign trade negotiations, in competition policy and in some aspects of coal, steel and agriculture. At the other end of the scale the pressure is already growing, at least in the UK and in France (and Spain), for the devolution of more power to sub-national units. Haphazard concessions to this pressure, such as are being discussed in the UK, could result merely in a larger number of levels of government, or even of smaller nation states, with inadequate organic links between them.

These existing trends to integration and to devolution suggest that the nation state is being found increasingly inadequate.

The Essence of Federalism

If it is accepted that different levels of government are appropriate to deal with different aspects of policy making, the essence of federalism is already there, and attention should be paid not to argument about the principle but to discovering the best system to adopt in the special conditions of the Community. Within this area it may be possible to consider, more usefully than in individual nation states, how to establish fairness between regions, and how far it is right to compensate for natural advantages and disadvantages.

More generally it may be objected that the recent accelerated growth of public expenditure and employment, with no readily discernible gain in representativeness and efficiency, finds a more obvious remedy in reducing the role of government than in proposals for introducing new levels of government to compete for the limited tax-paying capacity and patience of the citizen. The apparent growth of local bureaucracy since the reorganisation of local government, though much of the criticism may be the outcome of the effects of general inflation, has reinforced the suspicion about proposals for making the hierarchy of government more complex. Thus the devolution of power to Scottish and Welsh assemblies and possibly later to English regions is often regarded as a further mad proliferation of government, increasing its complexity without bringing any corresponding gains in effectiveness. In combination, the proposals for integration and devolution could well accelerate the trend towards less effective and less acceptable government.

The development of new approaches to the representation of various interests also causes considerable concern. Much has been written of the underlying threat of economic blackmail in the exploitation of their economic strength by organised interests. There are already many examples of the competitive use of the power of sectional interests to the detriment of the general good. There is also a natural repugnance to any brand of 'corporatism' because of its historical association with fascism. Awareness of these many dangers is indeed already manifesting itself in a refusal by individuals or small groups to accept political authority. People join associations to exercise political pressure in their own interests but that participation does not always result in an acceptance of the decisions which emerge from the political process. Thus society becomes more ungovernable and unstable. Given such individual responses, it would be irresponsible to embrace enthusiastically all innovations in government and industry. Attempts to introduce too many changes too quickly could produce an explosive social condition.

These criticisms have to be taken seriously. Any study of the federalist option must deal with the problems of bureaucracy, of human rights and of economic freedom, and these are included among the titles of later papers in this series. The influence on our thinking of existing federal systems is obviously important. But it should be emphasised that the conditions in which new political structures will emerge in the UK and in Western Europe will be radically different from those in which most earlier federal systems were created. For example previous systems in Switzerland, the United States, the Federal German Republic, have been concerned almost entirely with the relation of different sized geographical units to each other: the provinces, states or cantons and the "federal" centre. The smaller units have sometimes been differentiated by language but not by other functional characteristics. If our analysis is correct we now have to pay attention not only to geographical sub-division but increasingly to component units with a functional origin and functional loyalties. We have to consider whether and how they can be given some form of representative status and responsibility to match the power which some of them already have. In this area there is little guidance from past experience in democratic societies, though Yugoslavia has most interestingly attempted to combine geographical with functional federalism.

The Community is after all without parallel; it is and doubtless will remain a political system *sui generis*, a new political animal. Account must therefore be taken in the evolution of the Community of both the process of continuous change and the desire of many to conserve what was familiar. Much will depend upon the scale of change and the speed with which it occurs. Much depends also however upon the decisions which have to be taken daily and which endorse current trends and foreclose future options. There is therefore a vital need for a clearer conception of what future goals are or could be. Our purpose in the New Federalist Papers is not to propose the imposition of one particular formal federal structure or a particular time-table. It is rather to describe the options available in the Community in the search for the most acceptable method of allocating responsibilities among differing levels of government. Western Europe while not self-sufficient for all purposes, may be a unit which can combine concern with a large enough area with concern for diversity, human rights and individual participation both in government and industry, springing from a common culture and experience.

PART A

POLITICAL NEEDS AND INSTITUTIONS

1 The Community, the Nation State and the Regions

RODERICK MACFARQUHAR MP

In the aftermath of World War II, the leaders of the movement for European integration had the fresh memory of almost four million dead to spur their efforts. When the Six signed the Treaty establishing the European Coal and Steel Community in 1951 they stated in the preamble their resolve 'to substitute for age-old rivalries the merging of their essential interests; to create, by establishing an economic community, the basis for a broader and deeper community among peoples long divided by bloody conflicts; and to lay the foundations for institutions which will give direction to a destiny henceforward shared'. By 1957, when the Six signed the Treaty of Rome, memories of the holocaust had been softened by over a decade of peace and the preamble to the treaty talked less grandiloquently of pooling resources 'to preserve and strengthen peace and liberty'. Today, war between the historic antagonists of Western Europe, now closely intermeshed in the EEC and NATO and deprived of empires to quarrel over, appears unthinkable, and the need to dissolve nationalism in Europeanism less pressing. Yet, paradoxically, the very success of the movement towards European unity has led to a resurgence of European nationalism.

If a thirty-year cycle of world war, depression and renewed world war led to the flowering of the European movement, it is perhaps not surprising that the succeeding three decades of peace in Western Europe should have resulted in a more permissive attitude towards nationalism. But the pendulum has swung further. The major institution of European unity, the EEC, has helped foster European nationalism. Leaders of the Nine, particularly of West Germany, France, and Britain, find that although they govern only medium-sized nations, they are also representatives of the most powerful trading block in the world. The British Foreign Secretary may speak with only one tongue, but to outsiders he seems to talk in many languages and is treated with appropriate deference. *Europe des Patries* has become for some national leaders a satisfying blend of collaboration and independence.

Detente has also sapped the European urge. In the 1940s, 50s, and 60s, the Russians provided positive reasons—Czechoslovakia and the Berlin airlift, Hungary, and Czechoslovakia again—for West Europeans to unite in face of a common foe. The 1970s are not yet over, but already it seems as if Helsinki will symbolise Soviet activities in Europe for this decade. And even before Helsinki, ostopolitik together with economic growth, and the diminution of guilt feelings with the passage of time had undermined West Germany's *laager* mentality and thus the European urge of the most 'European' of the big three members of the Nine.

For the 45% of the EEC population that is under thirty, World War II is history and all that remains of the cold war is an argument between the Russians and the Americans as to whether they should be able to obliterate each other five times over, or only four. Their most important shared political experience was probably the student movement of the 1960s which represented a revolt against the bureaucratic structures and consumer values of Western society. Though most of them have been practising Europeans, wandering at will across national boundaries and associating freely with their peers, too many see the EEC as the symbol of all they distrust—mega-bureaucracy and the selfish exclusivity of rich, white consumers.

One must not exaggerate. The British referendum showed that a major challenge can still evoke passionate Europeanism from people of all ages. But in the EEC today, challenges are normally no more inspiring than all-night wrangling over the price of butter. Even when the big problems are posed, the solutions proposed are calculated not to alarm even the most cautious European leader. Inevitably such proposals fail to spark any wider enthusiasm for further progress towards European unity. We cannot say Europe is off course, for we do not know what the course is. A quarter of a century after the creation of the Coal and Steel Community, two decades after the signing of the Treaty of Rome, the urgent need is to return to first principles, redefine objectives, and chart a route by which we may reach them.

The case for federalism

The federalist case is based on the proposition that the nation state is an engine of war. The *European* federalist case is founded in the belief that the continent which shaped the modern nation state must set the example in superseding it.

The nation state is not the reason for wars; warfare is as old as history itself. But whatever the causes of war, in the modern era the nation state has become its organiser and beneficiary; and it was on behalf of nation states that millions of people gave their lives in two world wars. Both world wars started as intra-European wars with Britain, France and Germany as the principal protagonists. But some 75 nations were eventually embroiled, as well as many colonies that subsequently became nations, striking proof of the manner in which the European states involved others in their quarrels.

Europeans and their American descendants also gave birth to the doctrine of national self-determination. This contributed healthily to the dismantling of empire, but it also had the effect of sanctifying the concept of the nation state precisely when the nuclear era was making the institution otiose.

Five nations already have sufficient nuclear weapons to obliterate human civilisation. A sixth has exploded a nuclear device, and another dozen could easily do so. Confined to a few nations, nuclear weapons have reduced the

18

likelihood of world war, but proliferation could disrupt the stalemate. The world will only be safe when all nuclear and other modern weapons are under the control of a single authority, a world government, which could eventually dispose of them. Many non-federalists, if pressed, would accept the concept of a world government even if their vision of its nature varied widely; but there is little general interest in the idea in view of its apparent remoteness from immediate practical politics. Yet if a nuclear holocaust seems frighteningly less remote to pragmatic men of affairs, it is surely time to start thinking about a different 'unthinkable', world government, and the inevitably lengthy route to its achievement.

The UN is a symbol of man's realisation of the need for a world order, but it is unlikely to be a blue-print for its achievement. It is founded on the assumption that any group of people, however small, may band together or break away in nationhood, and it now embraces 145 members, of which the smallest, the Seychelles, has a population of 60,000. This expansion in the number of member nations perhaps makes the UN more prestigious, but at the cost of making its job of getting countries to live with each other in peace ever more difficult. The combination of national and nuclear proliferation is the greatest threat to global survival.

The trend to nationhood must therefore be reversed—and where more convincingly than in Europe, the cradle of the modern nation state. Hopefully, the creation of a United States of Europe will exhibit the declining value of nationhood and the increasing benefits of combination, and encourage the development of similar federations elsewhere. Certainly, it would be easier, ultimately, for a dozen political units—in a few cases existing nation states might be appropriate units—to negotiate a world order than for the 145 denizens of the Tower of Babel on the East River.

Of course the cause of European federalism has more immediate and more local justification. As the world struggles to evolve a new economic order, a united Europe, shorn of empires and without the incubus of super-power status, can pioneer fairer north-south relationships, while at the same time avoiding self-defeating intra-European competition for imported resources. Politically, a uniting Europe is more likely to convince the US of the continuing value of its commitment to NATO, and the USSR of the futility of attempting its subversion while at the same time increasing its independence of both super-powers. And if Washington ever opted for a strategy of fortress America, a united Europe would clearly be psychologically and diplomatically better fitted to absorb the shock and stand alone.

The obstacles to European federalism

But even if the continued desirability of a United States of Europe can be reaffirmed the obstacles to its achievement remain. Federal states are exceptions, and in most cases their achievement has been effected from above rather than below—for instance, at the end of empire in India and Nigeria—and they turn out to be federal more in theory than in practice. The primary characteristic of the genuine federations instanced by Wheare in his classic work— USA, Canada, Australia, Switzerland—is that they were effected primarily from below by states which had no pretensions to nationhood. Attempts by

19

modern nations to form federations have been few in number and disastrous in outcome—Malaya and Singapore, Egypt and Syria, Jordan and Iraq. Indeed the United Kingdom is probably the only successful example of the legislatures of two independent nations disolving themselves and forming a single nation (albeit unitary not federal) with a single legislature, and it took a century of living together under one crown before that was accomplished.

A European federation would be the first example of a federation from below entered into by well-established nation states. The obstacles will be considerable. In contemporary Europe we are nine nations speaking seven languages, attempting to unite after centuries of independent development and mutual strife. In the perspective of history, the establishment of a European bureaucracy and, hopefully, an elected European parliament within 35 years of World War II is no mean achievement; after all it took the American states 13 years from the declaration of independence to agree to form a federal union, and their peoples were only three million in number and of common stock, spoke one language, had no national pretensions, shared the same institutional heritage, and had all just fought a war of liberation on the same side.

Yet despite the progress so far made, a new strategy is almost certainly needed if the long march to union is to resume. One must hope that the transformation of the European Assembly in 1978 will represent a breakthrough. Yet direct elections will not produce a genuine legislature though they will confer a genuine mandate. But a mandate for what? To wrest power from national governments? Possibly, but if so the big guns will still be in the hands of the national governments, who will also, it must be remembered, be possessed of mandates of a more familiar legitimacy. The question arises: can there be ways of promoting the transfer of power from the national to the European level? Possibly: by the devolution of power from the nation to the region.

The importance of devolution

In the early post-Nehru years, prestigious Indian political commentators argued that an effective central government was inconceivable under their democratic federal structure made up of sixteen powerful, populous and often linguistically distinct states. They advocated the encouragement of 'subnationalisms' which could help splinter the states, believing that the central government would have more power if its interlocutors were, say, forty smaller regions. European federalists do not have the advantage of starting with a functioning central government, but there are signs that 'sub-nationalisms' may help to initiate a splintering of the old nation states which could be beneficial to their cause. In Britain, the process has already begun.

Writing just prior to what will be known as the devolution session of this parliament, it is hazardous to predict the nature of devolved institutions that will be enshrined in legislation in a year's time, hazardous even to assume that devolution legislation will get through the House of Commons. One can only outline one's own scenario. My belief is that devolution is inevitable, at least for Scotland, probably by legislation in the 1976-7 session, but if not, then later after bitter political struggle. If a referendum is held it may reveal a majority of Scots currently opposed to separation from England and the dis-

20

solution of the Union; but separate or not, a Scottish assembly is unlikely to remain for long without independent financial resources. If no taxation without representation was the slogan of the American colonists, no representation without taxation will be the cry of Scottish assemblymen of all political persuasions.

Wales will probably follow Scotland, but a pace or two in the rear. While popular sentiment in Wales at the moment seems to be quite opposed to any idea of separation and only tepidly in favour of devolution, the very vehemence of the Welsh opponents of devolution confirms the belief that once the process starts it will be irreversible and almost certainly will eventually exceed the bounds of the initial legislation which will confer less power upon the Welsh assembly than upon the Scottish one.

As devolution comes to Scotland and Wales, it seems likely that it will spark a demand from among the English regions for self-governing powers of some kind. The investigations of the Kilbrandon Commission revealed that even without the spur of nationalism, dissatisfaction with London rule was as great in the North-east and the South-west of England as it was in Scotland and Wales. Since then, economic problems have spread that dissatisfaction to the North-west and the West Midlands. Despite the negativeness of the government White Paper on the English regions, provincial Englishmen are unlikely to watch power being devolved to the Scots and Welsh without demanding a piece of the action for themselves.

The origins of devolution are diverse. Historically, the Scots went in with the English in order to gain commercial access to their colonial possessions. Now that the British Empire has been wound up after 250 years of successful 'trading', the original justification for the merger has disappeared and it is only natural that some Scots should question whether there are any other reasons for maintaining the partnership. The Welsh connection is older, closer and probably more beneficial to the smaller partner, but the Welsh people have retained a more than sufficient consciousness of identity to go it alone if need be.

Economically the justification for a strong central government is its ability to plan the economy and redistribute resources between rich and poor regions; the most recent comprehensive example of the latter is the DHSS decision to allocate more money to deprived regional health authorities at the expense of the better off ones. Redistribution is acceptable when the prestige of central government is high and/or the country seems well off. But in times of political and economic crisis, considerable dissatisfaction is caused. State subsidies to the motor car industry have made workers in other industries unhappy, and even within the car industry there has been dissatisfaction among Leyland employees at the support given to Chrysler. Under such circumstances, if Scotland and Wales take increasing control over their own destinies and wrest money-raising powers from central government, there can be little doubt that English local politicians, whatever their original attitudes to devolution, will seek to obtain greater control over economic decision-making for their regions.

Devolution also springs from the partly genuine, partly fashionable movement for 'participation'. Without over-estimating the real desire of people to spend the considerable amounts of time that genuine popular participation would demand, all MPs are aware that growing numbers of their constituents do join active pressure groups of various types, many of them concerned with local issues. I do not doubt that if power were devolved and the distance between Government and people was shortened physically and psychologically, there would be a substantial increase in popular interest and activity. This is not the case today with county and district politics only because voters correctly gauge that ultimately the decisions, and certainly the parameters of the decisions, are settled in Whitehall. After the costly disillusionment of the last reorganisation of local government, it would be unwise to place excessive hopes upon devolution from the purely administrative viewpoint; but if it were combined with the elimination of at least one tier of local government (probably the county) it should have beneficial results.

A strategy for European Federalists

From the European federalist point of view, devolution has one very great advantage: it must weaken the powers of the central government and bureaucracy, the main bulwark of *Europe des Patries*. While Scotland and Wales might envisage themselves as potential additions to the Nine, the English regions would be more likely and better advised in the long run to seek links with similar regions elsewhere in the Community in order to bring pressure to bear on Community institutions, over the heads of national governments if need be. If regional identity can be established, if regional concerns can be promoted, if regional loyalty can be encouraged then a start will have been made on ending dependence on the nation.

This would be to some extent a retrogressive step in an exclusively British context. Despite all the positive aspects of devolution, it would be unfortunate if the UK were divided into regions and its central government diminished without this probably inevitable process being used to European advantage. We need now a debate among European federalists on the proposition that regionalism should contribute to the erosion of the powers of national governments and that this is desirable in order to end the log jam in the process of Europeanisation. If the proposition is generally accepted, then a 'regionalist' strategy should be adopted.

In the case of Britain this would mean pressing the cause of devolution, taking a leading role in devolved institutions as they are set up, ensuring that they may have satisfactory financial resources of their own and attempting to establish links with other regions in the EEC and directly with EEC institutions, particularly through pressure on elected Euro-MPs. A similar programme would be appropriate to Italy where concern about the effectiveness of the central government appears to have engendered considerable authority for regional governments and some talk of a *Europe des Régions*.

France and Germany would present immense problems for they have strong central governments and heads of government, and France has a long centralist tradition. Clearly it would be naive to expect that one blast on the trumpet of regionalism would collapse the walls of nationalism. But on the assumption that the strategy is a long-term one, there is no cause for despair.

West Germany like Italy is a new nation by Anglo-French perspectives, and a divided one at that. It is also a federal state with fully functioning state governments, some with long historical roots, all with important powers in the fields of finance and education. Though the federal government is clearly supreme, nevertheless the regional units requisite for the regionalist strategy exist and indeed are far more plausible bases for the strategy as of now than the putative regions of a devolved Britain.

In France, the situation is more complex. De Gaulle saw the need for de-centralisation to regions; his countrymen did not and he went. Giscard seemed to favour regionalisation, but retreated a year ago, presumably under Gaullist pressure. But there are signs that the yeast of regionalism is encouraging fermentation in the French body politic. Breton nationalism and Corsican separatism have so far been contained, but if devolutionary concessions have eventually to be made there is almost certain to be a spill-over to regions with less sense of national identity, as is happening in Britain. Even without the nationalist component, regionalism is increasingly important. Though the regional law and decrees of 1972-3 were conservative in intent and effect, that they were instituted at all reflected an acceptance in Paris of the need to respond to a growing dissatisfaction with centralisation and an increasing desire for economic muscle at the regional level. Regionalism in France may be a tender plant but it is alive and federalists should nurture it.

The encouragement of regionalism in the smaller EEC members is less vital because they are on the whole more 'European', but it could be perhaps even-tually have beneficial side effects. If Eire were divided again into the three old counties and the government in Dublin were gradually to disappear, the bloody struggle of the IRA for a united Ireland would no longer have point. If Belgium were divided between the Flemish and the Walloons, Brussels would cease to carry the cachet of a national capital and could perhaps become a third region shared more amicably by the two peoples, like Chandigarh by the Hindus and Sikhs of the divided Indian Punjab.

The ultimate aim of the strategy would be a *Europe des Régions* in which the national governments gradually withered away making possible the develop-ment of a strong European government and the elimination of the national tier of bureaucracy. Admittedly, this would represent a departure from the tradi-tional European federalist vision in which the basic units were the nation states; but then no traditional European federalist has convincingly argued in recent years how a federal *Europe des Patries* might be achieved. And those who fear that new regions would be less able to stand up to a federal European government than experienced national governments may be right, but they mistake the problem. The worry is not that the federal government may be too strong, but rather that it will be too weak to accomp-lish the enormous tasks of building, integrating and managing a polyglot new state of 250 million people.

A federal government strong enough to control foreign affairs and defence, buttressed by 'economic and monetary union', in overall charge of major agricultural, industrial, and tariff policies, and with a budget large enough to assist backward areas, would have so much to occupy it that it would be able to discard the false doctrine that harmonisation equals Europeanisation and readily accept a substantial allocation of powers to the regions in the fields of education, health, social services and various aspects of 'home affairs'. More-over the inauguration of a *fédération des régions* would inevitably have been preceded by a long gestation period during which the regions' struggle with national governments for budgetary powers would have developed their economic muscles and political sophistication. Their rights could be further safeguarded by the creation of a second chamber, a senate of the regions.

A *Europe des Régions* should satisfy the desire for greater participation in government and decision-making at the grass roots. It would make political experimentation easier and safer. The prospect of the Italian communists participating in the Italian national government has caused understandable concern in other EEC capitals and in Washington. For one of nine member nations to 'go communist' would be a serious matter. But just as within Italy there is far less concern about communist control over Italian regional governments, equally no-one would worry much if half-a-dozen regions in a multi-region Europe were run by communists attempting to prove that they could do better than neighbouring socialist, liberal or conservative regions.

A *Europe des Régions* would permit the fruitful and vigorous survival of the positive side of patriotism—the shared sense of community and culture—and doubtless for a very long period, the English regions, for example, would tend to act in unison on many issues in the regional senate. But more, importantly, a *Europe des Régions* would gradually substitute an effective trans-European solidarity for the narrow nationalism of yesteryear. If a regionalist strategy were now to be hammered out, agreed and acted on by all Europeans who seek a European destiny, it could be the making of a great leap forward for our continent during its next 30 years of existence.

2 Institutions in a Decentralised Community

Ambitious Dreams and Painful Reality

HELEN WALLACE

A single decision-making centre for a united Western Europe was the goal ultimately sought by the founding fathers of the European Community. They hoped that the Paris and Rome Treaties had established a basic framework which would pave the way for the construction of strong central institutions. As the benefits of cooperation and common policies were demonstrated so, it was assumed, the member states would progressively cede greater and greater authority to the Community. Eventually the outcome would be a full political and economic union within which the old nation states would be subsumed. The ideals that lay behind these plans were certainly ambitious and optimistic. No-one believed that the construction of a united Europe would be easy, but back in the fifties the apparent inadequacy of the nation state and the obvious case for cooperation rather than conflict seemed to provide an irresistible drive towards unity.

Looked at some twenty five years later, however, the European edifice seems rather shaky. While some of the building blocks have been set in place the cement that should have bound them together in terms of political support has proved crumbly. There is no longer any consensus about which bits of the building to construct next nor even about its overall design. The European Community and its institutions survive but are compelled to fight to retain their.status or to extend their powers. The nation state has demonstrated an obstinate resilience that has proved difficult to erode or undermine. Yet at the same time within most of the member states of the European Community there are undercurrents of political change that challenge, even threaten established centres of power and the traditional constitutional framework. In particular the large economic and social interests have sought to increase their influence over government decisions explicitly as well as implicitly, and the regions have begun to assert increasingly vocal claims for a greater share in decision-making on both economic and political issues. All of these developments make the conventional models for institution building seem rather inappropriate as the basis for further reforms with the European Community.

Early Ambitions

The initial blueprint for the institutions of the European Community was beguilingly simple. The Commission was to be the centrepiece as a govern-

25

ment in embryo. It would act as the motor of integration by generating new ideas, by defending the interests of the Community as a whole and by putting constant pressure on the member governments to reach compromises on common policies. The initial scope for collaboration was defined by the Treaties, but progressively new areas of cooperation would be drawn within the competence of the Community. The Commission was to work in tandem with the Council of Ministers, composed of national politicians who would at first act as the spokesmen of their governments but in whom the habit of working together would induce a sense of shared responsibility for strengthening the Community. As the process of integration gathered momentum the Commission would become the indispensable core of the Community, establish itself as its governing force and win transfers of power progressively from the member states. The new Community would not be lost in a political vacuum but derive political support and legitimacy through a parliamentary assembly which would eventually be elected directly. The European Parliament would thus provide the power base for, and political control over, the Commission. Moreover the Community would suck into its orbit the aspirations of the big economic and social forces, partly through formal channels for cooperation such as the Economic and Social Committee and partly through a more informal network of close and regular involvement in policy discussion.

Out of this would emerge the new political system of a united Western Europe It was intended to mark a revolutionary move away from the traditional framework of the nation state, by creating a new European entity with its own central and supranational institutions. The touchstone of progress towards that grand design would be the transfer of power away from the worn out governments of the member states to a new and dynamic European level of government. Views as to what would happen to the component parts varied. Some looked towards a European federation in which the old nation states would be transformed into residual authorities with continued though reduced political scope. Others saw the Community as becoming responsible for all the most vital areas of policy-making, leaving the member governments to act as its agents. In spite of the radical nature of the blueprint the model of government envisaged for the new Europe bore a close resemblance to the conventional model of parliamentary democracy. The basic institutional pattern was fairly familiar in the balance envisaged among the main bodies. What would distinguish it from what had gone before would be its scale of operation and the replacement of individual nationalisms by a new European identity. The institutions envisaged for the Community would be highly centralised and tightly structured.

Existing Realities

Over the years, however, that ambitious blueprint has come to look more and more like a pipedream and to seem less and less in tune with the hard realities of political events. Partly this is a consequence of the over-optimistic timescale predicted for unification. More importantly though, developments inside the Community institutions, within the member states and in the international system as a whole have pointed up fundamental problems in the basic framework proposed for European integration. An initial difficulty stemmed from

26

the first policy goals set for the European Community. Harnessing the coal and steel industries of the Six, creating a customs union and the establishment of a common agricultural policy were all significant steps in active collaboration among the founder member states. They brought together a tightly knit network of officials, politicians and even interest groups into an impressive solidarity with a direct impact on these policy sectors and on the world market. They were not, however, the stuff of keen political debate in the sense of mobilising popular enthusiasm or recasting political structures. Repeated attempts were made to enlarge the political scope of the Community to include defence, economics and monetary union and wider political unification. Each attempt foundered on the chicken and egg argument that more authority had to be accepted at the centre before an enlarged scope was possible, yet that authority could not be established without a consensus on what its scope of action should be.

In the meantime the Community has gradually added to its range of competences in a diverse set of policy areas. The steady development of common policies envisaged in the Treaties has proceeded in a number of fields. New areas have been opened up, such as regional policy, or fisheries. Striking though the progress has been in many of these sectors it has not produced a cumulative extension of the central authority of the Community institutions. Each case has to be fought out anew; each round of negotiations in Brussels includes tedious and doctrinal arguments about how much responsibility can be permitted to the Commission and how much power the member states can retain over the conduct of the policy at issue. Moreover in a number of sectors, especially those that are the most sensitive politically, such cooperation as takes place among the member states is handled outside the formal framework of the Treaties and the Community institutions. There is no economic and monetary union, but there is a monetary snake managed by the central banks and governments of those member states able to stay inside its bands. There is no political union but there is extensive consultation among the Nine on foreign policy issues managed in concertation by their foreign ministries to which the Commission has only limited access. In yet other sectors such as energy new international institutions have been created as alternatives to and even competitors with the Community.

Why has this been so? Part of the explanation lies inside the Community institutions themselves. The Commission has proved unable to live up to the grandiose expectations of the founding fathers. The easy answer to this is that member governments have not given the Commission the chance to prove itself, yet to accept this is to close one's eyes to the problems of the Commission as an organisation. With some exceptions it has not attracted amongst its leadership politicians of a stature to take on the governments of the member states. The quality of its staff has not always been of a sufficiently high standard to win the ready respect of national civil servants. In spite of its small size the Commission has become bogged down in red tape and internal divisions that have undermined its capacity to act incisively or to project a dynamic image. However talented individual Commissioners or their staff the Commission as a whole has been judged by its average ability. The Commission has gained the unfortunate image of a remote bureaucracy at a time when bureaucracy has become the label that symbolises all the evils of modern government. However good the intentions of the Commission in making proposals for policy cooperation a benevolent bureaucracy is little better than a silk purse made out of a sow's ear.

Nor has the Council of Ministers crossed the watershed from being an odd amalgam of nationally-oriented politicians to becoming a Community-minded collectivity. On the contrary negotiations within the Council continue to reflect sharp political divisions among the member states that show no signs of diminishing in intensity. The popular image of the Community moreover derives largely from the conflict-ridden picture of protracted and often unproductive haggling among senior national ministers. The laborious procedures of the Council give little grounds for optimism that decision-making can be speeded up or yield more common decisions. There is a massive backlog of Commission proposals awaiting consideration, and the separate Councils that meet to bargain on different subjects—agriculture, finance, external relations and so on—behave as if their problems were the only ones that mattered to the Community. The Council as a body is unable to stand back from narrow preoccupations with short term interests and identify the main priorities for Community cooperation or to provide any direction on the longer term issues. The now regular involvement of heads of government in Community decision-making through the European Council has raised the threshold of expectation that a new era of purposive leadership may be around the corner, yet the gap between ambitious rhetoric and substantive agreement still yawns wide.

Marginal Influence

Momentum has also been lacking in the other Community institutions except perhaps for the Court of Justice. In an undemonstrative but imposing manner the Court has steadily redefined and extended the area of Community competence and asserted itself as the guardian of the interests of the Community as a whole against recalcitrant member states. Neither the European Parliament nor the Economic and Social Committee has achieved such success. Over the years the Parliament has shown itself a worthy but relatively ineffectual body of on the whole stolidly pro-European members. Its influence on legislation has been marginal, though its recent acquisition of a degree of real control over the Community budget has begun to provide it with some teeth. The decision by member governments to introduce direct elections may at last make the Parliament a force to be reckoned with though this will depend on the reaction of political parties, on the calibre of the successful candidates and on whether the new members prove capable of actively criticising and harrassing both the Council and the Commission. The Economic and Social Committee survives as a useful meeting place for consultation between the Community and the social and economic interests, but has failed to emerge as either a dynamic forum or as politically powerful. Indeed the most vocal and best organised interest groups have sought out other channels for influencing Community decisions through their national contacts, by informal discussion with the Commission and by pressing for the creation of new forums such as the Tripartite Conference on employment and economic policy.

The Limits of Political Convergence

The record of achievement on the part of the Community institutions has thus been patchy and disappointing. The addition of new tasks to the Community's area of competence has led to a proliferation of the number of bodies attempting to concert action rather than fostered the emergence of a strong centre of decision-making. The Brussels process has become complex and fragmented rather than the tightly knit structure envisaged by its founders. However, this also reflects the vulnerability of the Community to the buffeting of developments within the member states. During the fifties and sixties the European nation states recovered much of the confidence that had drained from them before and during the Second World War. Politicians and political structures reestablished themselves around the traditional centres of power rather than around the new European enterprise. Governments came but slowly to accept that unilateral action was only rarely viable and that collaboration with their neighbours was an unavoidable necessity. Yet this awareness of economic, political and security interdependence has not eroded the preference for national solutions nor for keeping open a variety of international options. The European Community is thus not the automatic resort of its member governments when they are faced with common predicaments or awkward issues. The Community may be the beneficiary, but only if it can demonstrate that it is the most appropriate arena for solving particular problems at specific points in time. Hence the member governments negotiating in Brussels continue to play their cards close to their chests and keep tight reins on the Commission's freedom of manoeuvre. This is a particular characteristic of those governments that believe their range of other options is wide. This leaves only the Benelux countries and Ireland generally in ready support of Community solutions for their own sake.

The reluctance of governments to acquiesce easily with Commission proposals is not, however. simply a product of blinkered nationalism. The economic, social and political issues that currently confront the European Community are far more intractable than those of twenty years ago. In a period of apparently steady economic growth and full employment governments did not anticipate the struggles over the allocation of limited resources, and the battle to contain still-rising popular expectations, which now marks domestic politics. Keynesian solutions to economic instability are under question; the social market economy is no longer so simple to maintain in balance. In a whole range of policies, governments no longer know what decisions to take. Such uncertainties within national governments necessarily make agreement at the Community level among those governments far more difficult. The growth and affluence of the fifties and early sixties made it look misleadingly easy for a European consensus on economic policies to follow on from a customs union. The political and social structures of the Six seemed fairly similar and certainly compatible. The member states appeared to have far more in common with each other than they had to divide them. This gave the impression that as long as a few kicks and pushes were made in the right places the Six would converge politically and economically into a single entity.

However, that period of optimism has been superceded by a period of turbulence and uncertainty. The international economic system has become increasingly fragile and vulnerable. At home governments have steadily extended their sphere of action and been drawn into more and more active intervention in economic management. Electorates have come to demand more of their governments in terms of welfare provision and financial protection. Yet the governments of Western Europe have found it difficult to respond to these increased expectations or to cope with the extra burden of work. More government has not apparently led to better government and it has certainly not enhanced the standing of or respect for government. Competing partisan ideologies may suggest alternative principles for action but rarely provide complete answers to the changing economic and political context. Nor have the resources of expertise available to governments yielded unambiguous advice on how to resolve awkward problems.

Consequently most governments have been forced back on rather rough and ready solutions to highly complex predicaments. Within each country different political parties have, of course, suggested varying courses of action. Just as important different branches of government have advocated different priorities for action. Faced with ambivalent advice and competing demands governments have found it difficult to see the long-term wood for the short-term trees. As a consequence the overall picture of the Community has shifted from one of six apparently homogeneous countries in the late fifties to an enlarged group of nine more disparate parts. This is only partly a function of numbers. Perhaps more significantly the degree of consensus about policies has diminished rather than increased, though the awareness of common problems has been sharply accentuated. The dissensus reflects great divergences in economic performance, but also considerable variations in political circumstances and the distraction of awkward domestic preoccupations. Not only are the member states of the Community different from each other but there is increasing evidence of diversity and even dissension within several of them. Any further enlargement of the Community would necessarily increase rather than decrease its economic and political heterogeneity.

Inappropriate Proposals

The overall consequence for the European Community has been that the waters of collaboration have become more and more muddied. Governments often resist Commission proposals because they do not know what to make of them or because different groups and agencies in their own countries are offering conflicting opinions. The Commission's proposals frequently seem inappropriate because they grapple with only part of the problem under discussion or because the Community lacks the economic resources or political clout to make the proposals viable. There is great uncertainty about which problems to tackle and in what order. Does industrial collaboration presuppose a concerted economic approach? Can regional disparities be reduced without major changes in economic structures? Should the Community go first for macro-economic cooperation or for small bits of common policies that might one day add up to a single economic approach? Part of the explanation for these dilemmas is that they depend on a mixture of economic assessment and political judgment. They require time for the steps taken by the Community, however tentative, to produce results. Perhaps most of all they depend on the capacity of the member governments and the Commission to agree on how much they should try to do together and on which priorities to single out for immediate action.

The implication is that grand blueprints for institutional reforms are unlikely to provide any panacea for all of these problems. Occasional attempts are still made to go back to the drawing board and sketch out yet another scheme for strengthening the institutions of the Community in one way or another. The Tindemans exercise on 'European Union' although not in the mould of the old grand designs represented one further effort to focus the attention of member governments on the institutional problem, but reactions to its professedly modest proposals suggest a flagging conviction on the part of those involved that even such changes could provoke a great leap forward. Enthusiastic supporters of the Community may pin their hopes on the direct election of the European Parliament as a catalyst for political unification, but few believe that even this will yield rapid results. The lessons of the past twenty years suggest that to concentrate primarily on the institutions of the Community is to avoid facing up to the wider economic and political problems involved in constructing a united Western Europe. However, to admit this is not to imply that no institutional reforms are necessary. On the contrary the way the institutions operate can either facilitate or obstruct constructive agreements among the member states. Our overriding concern should therefore be to identify more specific and perhaps more modest reforms that would improve the atmosphere of Community negotiations and foster the image of a Community that is responsive to its wider constituency.

Lessons for the Future

The first and perhaps most important lesson is that it would be misguided to continue to press for a highly centralised super-government in Brussels. Given the evident difficulties of national governments in coping with their commitments there are few grounds for optimism that a European-wide government on a grand scale would be any better able to avoid the same pitfalls. Indeed the larger the scale of operations the greater the dangers of overload and confusion. Besides, a single decision-making centre of the kind repeatedly advocated in the past with the breadth of responsibilities often demanded would require a massive increase in both human and financial resources. The present climate makes such an increase both improbable and unpopular. Any significant extension of the bureacracy in Brussels would give fuel to the claims of those who argue that big government is bad government. At a time of widespread retraction in public expenditure within the member states it is also unrealistic to expect that a sizeable increase in financial resources would be forthcoming. Furthermore to push more and more responsibility towards the centre would be to risk charges of remoteness of decision-making at a time when the tenor of many political developments is towards making government more accessible and more localised.

The second key lesson is that the time has come for a radical reappraisal of which policy functions should be dealt with at the European level. In the past enthusiastic Europeans and the Commission itself have promoted the argument that the Community should be actively involved in an ever larger number

31

of policy sectors, from monetary union to common rules for the production of beer and bread. Already the fervour for indiscriminate harmonisation has abated, to be replaced by a more modest standardisation of rules concerning cross-frontier movement of goods and people. However this reassessment needs to be taken further. The guiding rule of thumb should be that the European Community should concentrate its scarce resources on performing a smaller number of tasks rather more efficiently. Just as within the member states the advocates of decentralisation are calling for more local or regional decision-making, so at the European level only those policies should be promoted that cannot be dealt with by more accessible institutions of government.

This would limit the functions of the European Community to two spheres of operation: the direct management of a select number of transnational policies and the coordination of a range of other activities to ensure that nationally or locally administered policies were mutually compatible. In other words there continues to be a strong case for a direct Community responsibility for monetary regulation, for commercial negotiations with third countries and for political, economic and perhaps security collaboration on issues that governments cannot handle alone or where concerted action by a European block could be an asset in international bargaining. In a variety of other sectors there is room for selective involvement by the Community in identifying a European dimension, but one which would permit latitude and flexibility to the member states*. This could, also, be developed through extending the principle of the use of directives rather than regulations as the legal instrument through which Community policies were enforced. Such a pattern of policy-making would continue to require an active involvement on the part of national ministers and officials and also of regional representatives. The necessary dialogue among different levels of government would however be less threatening and thus breed less suspicion if the Community institutions were attempting to act as catalysts for concerted action rather than apparently seeking to take over the direct responsibility for themselves.

Institutional Reforms

The corollary of these arguments is that it does not necessarily follow that precisely the same division of institutional responsibilities need apply in all policy sectors. Different institutional mechanisms are appropriate to different kinds of activity. In other words the success or failure of Community solutions should not be judged solely in terms of whether the Commission has won a direct managerial role. In agriculture the management committee system has worked well to interlock the Commission and national administrations. In the monetary sector cooperation among central banks operates smoothly and unostentatiously. In the discussion of regional economic development the regions should themselves have a direct role in policy formulation. In the debate on problems such as unemployment the large economic

---

* *See for example the proposals made by John Marsh in Chapter 12.*

32

corporations can reasonably expect more attention and more opportunity to articulate their claims. The pattern that would emerge would perhaps be rather untidy , but it would not necessarily be less productive than the traditional attempts to force the treatment of all policy issues into the same mould.

This is not to say that institutional reforms are unnecessary. On the contrary improvements in the workings of the present institutions are urgent and long overdue. Indeed they are a prerequisite for convincing governments that the Community framework is administratively competent to perform even a limited range of tasks, and for persuading the citizens of the Community that it is more than a remote and insensitive international bureaucracy. The sheer difficulty of reforming the internal structure of the Commission and the struggles which accompany each change of Commissioners to effect only minor alterations in functions and personnel demonstrate its rigid bureacratisation. It is absurd that so small a body should allow itself to become so bogged down in red tape that it is slow to respond to new demands and unable to coordinate different policies. The efforts made by individual Commissioners and their officials are all too frequently undermined by excessive respect for laborious procedures. In addition the Commission needs to develop a more sophisticated capacity for long term planning and for systematic target-setting. Recruitment and the deployment of personnel need to be freed from the constraints of 'geographical quotas'. Shorter term contracts might offend against the principle of a European career service, but they would allow far greater flexibility and room for regular exchanges of staff with national and regional authorities in both directions.

The Problem of Accountability

Similarly the Council of Ministers suffers from time-consuming and contorted procedures. One of the oddities of the European Community is that ministers allow themselves to spend so much time on ritual argument rather than on constructive discussion. Fewer but tougher proposals from the Commission would help, as would a greater willingness to delegate detailed negotiations to officials in the Committee of Permanent Representatives and the other Council committees. Majority voting on the major issues may not yet be acceptable but limitation of the requirement for unanimity to these would enable more speedy decisions on many of the less contentious areas of negotiation within the Council. Perhaps most urgent is the need to prevent separate Councils from going off at tangents without considering overall priorities. It has become apparent that specialist ministers are not prepared to accept their colleagues from foreign ministries sitting in the 'General' Council as the arbitrators and mediators in Brussels. The experience of the European Council so far does not give grounds for optimism that it alone can pull together the different threads of Community activity. A greater emphasis on the role of the Presidency of the Council in promoting debate on priorities would make for some improvements. Six monthly debates on long term priorities should not mean simply adding to the list of items to be considered; they should also produce hard decisions on which items to abandon until a more appropriate moment. Moreover the Council should make a serious attempt to grasp the nettle of Community expenditure. This requires not just a pruning of the proportion of money spent on the common agricultural policy, but regular reviews of Community spending programmes through a systematic and more flexible budgetary process.

The problem of accountability is obviously crucial. The enhanced authority which direct election will confer must be used not simply in supporting the Commission against the Council but also in constructive and critical examination of the whole range of Community activities. The Community has got to prove itself strong enough to stand a vigorous debate in which alternative political programmes are presented and opposition to conventional Community wisdom is expressed. Nor should the representation within the Parliament of particularist interests from the various regions of the Community be seen as a drawback. Active promotion of minority causes or special pleading for specific regions would be a positive asset. However, a more representative and critical Parliament will not automatically lead to more effective scrutiny of Community activity. The untidy and opaque character of Community decision-making makes it hard for even the most determined parliamentarians to react quickly to new proposals or to keep abreast of existing policy programmes. Fewer legislative proposals would enable members of the Parliament more easily to concentrate their attention on the political implications and the time is long overdue for the Parliament to have a direct voice in new legislation. The budgetary powers recently won by the Parliament have constituted a step towards discussion of spending priorities, but these need to be strengthened to allow a more systematic examination of the budget well in advance of expenditure rather than hasty criticism at the last moment. Similarly the Parliament must become more actively involved in a critical assessment of the current programmes of the Community in terms of the allocation of resources and the effects of those policies.

Developments of this kind within the context of the existing institutional framework would all go some way towards improving Community decision-making. They are, however, inadequate to meet the charges that the Community is remote and inaccessible to influence except from member governments or the large and well organised lobbies. Rather more extensive changes are required if the interests and problems of particular regions in the Community are to be effectively ventilated. European federalists have long advocated moves towards a 'Europe of the regions' in which the nation state would tend to become the redundant level of government. So drastic a change is not an immediate prospect, partly because of the resistance of national governments and partly because the pattern of regional assertion varies markedly from one member country and region, to another. However, various intermediate possibilities could help to involve regions more actively in the Community decision-making more sensitive to differentiated regional demands.

The Commission must make itself more explicitly accessible within the member states outside national capitals. Regional offices on the pattern of Cardiff and Edinburgh are one means of doing this, but these would need to be supplemented by regular consultations with regional interests on the spot and not just with the more adventurous regionalists who find their way to Brussels.

Most important, there should be a direct dialogue between regional interests and the Community on those aspects of Community policy that have an immediate impact on the regions: on regional policy, social policy, the structural dimensions of agricultural policy, etc. So far member governments have resisted this, and impeded the efforts of Commission officials to gain direct access to the regions. Applications for Community cash at the moment depend on national authorisation and national priorities. Often opinions voiced in regions themselves express dissatisfaction with a carve-up of resources on which they have little or no influence, and which leads them to tar the Community with the same brush as national governments. A regular regional contribution to assessing the utility of past expenditure and discussing future resource allocation, would go some way to mitigating the suspicions of Brussels as a remote bureacracy. It might also produce a more effective distribution of scarce resources.

For the moment there is no single model for regional consultations that could be applied in all the member states, but that is no excuse for further delay in opening up a dialogue between the regions and the Community institutions. Germany and Italy have a regional tier of government and would therefore prove easier targets in the first instance. But in most of the other member countries there is a variety of regional institutions able to inject relevant views into the debate about Community policies. Irrespective of their formal status those various bodies should have the opportunity to influence the development of the Community through pressure on governments, through their European MPs, and through direct discussions with the Commission and key committees of the Council. The greater visibility that the Community would gain from such a dialogue would clearly foster a more sensitive image for the Commission. It would however, also serve the interests of member governments by helping them to explain the relevance of the European Community to their narrower domestic preoccupations.

The Important Criteria

The logic of these suggestions is that reforms within the European Community are more likely to be both acceptable and workable if they steer an intermediate course between ambitious blue-prints and minor procedural adjustments. Three important criteria should guide such reforms. First, the emphasis should be on medium-term changes that have some chance of gaining acceptance from governments without seeming so drastic or threatening that they are consigned to the already large repository of well-intentioned but over-simple blue-prints. This does not mean that all reforms should be tailored to protect or enhance the powers of national governments. But it does imply that reforms must be cast in such a way that governments can be carried along even in spite of themselves. Secondly, the focus should be on equipping the Community to handle successfully a limited range of important functions. This implies building on those established mechanisms that have proved relatively effective in promoting consensus and admitting that others have failed to take cooperation further. Thirdly, there should be a major effort to draw into the Community nexus key groups and interests that are currently deprived of influence over decisions which in practice directly affect them. Of these the most important are the regionally oriented interests that perceive the Community as compounding national trends towards increasingly remote bureau-cratic and insensitive governments.

Reforms which give greater influence both to the Community and to the regions, and which establish direct communication between them are perhaps the only available stepping stone towards a truly federal system. The practice of such consultation could encourage the growth of a variety of centres of power with functions distributed on a flexible basis that can change over time in response to changing needs and demands.

The old institutional model of the 1950s is neither appropriate to the current tasks of government nor in tune with demands for more accessible decision-making. A Community the success of which is measured in terms of the transfer of power and authority to Brussels will not be one which will be accepted as legitimate by those rising generations in Europe who do not remember the supranational fervour of the Resistance and the post-war years, and whose criticism of the nation state itself is that it is remote and bureau-cratic. A more modest Community with institutions designed not to supplant the nation state but to add an extra level of government to manage only those functions which cannot be handled nearer the people is far more likely to gain acceptance. The virtue of federalism as a strategy for building a United States of Europe should be not to press for cumulative and indiscriminate transfers of power to Brussels, but to devise the most effective framework for sharing power among the different levels of government from the local to the European.

3 Why a Federal Britain?

TOM ELLIS MP

Contemporary politicians are often made acutely aware of the immediate, practical and direct nature of their calling. The electors' demands are commonly short-term and simplistic and the pressure is so great to respond to the clamour of the moment that consideration and analysis of more deep-rooted, complex and less immediate matters are inhibited. Thus, when an issue of fundamental significance which has been developing over many years suddenly becomes apparent, the response of some politicians to the issue can be less than considered, their assessments superficial and their actions misdirected.

A topical example in Britain is devolution, an issue of importance now seemingly argued in terms either of the electoral effect of the government's proposals on the major parties and on the Scottish National Party, or of the creation of an unwanted tier of local government, or of the opportunity they present for establishing a separate, sovereign nation-state in Scotland on the classic nineteenth century European pattern. Political developments in Scotland and Wales of course mirror the attitudes, aspirations and beliefs of the people of the two countries, formed over the years consciously or unconsciously by the complex interplay of a great many economic, cultural, sociological and historical facts and myths, not to mention the intangible yet real influence of a particular ethnic society and its sense of nationhood.

This essay considers in general terms aspects of three separate factors behind the immediate demand for devolution to Scotland and Wales and then considers how they might lead to change of a fundamental, and in my view, welcome, kind in Britain.

Failure of Governments to Cure Regional Poverty

For most of this century the Scottish and Welsh economies have been substantially weaker, both qualitatively and quantitatively, than that of England and as a consequence the two countries have experienced continuing levels of unemployment and emigration manifestly greater than those of their dominant partner. Both countries have featured prominently in all the regional development policies introduced by successive British governments and it is not without irony that apologists for the centralist British nation-state have enthusiastically pointed to the aid forthcoming to each development area from the central government under these policies. Nor is it any less ironic to note how

37

the original frankness of the term 'Depressed Area' has modulated with changing attitudes into the euphemistic 'Development Area'. It is only recently however, and then only in the development areas themselves, that the presumed efficacy of this centrally-determined aid has become something less than accepted wisdom and has been questioned at a more fundamental level.[1] At the same time the objectives of regional policy also are being assessed a little more keenly for their true worth.

Policies are adopted by governments, one imagines, in order to reach objectives. It had been assumed that the broad objective of regional policy was the elimination over time of regional disparities and disequilibria. Experience over 40 years has now accumulated since formal regional policies were first introduced in many European countries and the disappointing fact is that except in a very small number of special cases regional inequalities have not only failed to lessen but have in some instances actually increased. The lack of success therefore of regional policies across Europe in reaching supposed objectives has led to a growing scepticism in the development areas about those very objectives.

There is, of course, a ready acceptance that, just as in the various countries and in Europe as a whole, individual development areas since the war have also enjoyed economic growth and increasing material well-being. But whereas this policy of overall economic growth adopted by so many governments as the elixir of their political lives may be appropriate to the generality of national politico-economic problems, it has become clear that it is not merely in itself inadequate for regional problems but by its very nature might even be injurious. Although poor regions have become richer, some rich ones have become even richer still so that the disparities not only remain but have increased. The first annual report of the European Communities' Regional Development Fund points out, for example, that in 1975 the gross domestic product per head was six times greater in the richest regions of the European Community than in the poorest ones, whereas five years earlier it had been only five times as great. It is argued in the poorer areas therefore that if it is not possible to introduce positive policies sufficiently effective to enable them to catch up with the ever-growing richer areas, negative policies designed to limit growth in the richer ones must be applied with greater vigour.

National governments are unwilling to do so, partly because of the political problems which would arise in the richer areas but mainly because it would mean departing from the magical formula of ever faster growth for the country as a whole. The arguments are advanced that national economic growth is a prerequisite to growth in the development areas and that national economic growth is impossible without growth in the richer areas. Typical official attitudes are summed up in the following quotations:

'Although regional policy is a factor in the decisions made by industry about the creation or maintenance of employment and the location of investment, it is not the only one or the most important. Industrialists are concerned above all with the prospects for the national economy and the government measures

---

[1] See Barry Moore and John Rhodes, 'Evaluating the Effects of British Regional Policy', Economic Journal, 1974 for a detailed economic appraisal of national regional policy in the UK.

likely to have the biggest influence on them are measures directed at demand management in the economy as a whole'.

'To apply an effective regional policy based solely on incentives would be costly to the Exchequer; and to base it solely on direct controls by government would be costly for the firms concerned'.[2]

The conclusion which in the development areas is beginning to appear inescapable is that central governments do not have the political will or capacity to reach the objective of national economic parity across the regions of their territories. The real problem, that of relative deprivation, in practice therefore has become intractable. All the more galling are the few exceptions proving the rule, West Berlin, for example, whose economy has prospered in relative terms because the political will has existed in Bonn for the obvious political reasons.

The growing appreciation in Scotland and Wales of the seemingly intractable nature of the problem under the present political structure of the United Kingdom has led to an increasing acceptance of those economic theories which postulate an inherent conflict of interest between rich and poor areas, that a rich area needs a poor area alongside it for its own sustenance. Conclusions reached by Hirschman from research in Venezuela are increasingly quoted, as are Gunnar Myrdal's theories in respect of undeveloped countries in South East Asia for example, and the 'growth-pole' theories of industrial development evolved by Perroux in relation to Western industrialised countries.[3]

Measures of Deprivation

Concealed within this failure to attain regional parity on broad quantitative economic grounds are the equally significant qualitative and demographic inequalities which impinge on the public consciousness even more vividly in Scotland and Wales, contrasting with the almost total disregard of qualitative and demographic factors by central officialdom. The Expenditure Committee of the House of Commons, for example, published an assessment of Regional Development policies in 1973 which, painstaking though the Committee's Report was, could hardly be regarded as comprehensive or even mildly imaginative with its complete neglect of qualitative considerations. A minor consequence of this centralist attitude are the scornful references in the development areas to the 'branch factory syndrome'.

A Welsh example of this qualitative aspect of the regional problem of relative deprivation which puts flesh on the bare statistical bones is contained in a study commissioned in 1973 by Y Gymdeithas Wyddonol Genedlaethol (National Scientific Society). The Society examined scientific employment in Wales and found grave shortcomings.[4]

The study discussed the two categories of scientific employment, one dependent on specific communities, and their day-to-day requirements, the other without direct links to a particular community and therefore untied to a particular location. The second category of appointments are attractive to science graduates and provide research facilities not normally available to those in the first category.

---

[2] *'Regional Development Incentives'*, Cmnd. 6058, May 1975.
[3] See Stuart Holland, Capital and the Regions, *Macmillan 1976.*
[4] *'Scientific Employment in Wales'*, Aberystwyth 1973.

The study showed that the proportion of British graduates in the physical and biological sciences produced from Wales in 1972 was slightly greater at 5.15 per cent than the Welsh proportion of the population of Great Britain. However, of some 99 government research establishments in Great Britain employing a total estimated graduate staff of 13,825 only two small ones were located in Wales employing an estimated 50 graduates. Following a similar pattern not one of 38 industrial research associations was located in Wales and of 26 research establishments attached to nationalised industries and other public bodies, two (a British Steel Corporation laboratory employing 13 graduates at Swansea and a small Post Office laboratory at Cardiff) were located in Wales.

Another indication of the lack of scientific opportunity in Wales was afforded by the 458 UK graduate posts advertised during 1972 in the scientific journals 'Nature' and 'New Scientist', of which only three were located in Wales.

Total government expenditure on research and development in 1970/1 was £645 million.[5] Complete figures for separate Welsh expenditure are not available (*sic*) but the National Scientific Society's report claims conservatively that it would be surprising if it exceeded £8 million.

The Report, which contains much evidence of this kind, concludes depressingly, 'the chance that a science graduate will obtain a satisfactory research post in Wales outside the University are poor; in the case of the biological sciences they are almost non-existent'.

The young Welsh science graduate, forced to leave his native country if he wants to pursue a research career, provides striking human evidence of the qualitative deprivation of a development area. The effect is all the more significant where, as in the case of Scotland and Wales, the development area is largely codeterminous with the nation. In Wales during the last two decades, not only has the population growth been half that of England but the population balance has worsened. Wales has a higher proportion of old people, labourers and unskilled workers than England and a smaller proportion of economically-active people and professional workers like managers, scientists, directors, lawyers and accountants. Thus the economic failure demonstrated by net migration has been compounded by the emigration of the ablest young Welshmen. In quantitative terms the demographic trends between the two world wars have continued and the mass emigration from Scotland and Wales in the 1920s and 1930s is not to be regarded as a historical aberration. The change in the overall employment pattern in Great Britain during the last decade is summarized in the following quotation:[6]

'Had Scotland, Wales and Northern England secured 42 per cent (their share of Great Britain employment in 1960) of national employment growth during the 1960s, they would have experienced a growth of 270,000; in fact their employment fell by 100,000. Of the deficiency of 370,000, 180,000 was attributed to developments within the services sectors; 120,000 was attributable to the primary sector largely arising from the disproportionate

---

[5] 'A Framework for Government Research and Development', Cmnd. 4814, 1971.

[6] 'Regional Development Incentives', Cmnd. 6058, 1975.

dependence on coal mining; and only 70,000 to the manufacturing sector'. This loss of jobs was matched during the same period by an increase of 6 per cent in employment in the South and Midlands of England.

Changing Social Structure

A second factor behind the demands for devolutionary measures for Scotland and Wales can be described loosely as sociological. It is clear that the comparative disadvantages of the Scottish and Welsh and other regional economies have been present for at least 50 years and could have been advanced at any time, rightly or wrongly, to justify a disillusion with the centralised political structure in Great Britain. It is only during the last decade however, and then only in Scotland and Wales, that public reaction has begun to express itself strongly, for example by support for the nationalist parties.

A large number of factors could have played some part in stimulating this political response:—the decline in Britain's economic standing, the loss of empire, North Sea oil, entry into the EEC are four which immediately come to mind; but a deeper-seated and more general cause must be found to explain the same development in many of the regions of Europe. The key to the problem is to be found in the fundamental changes which have been occurring since the war to the social structures of the countries of Western Europe. As a result of these changes the nature of political power, in particular of its location, is itself changing and manifesting itself in the demands of the economically disadvantaged regions, especially those where a distinct sense of nationhood is helping to quicken the process. Social change since the war has been great and many material factors have contributed; increased wealth, mobility, education, mass communication and so on; but none has been as significant or as far-reaching as the change in the nature of decision-making and it is important therefore to clarify the revolutionary nature of this change and its effect on society.

Hierarchical Decision-Making

Decisions can be conveniently classified as being programmed or non-programmed.[7] Programmed decisions are those to which the decision-maker is automatically committed by the framework of circumstances surrounding the situation calling for a decision. An income tax inspector deciding on a taxation problem is committed to his decision by the taxation laws, however complex they may be, which he applies with a professional competence. He makes a programmed decision. Similarly a car driver deciding to change gear on going uphill is committed by the steepness of the hill and the power of his engine.

Programmed decision-making formed the foundation of the ecclesiastical and military hierarchies, both early examples of large-scale organisation. Their rules, designed to cater for every situation on which a decision might be taken by functionaries at various levels in the organisation, were laid down by the small group holding power at the top of the hierarchy. The philosophical basis of the method is inductive, being expectant on the basis of past events, and accordingly programmed decision-making is best suited to static or slowly

---

[7] *T. Burns and G. F. Stalker,* The Management of Innovation, *Tavistock Press 1963. This book gives a definitive treatment of the ideas on which this section is based.*

changing circumstances where situations recur and can be anticipated. The functionary then faced with a situation calling for a decision is expected to respond precisely to the specification laid upon him either by applying the rules appropriate to his level or, if the situation is outside his competence, by referring it up the ladder to his superior.

As industrial undertakings slowly became more complex towards the end of the 18th century and increasingly during the 19th century, industrial management modelled itself on these highly experienced ecclesiastical and military hierarchies. In due course the industrial environment set the tone of Victorian society, a society whose dominant ethos was hierarchic, authoritarian and conformist, and one whose attitudes and prejudices continued unquestioned until the end of the second world war. Lord Tennyson captured the mood in a celebrated couplet from his hymn of praise to the Light Brigade: 'Theirs not to reason why, Theirs but to do and die'. It is interesting to speculate exactly when in a comparable circumstance during the past 30 years such a couplet would first have been thought to reflect an attitude more stupid than praiseworthy.

The political structure reflecting the social ethos as it developed during the 19th and early 20th centuries was pyramidal and characterised by the location of political power increasingly at the top of the pyramid. It was because of this clear location of power that, during the second half of the 19th century, one could talk meaningfully about the sovereignty of a nation-state and of its parliament since it meant that the national government at the apex of the pyramid was the ultimate arbiter of all decision-making within its territory. In turn the social ethos received powerful reciprocal reinforcement from images of Imperial splendour which confirmed the practical success of the hierarchic dispensation of authority. All decisions for the better governing of the governed were programmed from a central fount of wisdom and authority.

The Dispersal of Power through Science and Technology

There was worm in the wood however. Industry began to use science not simply for purposes of quality control but deliberately and positively for producing innovation. This novel development, which was a trickle in the 19th century, became a torrential flood after 1945. Thus, rapid technical and commercial change became a common industrial feature especially in advanced technology industries like electronics, and the inductive method became inappropriate as a philosophical basis of management. Situations calling for decision arose frequently at all levels for which no rules existed. The man confronted with the situation at whatever level had therefore to use his judgement in deciding what to do. He had frequently to make non-programmed decisions and the evidence now is amply documented that those firms prospered in changing circumstances who were able to adapt their management structure to cater for this innovation and those foundered who could not.

At the same time industry, especially in the fields of advanced technology, has become knowledge-based. Knowledge has become a fourth factor of production to be added to the classical triumvirate of land, labour and capital. As such it must be spread broadly across the mass of the people rather than be held in a few hands.

The revolutionary nature of these changes was not at first appreciated either in industry or in society more generally. But since knowledge in modern society is both synonymous with power and conducive to its being exerted, the new proletariat is now in the remarkable position of being able not so much to establish a dictatorship of the masses as to insist upon a democracy for the masses. Jack has now become as good as his master. The pyramid of power is in the course of collapse and we are facing the need to change from a vertically structured to a laterally structured society.

Our problems have become those of interdependence because power is no longer localised. The real political issue therefore is not Aneurin Bevan's of where to find power (even in his day the seat of power, as he himself admitted, was becoming something of a mirage) but how to differentiate between various facets of it in their various locations and how best to exercise these facets of power. The solving of this problem of course will not be easy but it is already clear, in the European nation-state at least, that for the multifarious purposes of modern government it will hardly be achieved on a basis of the political structure inherited from the 19th century, with the seat of power clearly located at the apex of the political pyramid and the all-embracing edict from the central bureaucracy as the determining instrument of government.

The centralist approach, which must be clearly distinguished from the not necessarily related problem of size, is no longer adequate, first because it is psychologically unacceptable, and secondly because it lacks the flexibility of response for coping with the pace at which modern societies are changing. A pointer to the way ahead is provided by those industrial firms, including very large ones, which have adapted successfully to the new environment. Their success has stemmed from new management methods designed to function within the laterally structured society of the firm with its preponderance of non-programmed decision-making. Authority and responsibility have been devolved and the new virtues, replacing the old ones of authoritarianism and rigid conformity, are flexibility and commitment, not in a loyalist sense to the immediate superior in the line of command, but to the overall objective of the firm.

Similarly in government we have come to the end of the hegemonic order within the nation-state, a development which of itself provides a justification for federalism if only to secure the decent burial of the hegemonic corpse.

The Sense of Nationhood in Scotland and Wales

A third factor playing a substantial role in the contemporary British political scene is an historical and ethnic one: the sense of separate nationhood held by Scottish and Welsh people. A great deal has been written on the profoundly complex subject of nationhood and the more readily comprehensible political nationalism which is sometimes confused with it. This is not the place to explore in depth the psychology or history of these phenomena. A notable brief historical analysis of some aspects of Scottish nationalism has been provided by Tom Nairn in an essay published recently.[8] He looked at the 'curious quasi-national legacy of North Britain' and suggested reasons why the potential

---

[8] 'The Red Paper on Scotland', Edinburgh University SPB, 1975.

classical development of nationalism in Scotland during the early stages of capitalist development did not take place. Nor did it take place in Wales for different reasons. There the potential for the development of nationalism was in some ways even greater and was recognised to be so as Robert Griffiths has pointed out:

'Here the late arrival of the Industrial Revolution, postponing as it did the indigenous bourgeoisie's embrace of the Union, and the remarkable resilience of the Welsh language, have retarded the emergence of a West British sub-culture as a credible alternative to Welshness. This was recognised in the life of the British industrial state. Consequently a policy of direct anglicisation was undertaken: socio-cultural autonomy in the Scottish mould might have proved too risky in Wales'.[9]

However, despite the attempts of state officialdom completely to assimilate the Welsh into a pattern of Britishness, and despite its tolerance of things Scottish together with the retention in Scotland of the trappings of national identity such as a legal system, an established church, at least the vestiges of a financial structure and so on, it was the Welsh who retained a distinctive sense of nationhood least compromised by Britishness. In Scotland there developed a Scottish-British ambivalence, a neurosis of the national psyche strengthened if not brought about, according to Nairn, by the development of a cultural sub-nationalism:

'. . . the old regime and its intellectuals had crumbled away without firing a shot: they were overwhelmed by the burgeoning growth of the Scottish Indus-trial Revolution and the new entrepreneurial bourgeoisie linked to it. No prolonged cultural subversion was required to pull down its bastions. William Ferguson notes "The decline of the specifically Scottish intellectualism which throughout the 18th Century had without conscious effort sustained the concept of a Scottish nation". This decline was not to be counterpointed by the rise of a new "specifically Scottish" culture, less intellectualist and more romantic advancing the new concept of nationality appropriate to the age . . . A national culture in that sense which had become newly important, entailed an intellectual class able to express the particular realities of a country in a romantic manner accessible to growing numbers of the reading public . . . The relationship between civil society and State in Scotland precluded a fully national culture in this sense'.[10]

What in fact happened was that the country produced a 'stunted, caricatural version of it,' what Nairn has called a cultural sub-nationalism, embarrass-ingly illustrated by the massive output of the Kailyard school of mawkish parochialism and 'ben and glen' romanticism.

'For Kailyard is popular in Scotland. It is recognisably intertwined with that prodigious array of Kitsch symbols, slogans, ornaments, banners, war-cries, knick-knacks, music-hall heroes, icons, conventional sayings and sentiments (not a few of them pithy) which have for so long resolutely defended the name of "Scotland" to the world. Annie Swan and Cronin provided no more than the relatively decent outer garb for this vast tartan monster. In their work the thing trots along doucely enough on a lead. But it is something else to be with

[9] 'Planet 32', Tregaron, Ceredigion.
[10] 'The Red Paper on Scotland', p. 36.

it in a London pub on international night or in the crowd at the annual Military Tattoo in front of Edinburgh Castle. How intolerably vulgar! What unbearable, crass, mindless philistinism!'[11]

But it nestled snugly for a century and a half in the warm glow of rampant British imperialism and subsequent post-imperial nostalgia and partly accounted for the approval benignly accorded to Scottishness, in comparison with the more prudent attitude shown towards Welshmen by the British establishment over this period. It is this neurosis, this ambivalence of identity, recognisable by such symptoms as the alternate soft-harsh responses characteristic of an absence of self-assurance, the abrasive militancy and the maudlin sentimentality of Clydeside for example, which posed the fundamental post-war pre-oil political problems in Scotland even more than the economic issues.

In comparison, post-war Wales seemed to be in the rudest of political health. Wales, much more than Scotland, succeeded despite, or perhaps partly because of, the continuing assaults first of all directly by the state during the 19th century, and later more directly by commercial and other interests, in retaining her national cultural tradition comparatively inviolate, indeed in sustaining a major renaissance in the 20th century even if this was little understood or appreciated outside. It is true that four-fifths of her people have lost their native language, the main vehicle of the national identity, but the very belief that, given adequate governmental assistance, the language's decline has been halted is itself a political medication. Thus the contemporaneous political cynicism and malaise arising from a combination of blatant materialism and British pretentiousness increasingly apparent in its rapidly crumbling world have in Wales been partly sublimated by the intense and manifestly 'national' contoversies surrounding the Welsh language and the many institutions caught up in the arguments. Also the seduction of the native Welsh aristocracy to London and its Tudor court as long ago as the 16th century resulted in Wales for two hundred years being a leaderless and peasant country, and left the soil fallow in which grew in due course modern Wales' distinctive and untrammelled awareness of its nationhood (and partly enabled her to avoid the Scottish experience). The process of educational self-help during the 18th and 19th centuries produced not only the first classless nation of modern times with leaders genuinely of the people but also at an early stage developed the democratic arts appropriate to the laterally structured society of Welsh Wales. There was no Welsh patrician involvement in the development either of capitalism or of Britishness since there were simply no Welsh patricians, and thus uncertainties of identity arising from such a source did not exist in Wales as they did in Scotland to nag and undermine the national awareness.

This awareness and its potential for developing at least into something more recognised and recognisable institutionally, if not into a nationalism in the classic mould, was thus greater and less neurotic in Wales than in Scotland. This was evidenced by the much earlier response of the Labour Party in Wales, at the time in an extremely dominant position, to social and political developments. Although it was much too late in the day for asserting a classical nationalism even if it had wished to do so, the Welsh Council of Labour began

---

[11] 'The Red Paper on Scotland', p. 39.

45

seriously to study the problems of devolution in the late 1950s and early 1960s and committed itself publicly in 1964 to a prudent though potentially substantial programme. Movement in Scotland on the other hand became noticeable only after it had been lubricated by a drop of oil and, although it now proclaims itself more stridently than its Welsh equivalent, it would be a mistake because of this to imagine that the Scottish demands are necessarily more soundly based than the Welsh ones and therefore deserving a greater measure of accomplishment.

A comparative study of the government's proposals for Scotland and Wales suggests however that the mistake is being made. It appears that the detailed practical proposals for establishing a Scottish Assembly, desirable in itself, are being so conditioned by electoral pressures that they may well prove to be less satisfactory than might have been the case. The comparison also illustrates the pragmatism in the political process as it has developed and the shortcomings which can follow when governments fail both to take a view themselves in sufficient depth and to educate their electors to the true needs of the situation.

The Pressures for Change

I have described briefly three aspects, economic, sociological, ethnic and cultural, of the political scene in parts of Britain. They have existed in Scotland and Wales, over several years sometimes clouded, now increasingly clear and dynamic. They are bound to influence, indeed are influencing, the political structures of Britain.

The peculiarly fruitful interplay resulting from their timely concurrence, each strengthening the other so that the whole has become greater than the sum of the parts, has produced in both Scotland and Wales a confidence and an insistence on 'the national identity', however vaguely understood, which would have been derided in the London of 12 years ago, where a great British political party was still intent on claiming for Britain 'a seat at the top table', from which to join in running the affairs of the world. Similar developments have been taking place in other European nation-states and of course the creation of the EEC, itself reflecting many far-reaching changes of circumstance, is a fourth factor which will add its own considerable influence to further developments within the nation-state. Apparent also is the post-imperial disintegration of the conventions, myths, taboos and prejudices, not to mention the more direct economic and political inheritance of imperialism, which successive British governments have striven so hard to retain. It seems clear therefore that the pressure for change in the British political structure is now so firmly set as to be irresistible, that the pace of the change will be hectic and that the change will ultimately be fundamental.

In the light of this one views with some apprehension the present schemes for Scottish and Welsh devolution. The suspicion that these are no more than palliatives for dealing with a half-understood 'threat to British unity' is confirmed by the opportunistic differences between the proposals for Scotland and Wales. In particular, the pragmatic approach of the government and its refusal to countenance more fundamental change outside the constraints of the political philosophy of the nation-state give rise to concern that a failure to meet the real needs will increase the atavistic hankering for outmoded political structures already being demonstrated in some Scottish and Welsh quarters. The pragmatism, cautious in respect of Wales, is less cautious in Scotland where electoral pressure is greater. Here the proposals fall between the two stools of a limited devolution of executive power within the nation-state and the much greater devolution of political power appropriate to a federal system, both feasible in themselves but hardly in combination. The retreat from the 'governor-generalship' role originally announced for the Scottish Secretary of State was an early example of an initially clear-cut adherence to the principles of the British nation-state later being fudged.

A more practical example of problems ahead lies in the financial and fiscal aspects of the scheme proposed for Scotland whereby massive amounts of money will be made available to the new institutions of Scottish government as a block grant 'settled as part of the annual public expenditure review for the United Kingdom as a whole'. This means that a Scottish administration will be authorised to allocate or spend an annual sum of over £2000 million without having any responsibility for raising it, at a time when the Layfield Report has posed this very issue so starkly as to throw in doubt the whole future of local government as we know it. A further ominous Scottish feature is that the electoral pressure there is largely opportunist and fuelled by a nakedly materialist and short-sighted reliance on North Sea oil, with the SNP seemingly satisfied with the reactionary policy of attempting no more than to establish a Scottish nation-state in the classic 19th century European pattern. It is not without significance that the party was ideologically opposed to British membership of the EEC and only prepared to consider membership for an independent Scotland, subject to conditions being agreed. The SNP has similarly refused to associate with the Basques, Bretons, Catalans, Welsh and other groups in the newly-formed 'Bureau of Unrepresented Nations' established in Brussels. A final irony in the government's position is its insistent reassurance that the devolution proposals present no challenge to the existing world of local government.

The Case for Federalism

We are thus in danger of missing an opportunity for political restructuring consonant with recent social change. Moreover in our anxiety not to jeopardise 'the unity of Great Britain' we are in danger also of actively following a policy conducive in its muddle-headedness to that very end. The confusion arises from the idea of granting minor concessions which might or might not be appropriate for the supplicants but all within the absolutism of a supreme sovereign power residing at Westminster, when in fact this concept is utterly at variance with both the political reality and the sociology of Europe. It is this confusion which gives rise to the question 'ought we to devolve or not?' The political reality of Europe of course is that of increasing interdependence at many levels, nationally, regionally, sectorally, politically, socially, economically and thus it is the question 'what ought we to devolve and what ought we to centralise?' which is more aligned to this interdependence and is accordingly more intelligent. The centralisation of government in Great Britain and France is less well adapted to dealing with this question and clearly is now an anachronism in comparison with the more appropriate governmental structures of other members of the European Community and of the USA, Canada, Australia and elsewhere.

The first step therefore towards strengthening our unity must be clearly to appreciate the warring antinomies contained in any proposal for a meaningful modern transfer of political power, outwards or inwards, while at the same time retaining 19th century political philosophy of the unitary nation-state. The rule applies as much to the 'region' within the nation-state as it does to the nation-state within the European Community. The criticism to be levelled at Plaid Cymru and SNP therefore is that, in responding to modern political pressures, they seek to adopt for their own countries the same historically outdated political structure which they want to destroy in Britain.

One must look elsewhere for the system most likely not only to maintain British unity but generally to provide a stable political, economic and social structure in Britain and in Europe. The Victorian idea of stability was a static one. It was synonymous with immobility which led in due course to the concept of permanence, that most dangerous of Victorian concepts. The concept rested on the twin pillars of guarantees provided by military strength and the preservation of the status quo through an organisational structure based on programmed decision-making and the swift reporting upwards of any deviance. In Europe today both are outmoded and permanence has become a chimera while the emptiness of nation-state guarantees are matched by the vain attempts at hierarchical political structures to exercise their inappropriate hegemonic control. Stability now is more a dynamic continuity in an environment of change and the political problem is to devise a structure allowing for this dynamism while at the same time accommodating the centralist constraints of modern technology. Curiously there are echoes of the old argument between Marx and Bakunin in the new situation where dangers arising from the State's involvement in the modern technological process resemble those foreseen by Bakunin over 100 years ago in the political relationship between society and the Marxist state. A former Labour member of Parliament captured the essence of the problem when he said 'Bureaucracy will destroy socialism'. All the signs now point to a lateral structure for a solution.

The ethnic accentuation of the dangers are outlined by Robert Griffiths: 'The point is that this conflict between State and society is all the more exploitable and combustible in Scotland and Wales because here are two national societies seeking to survive within the social, cultural and political order, the State, in fact, of another nation. As that order is declining, so the potential and actual conflict increases between its stout defenders and the two growing national movements bent on hastening its demise'.[12]

The essential for the new political structure must be an absence of hegemonic control, whether in government or any other institution. The old adage 'Divide and rule' therefore acquires an entirely new significance and, in its federalist sense, a new wisdom. The wisdom lies in appreciating the problem of reconciling large scale economic interdependence and its attendant technological centralism with democratic control and the expression of social identity. It is in federalism that the necessary flexibility, the new dynamism, will be found and it is not an accident that the organisational structure of the more dynamic and

[12] 'Planet 32', p. 39.

successful of the giant multi-national corporations is in the narrow context of their own affairs, federal. Nor is it an accident that West Germany, the most successful member of the European Community, is itself a federal country.

As an academic exercise one could fashion a possible federal structure for the European Community complete in all its details and having as its constituent members the most appropriate or 'natural' regions of the Community. In such a scheme England, Scotland and Wales would take their place as the regions of Great Britain. The problems arising from variations in population sizes between the three countries would be lessened in the European context since the other 'natural' regions of comparable population sizes would neutralise the potential English hegemony. In practical political terms however not only is such a structure in any case unlikely for the forseeable future but the impracticability for the moment of conjuring a Federal Europe from air at one stroke inevitably condemns such a plan to the academic.

To talk of federalism in Great Britain however is now legitimate practical politics. There are many existing federal states in the world to guide one in choosing the combination of practicalities best suited for a Federal Britain. It seems clear that for this purpose England would need to be divided into regions and, while some might pour scorn on the idea of 'artificially' dividing the country, this might well be due more to prejudice in favour of the nation-state principle and à hierarchic structure than to any real objection on grounds of 'artificiality'. It is not without significance that some regions of England, notably the North-East, are already echoing, if only faintly, arguments heard in Wales some years ago. For example one notices in the North-East at the moment concern about the corrosive spread of an 'anglo-american mass mono-culture' which threatens the region's identity. There exists also a clearer awareness and concern about potential advantages accruing to Scotland and Wales in straightforward economic and materialist terms following the establishment of their directly elected regional assemblies.

As a consequence the existing regional awareness is being strengthened and it will seek to express itself politically. The practical problem is how best to reach a federal position assuming the general acceptance of the principles, that is to say how to accomplish 'the distribution of powers and responsibilities to appropriate political levels and types of institution, both up and down the scale, so as to combine representation and authority, union and diversity, organisation and freedom'.[13]

The gradual road from devolution to federalism
The English genius is gradualist and empirical and it is along the gradual road one would expect to travel best. For this reason, and reasons connected with not a few practical problems which one could otherwise foresee, an appropriate first step is limited devolution on the proposed Welsh pattern with the introduction of unitary local government authorities in each region, a proposal made several years ago by the Welsh Council of Labour. Two essential additional requirements are: first, the financing of the administration at least partly from direct regional sources; and secondly, a clear commitment to a developing federal structure through the gradual transfer of appropriate

[13] 'The New Federalism' (Introduction, above).

additional powers and responsibilities to the region as rapidly as they could be adequately absorbed, while at the same time continuing with the similar process which has already started in respect of the European Community. Under the present proposals for Scotland, for example, a breach of Community competition policy, through Scottish Assembly measures judged to be unfairly favourable to a Scottish enterprise, could result in a constitutional crisis, if the UK government, a party to the Accession Treaty, were arraigned before the European Court and were yet unable to insist directly on an abandonment of the measures instituted by the Assembly. To avoid this risk consistency must be maintained between devolution of power in the UK and the evolving relationship with the Community.

The replacement of the classical nation-state upon which the European Community at the moment bases its legal existence will be best done empirically and gradually rather than by transmogrification. A clear understanding of the philosophical purpose involved and the political will to give it effect are vital. The worst eventuality would be a half-understood, half-hearted, half-cock policy which in the end would be truly divisive.

4 The Future of Community Law

NEVILLE MARCH HUNNINGS

When thinking of the nature of Community law, both as it is now and as it might develop, one has to remember three things. The first and most important is that the law of the European Communities is merely one emanation of a wider phenomenon: the developing law of Western Europe as a whole. Technological and social change has been so swift and radical that the existing legal structures are unable adequately to cope and fundamental reformulations have become necessary in practically every branch of law. This applies whether the country is rich or poor, north or south, Latin or Germanic, Mediterranean or Baltic, common law or code law. Willy nilly we are now watching the pragmatic emergence of a new European Law. On the one hand this is happening because basically similar solutions are emerging for similar problems in essentially similar societies. On the other hand, the development is being assisted by such European institutions as the Council of Europe, the Nordic Council, Benelux, the UN Economic Commission for Europe, and even such bodies as the OECD. The European Communities have a special place in this pattern because of the intensity of their law-making, the peculiarly imperative motivation of their legislative organs and because, although in one sense they constitute a quasi-state, they also represent an inter-state harmonising process of a particularly insistent character. This creates its own centripetal force and already we see peripheral countries not only seeking to join the Communities as full members but even, while remaining outside, wishing to align their own legal developments in some respects to the developments being worked out within the Communities.

The reverse of this phenomenon constitutes the second point. The most important area of development in public international law at present is the field of international economic law, which of course forms the central core of the legal concern of the European Economic Community. This international dimension is related to the swift post-war emergence of political awareness of a 'rich and poor' syndrome in international society, comparable to the rise of the trade union movement and socialism within the European nations some 70-80 years ago and the creation of the 'welfare state' some

51

30-40 years ago. Again, the process is being assisted by a number of institutions which represent either the special interest groups in the world community—the OECD for the rich states (i.e. Western Europe plus the United States, Canada, Australia and New Zealand plus Japan) and UNCTAD for the poor states (including some which are not so poor), or the organs within which the two groups can work out their economic co-existence, such as the GATT, the International Monetary Fund, and the World Bank. The United Nations itself serves not only as the main political forum but also as the umbrella for the flying of such kites as an international taxation system (arising in the Law of the Sea Conference) or commodity regulation. The Community is consciously adapting itself to this external pattern, not only in its foreign relations and participation in bodies such as the GATT and UNCTAD, but also in its legal work. Thus its unification of weights and measures throughout its territory is aligned on the international standards system; its adoption of a Community Patent Convention is like a Chinese box, enveloped by the European Patent Treaty which in turn is part of the world system instituted by the Washington Patent Cooperation Treaty. Euratom operates within the context of the International Atomic Energy Agency, a UN specialised agency, and the latter's inspection procedures have recently been adopted by the Community.

The Legal Power of the Community

Finally, and most paradoxical of all, is the peculiar nature of the Community's constitution. The Community is not a federal state in the classical sense and never will become one. Neither is it a confederation, although its position is similar to that of the confederation of the Thirteen States in the decade before 1789. It will develop into a new political form for which the word 'Community' is quite adequate and indeed accurate. Nevertheless, the greater power of its member states is legally very much less secure than is generally realised. In fact, the Community even now has greater legislative powers than any federation existing in the world today. This is because the founding fathers, or rather the founding states, did not have the full courage of their convictions and consequently, through not accepting the imminence of a federal-type structure, failed to include in the Treaties any legal self-protection, any real division of powers between Community and member states. The legislative powers of the Community within the areas covered by the Treaties (and with a generous interpretation those are vast indeed) are unlimited and it remains in the hands of the courts to determine whether and to what extent the member states have retained powers over human rights, national sovereignty, even national territory, not to mention such classic areas of federal conflict as the tax power and foreign relations. In all these fields one or other Community organ has claimed Community priority to at least a significant degree, and it is not really possible to postulate any branch of legal activity which is clearly reserved to the member states in a way which is judicially enforceable. To that extent, the Community when it reaches fruition and whatever its ultimate form will, in its legal powers (as opposed to its political organisation), be equivalent to a unitary state and not to a federal one. The 'federative' element is to be found in the institutions; but that has

52

the corollary that the true battlefield will always be political and not legal. Perhaps after all the British Government has been right, albeit rather gauche, to fight all its Community battles on an openly political, even *realpolitik,* level. And perhaps that is what was wrong with so much institutional and academic comment on 'European Union' during the Tindemans debate: a failure to understand that, with all the legal dice loaded heavily in favour of the Community, it was necessary to keep some form of institutional balance the other way. Although the centralising monarch is happy enough at present to ally itself with the people in order to defeat the barons in their fastnesses in London, Paris, Bonn and the rest, the lesson to be learned from history is that once the power of the barons has been broken the monarch rapidly becomes absolute, even tyrannical, and a revolution becomes necessary to cut him down to size.

The Future of Community Law

Against this background, then, what can one discern of the future nature and role of Community law? What is its genius, its essential and peculiar features? How is it created and to what extent is it likely to be responsive to the expectations of society? Can it bear the main weight of a major legal system or must it remain marginal, even if superior, a mere super-structure resting on a firm base of national legal systems which themselves carry the day-to-day burden of creating and administering law and justice? Indeed, to what extent is Community law to be concerned with justice at all?

Perhaps the first thing to note is the economy of means—which also applies in most other areas of Community endeavour. Not only is the Community executive branch concerned almost entirely with policy and legislative functions and not with executive duties at all, but so also is the case with the administration of justice. There is only one Community judicial organ, which has a multitude of functions, but which is not supported by a network of inferior tribunals. There are no 'federal courts', as in the United States. The application of Community law to every-day situations is left to the existing courts of the member states, as in most of the major federal systems outside the US. Where the Community system differs, even from the latter however, is in the relationship between the European Court of Justice and the national courts. It is not like the Australian High Court or the Supreme Court of Canada, the Swiss Bundesgericht or the Bundesgerichtshof of the Federal Republic of Germany, in that it is not hierarchically superior to the other courts in the system, it is not a court of appeal or cassation. It is at all times a court of both first and last instance, except in so far as it could be regarded as hearing 'appeals' from Community organs acting in a quasi-judicial capacity (such as D.G.IV in anti-trust cases). The relationship with the national courts at all levels is a strictly horizontal, fraternal one; elder brother perhaps, but certainly not fatherly.

As a consequence the impact of Community law and even its development through the case law is more in the hands of the national courts than is usual in a federal system. One may persuade a national court to refer a question of interpretation or validity to the European Court, but there is no Community appeal against the former's refusal to do so. This near monopoly possessed by the national courts is even reinforced by the European Court itself, which has applied Articles 173 et al. of the EEC Treaty very restrictively, so that it is extremely difficult for a private person or company to manage to bring an action directly before the European Court, let alone with any chance of success. Since in any legal system it is private litigants who take the initiative in enforcing the application of legal rules, while public enforcement agencies are more likely to be affected by considerations of a wider expediency, this lack of direct access to the sole Community tribunal could have a seriously inhibiting effect, especially as the main bulk of 'lawyer's law' already takes, and will increasingly do so in the future, the form of directives and legislative treaties which are for the most part not directly applicable. In such a situation, there is great scope for political or at least policy reasons to slow down the Commission's enforcement role; and while such a lack of officiousness can be evidence of a welcome realism and flexibility, its merit weakens when such understanding of governments' difficulties takes place at the expense of private rights.

Enforcement of Community Law

The problem with which we are faced is this. Regulations and the provisions of the Constitutional Treaties are applied directly by the national courts and there is relatively little difficulty in enforcing them in the same way as national laws are enforced. The only new dimension is that of unifying their interpretation through Article 177 references to the European Court of Justice. In the case, however, of directives, legislative treaties (such as the Enforcement of Judgements Convention 1968, or the Community Patent Convention 1975) or international treaties (such as the free trade agreements, or association agreements), there is need for some form of transformation into directly applicable law. In the case of international treaties, this should take the form of Community legislation; in the other cases it should take the form of national legislation. At present, private persons who stand to benefit from any such provisions have no standing to force either the Commission or the member states respectively to legislate. The only organs which can do that are the member states exerting political pressure on the Commission or the Commission bringing an action under Article 169 against the states. In both situations there is a marked reluctance to enact the implementing legislation, with if anything the Commission being the more remiss in complying internally with its international obligations. In both circumstances there is an ingrained reluctance to interfere too readily with the other agency.

One solution with regard to the enforcement of directives is the development of Community constitutional law so as to make them directly applicable. This is already being done by the Court of Justice, and the process can be expected to continue. But it has one seemingly in-built limitation. The theory behind this development seems to be a sort of *estoppel*, member states should not be entitled to plead their own failure to implement when a directive is pleaded against them. This has the consequence that their direct effect can only be used against the state organs, that is can only give individuals rights but never impose duties upon them. This can be serious in, for example, the sex discrimination directives which are intended to apply mainly against private defendants (employers), and the only basis on which such non-implemented directives could be applied directly would be by using them as a guide to the interpretation of other relevant legislation.

This approach to the potential direct applicability of directives, that it gives individuals rights but not duties, is supported by a well-nigh unanimous doctrine. But there is another way to look at it. It has always been striking that directives as defined in Article 189 EEC were intended to have an effect which was exactly the same as that of international treaties under British constitutional law. Britain is in this respect a 'dualist' state; that is, treaties, like directives, have no effect in internal law unless their provisions are embodied in national legislation, either piecemeal or *en bloc*. The continental approach is, with some variations and gradations, 'monist'; that is treaties when ratified become effective both internationally and internally through the same act, and the provisions which are valid in internal law are the treaty provisions themselves and not their reproduction as part of a national legislative text. As the European Court gives certain directives direct effect, there is a shift in attitude to directives from the pure 'dualist' approach of Article 189 towards a more 'monist' approach which perhaps comes more naturally to many of the judges of the Court. If this unexpressed motivation were the real one, in spite of the rationalisation through the principle of *estoppel,* then there would be no reason to restrict the obligations arising from unimplemented directives to state organs, and directives might then become usable in purely private litigation. The European Court seems to be moving in this direction in its recent decision in the *Federation of Dutch Industries* case ([1977] 1 C.M.L.R. 413).

Direct Legal Action

Another solution would be to develop the direct legal action. At present, it will be recalled, individuals have no standing to sue their own or any other member·state before the Court of Justice for breach of their obligations under Community law. Such high constitutional litigation is reserved to the Commission under Article 169. Consequently, a private party has no means of forcing a recalcitrant or lethargic state to enact legislation to implement a directive. But many states, faced with analogous problems under their own national constitutions, have used the office of *ministère public* or public attorney to bring actions on behalf of individuals or even a class of individuals which they are not entitled to bring themselves. In England, this function is performed by the Attorney General in the 'relator action'; he brings the action but the real plaintiff in effect is the private party on whose behalf the action is brought. The proposal made here is that the Commission should use its powers under Article 169 to bring 'relator actions' against member states openly on behalf of private litigants, instead of bringing such actions solely in its public law political capacity as 'guardian of the Community spirit'. It is significant that such an approach was adopted very early by the European Commission of Human Rights in bringing cases before the European Court of Human Rights on behalf of the complainant (who had no standing before the Court) even though it (the Commission) did not necessarily share the complainant's view and may even indeed have already ruled against him.

The reverse problem of the Commission's arrogance in disregarding its international obligations (apart from customs tariff provisions, it has made virtually no attempt to implement legislatively the free trade agreements with the EFTA countries or the special agreement with the Lomé Convention countries) may also be solved by the European Court adopting a 'monist' approach and holding that those treaties are not only binding on the Community but also confer rights (and obligations) on individuals which they can enforce in the courts. The Court has delivered a number of judgements indicating that it will adopt that view (the most recent and strongest being *Bresciani* v. *Amministrazione delle Finanze* [1976] 2 C.M.L.R. 62) and the Commission may have refrained from legislating to implement these treaties precisely because it assumed that they would be held to be directly applicable.

The Extension of Community Law

These issues are important because of the changing nature of Community law, both in its style and in its subject matter. In its first phase, the Community's legislation almost exclusively took the form of regulations dealing with technical matters such as customs, social security, manufacturing standards and freedom of establishment (these latter two account for most of the directives issued in this period). Only the anti-trust regulations could be said to belong to a more central field of law. But since the late 1960's a major qualitative change has taken place. Using harmonisation of standards and freedom of establishment as its standard-bearers, the Commission has now pushed through the Council laws on banking, insurance, doctors, taxation, company law, sex discrimination, civil procedure, patent law; it has introduced or is planning legislation on trade marks, bankruptcy, private international law, stock exchange transactions, unfair competition and trade practices, consumer protection, criminal investigations, protection of the environment, labour relations, worker participation in industry, social welfare, advertising, lawyers, architects, the law of the sea. In other words, the Community has now entered a phase in which it is ready to involve itself in any and every branch of law. It is no longer wise to do what so many legal practitioners have done and ignore Community law 'because it only has to do with commercial law'. It is becoming of direct concern to the ordinary citizen and not just to the trader. And this has two major consequences.

In the first place, the citizen is ill-placed to master this new element in his social life. For the most part he is blissfully unaware of it, even in the Six original member states. He can neither plan his actions so as to avoid the more unpleasant effects nor take advantage of those aspects, and they are many, which are to his benefit. The problem of legal information may be only one part of the wider problem of Community information generally; it may also be part of an increasing inability to keep track of legal rights and duties on a national level, which results from the constant stream of changes and new experiments, whether politically biassed or not. Greater involvement of the citizenry in the law of the Community is an essential principle, and without it there is a serious risk of public alienation, with consequent dangers of oligarchic attitudes consolidating at the top. In large part, the solution must lie in the hands of the legal profession, which must at all levels be quick to spot a Community factor and advise its clients accordingly. That is why much of

Community law is being influenced by German lawyers and why so many of its recent developments in the field of patents and trade marks have had a strong English dimension. But legal advisers, especially perhaps those who are far-sighted enough to become skilled in Community law, reach only a small segment of the population. To reach the others, it is necessary for legal awareness of the Community to be passed on through neighbourhood law centres, social welfare services, trade unions, citizens' advice bureaux and other similar bodies.

Public Opinion and Community Law

The other consequence of this activist phase of Community law-making, and linked to the first, is the nature of the involvement in it of the general public and indeed the responsiveness of the law-making organs to public opinion as such. There is said to have been much adverse reaction within other member states when Commission President Jenkins reacted swiftly to public outcry in Britain against further cut-price sales of butter to Russia early in 1977, on the ground that he should not have been so sensitive. The Community is used to reacting to special interest groups but, in spite of lip service, it has not normally paid any real attention to public opinion. This is seen in the traumatic experience undergone by the Commission following its proposals to harmonise standards for 'Euro-bread' and 'Euro-beer'. The widespread public outcry and ridicule, together with the taking over of the relevant Directorate-General by the new Danish Commissioner Gundelach, led to those proposals being dropped; but the Commission is still referring to the experience several years later.

This sort of involvement of public opinion in law-making is what is expected in a tight parliamentary system. But the European Assembly is too far removed from the electors to enable its members to respond to their constituencies when they are sitting in Strasbourg or Luxembourg, even though those same members may be quite adequately sensitive when they are sitting in Bonn or The Hague or Rome. The situation may change slightly when the European Assembly is directly elected, although it is unlikely to be as significant an alteration as many people expect. Indeed, if the French idea of a single multi-member constituency covering the whole country is widely adopted, there will be virtually no change at all, for the individual members will still be chosen by the party, as they are now, and distributed according to the party strengths in the country, which, assuming perhaps unrealistically that national parliaments reflect such strengths, is also done now. In any case, members of the European Assembly inevitably acquire such specialist knowledge of Community affairs that they become 'experts' and so again become to some extent psychologically immune from less expert public opinion.

A less political and more technical method of approaching this problem is to consider the actual process of law-making. At present, the dominant initiative in nearly all Community legislative effort is official rather than political or social. If the idea originates in the Commission it will normally be self-generated; if it was inspired by the Council, or the member states through Coreper, there is more likely to be a remote political motive in some of the member states represented on it, but such Council suggestions to the Commission are usually kept so quiet that practically no political capital can be made out of them. The formal procedures thereafter are also dominated by officials, especially as controlled by Coreper, both in the Council and in relations with the Commission. The two bodies which are not so dominated, the European Assembly and the Economic and Social Committee, carry out most of their business in committees whose proceedings are secret and whose reports are uninformative. There is thus practically no opportunity for public opinion to become aware of Community legisation (plenary debates in the Assembly are not yet of such quality as to perform that function) except when the Assembly or the *Official Journal* publishes a draft some time after it has been submitted to the Council, and when it is published in the *Official Journal* after it has been enacted into law. To be sure, there is a great deal of informal publicising. The Commission circulates drafts quite widely to special interest groups, who themselves will consult their members. Even a private citizen, if he knows the right official to ask, can obtain drafts without much difficulty. But this is all on a fairly confidential basis. It does not solve the problem of involving public opinion in law-making.

To some extent, a greater 'flair' on the part of the Community services would help (the long-awaited Commission memorandum on trade mark law was published in the summer vacation, of all times!). But more than that, a more open justification is required of the need for the legislation and for the form which it takes. There are various methods of doing this. There is the advance warning, as developed in the British 'green paper' system; a discussion document setting out the ideas which are circulating within the department but before they have taken shape, put on sale to the general public and positively inviting a response; Commissioner Gundelach experimented with this in the Green Paper on Employee Participation and Company Structure, and similarly with the Memorandum on Trade Marks. There is also the 'white paper'; the firm statement of intention to legislate and the lines along which the legislation is to be drafted. This technique too is applied by the Commission, but more often in the form of a press conference or parliamentary reply than in a closely argued pamphlet.

'Royal Commissions'

This lack of substance is found in most Community legislative documents, and for that reason the adoption by the Community of a device which is particularly prevalent in Sweden and the United Kingdom would make an inordinate difference both to the quality of legislation and to public awareness of it, namely, the Royal Commission or special committee system, in which a number of persons with experience in a variety of relevant fields are appointed to examine the implications of a proposed legislative change or innovation, taking written and oral evidence from anyone who offers it, and publishing a detailed report and perhaps also the evidence containing a full survey of the existing situation, the reasons for change, proposals for change, the reasons for choosing them and rejecting the alternatives, and possibly also a draft of a proposed legislative instrument.

The publication of such a report, apart from its intrinsic value as a source of background knowledge about the subject in question, creates greater public confidence in any subsequent legislation to the extent at least that the alternatives have been adequately considered. It also provides a much sounder basis for a second round of representations from interested parties. There are, however, two elements which are absolutely essential for the successful use of such a committee report: the members of the committee must be drawn from a variety of relevant sources and the committee must draw much of its impetus from the evidence it receives or acquires. The Commission has from time to time appointed experts to prepare reports on special topics which it hopes to make the subject of eventual legislation. Professor Sanders' report on the Statute of a European company, and Professor Ulmer's report on the laws of unfair competition are notable examples, and their content was of a very high quality, as one would expect. But their grave defect was precisely that they were pure academic studies. When legislating on a Community-wide scale, with so many differing legal systems, let alone different detailed provisions, it may be necessary to precede any incursion into a major field of law by a factual academic comparative law study, although even that is done far too seldom in the Community, which refuses to follow the good example in this of the Legal Directorate of the Council of Europe. But that is no substitute for the practical consideration of legal policy which is carried out by the typical Royal Commission, and which can usually take more or less for granted the straight exposition of the relevant current law. It is noteworthy that the report of the Cork Committee, set up by the British Government to examine the draft EEC Bankruptcy Convention along usual British lines, is said to have had a resoundingly favourable impact on the Commission and in the other member states as a means of subjecting the issues to a wide-ranging examination. It is also significant that the nearest approach of the Community to such a technique, the Vedel Committee which considered the workings of the Community Constitution, is also the one which has had the greatest impact, even though that impact was lessened by the self-contained nature of the Committee, no evidence being taken from outside and its multinational membership being, as usual, primarily academic.

The Danger of Uniformisation

But while the procedure of law-making is important, the content of that process should not be ignored. There are a number of significant factors to be considered here. The 'constitutional treaties' lay down certain fields in which the Community is under an obligation to legislate, such as customs and agriculture, or where the implementation of 'common policies' necessarily requires legislation. The 'common policies' are in fact the nearest the treaties get to a clear division of powers between Community and member states. Outside this compulsory legislation there are wide optional powers, culminating in the catch-all Article 235. In view of the lack of a proper federal list of central powers, state powers and concurrent powers there is relatively little guidance as to the use of the Community's optional powers except for such phrases as, in Article 100: '. . . such provisions . . . as directly affect the establishment or functioning of the Common Market'. Consequently it is possible by taking a long teleological view to claim that practically all law affects the functioning of the Common Market in some way and therefore is meet for communitisation. The most obvious example of the aspects most probably in the minds of the framers of the treaties is inconsistent manufacturing standards, where any policy differences, for example on safety, between the different state laws are insignificant when compared to the resultant hindrance to the free flow of goods. The other extreme is immortalised in the 'Euro-bread' fiasco. In fact, the Commission has now moved from a fairly rigid and doctrinaire insistence on uniform laws to a more flexible adoption of 'optional harmonisation', at least in the field of movement of goods and trade practices.

But a more basic issue is hidden here. The fundamentalists tend to say that any divergence between national laws in areas covered by the Community automatically distorts competition and is incompatible with the Common Market. They therefore aim at a single centralised set of legal rules almost as a matter of dogma. This is a false position for various reasons. First, several federal states have wide differences in the local legal rules without feeling a dogmatic need to remove them. Second, such an approach places uniform laws above good laws, especially when allied to the lack of adequate pre-legislative consideration discussed above. Third, and most important, the present is a period of very active social, political and technological change and consequently also of far-reaching law reform. Such a period is the very last in which any attempt should be made to codify the law and reduce it to a single text. It is a time when legal experimentation should be encouraged, when German worker participation *(Mitbestimmung)* can be subtly modified in the French *réforme de l'entreprise,* tried out in quite a different form in the British Bullock Report, and adopted in yet another form in the Swedish *medbestämmande* law, culminating in the extreme proposals for employee funds in the Swedish Meidner Report. For the Community to stifle such essays by providing at this stage for one particular form in its unifying company law directives would have been the height of folly.

The key factor here is the languor of the Community law-making process and the even greater difficulty experienced in changing its laws which have already been passed, derived in part from that very lack of sensitivity to the public. This results in Community law having a freezing effect which is totally incompatible with both the principle of law reform and the need to adjust rapidly to swiftly changing legal situations, to experiment and to change again when the experiment does not quite succeed. It is in fact this diversity in unity which has always been Europe's greatest gift to the world, creating as it does a liveliness and inventiveness which could all too easily be damped down by ill-considered uniformisation. This applies in law fully as much as in other areas and is to be feared in all branches of law in which the Community does not have a direct interest in change. In the latter, however, anti-trust law, movement of goods, agriculture, there will be adequate self-interest to stimulate change when change seems necessary to promote Community interest. But the Community has no interest in patent law or company law or the law of agency beyond that of ironing out the differences in the interest of freer commerce across national frontiers; hence, it is fairly neutral as regards the precise legal rules chosen to be incorporated in such instruments, and is relatively unconcerned if they should turn out to be less good than they might have been.

Community case-law

The codifying spirit is not, however, peculiar to legislation. It also applies to judicial attitudes. The European Court of Justice passed its formative years in the company of judges nearly all of whom had been trained in the judicial attitudes proper to a codified system of law, even though in fact the Court had been modelled on the one major court in the Six which was not code-influenced, namely the French Conseil d'Etat. But, however much the judges may have been inclined to approach their task along the lines familiar in a code system, they simply could not do so because there were too many gaps. We have therefore seen the inexorable development of the Court of Justice into a pure common law court, creating law where none previously existed, drawing general principles out of the air common to all the ten legal systems, proceeding from case to case, and indeed being led sometimes to enunciate principles in a form which it might have preferred to avoid merely because of the accident of litigation. Although its judges are not such political appointees as the Justices of the United States Supreme Court, it is to the latter that the Court of Justice is most nearly comparable, even to the extent of introducing the American doctrine of 'prospective overruling' in *Defrenne* v. *Sabena* [1976] 2 C.M.L.R. 98, a doctrine which is peculiar to the common law world. It has already passed its *McCulloch* v. *Maryland;* it has not yet met its President Andrew Jackson who issued the challenge: 'You have given your judgment, now you enforce it!', but when it does it can be expected to survive it as successfully as the US Supreme Court. It has shown an amazing skill in developing the law and ensuring its respect by very proud administrations. And it has now built up a body of tradition and style and practice which is likely to endure even through periods of legislative super-activity. Community law is and will continue to be what the Court says it is.

5 Promoting a European Identity

ERNEST WISTRICH

WHAT is it that makes people identify us with Europe? What are Europe's characteristics which distinguish our continent from others, and which command a greater allegiance than relationships with peoples or countries beyond our continent? Geographically we are a peninsular off the Asian land mass. Our populations are drawn from several families of nations, including Anglo-Saxons, Celts, Latins, Slavs and others. Apart from many individual dialects, Europeans speak more than 30 distinct languages. Links between Britain, for instance, and the so-called white Commonwealth are closer than with the countries across the narrow English Channel. The same applies to the sense of kinship that France enjoys with French Canada, or indeed most Europeans with their equivalent ethnic groups in North and South America.

Our European past, as taught in our schools, is just a long litany of internecine conflicts and wars. And yet distinct European values have been indelibly shaped by our common cultural and historical heritage such as Greek thought, Roman Law, Christianity and the Middle Ages; more recently, the Renaissance and its immense cultural influence upon architecture, literature, the arts and music, the age of reason, the industrial revolution, imperialism and social democracy. In our present day, apart from Western Europe, no more than a handful of countries in other continents enjoy similar standards of human rights and pluralist democracy. The populations of most of these derive their ancestry from Europe and enjoy similar cultural values.

In this broad sense there is a European identity, but one with which only students of history are likely to associate. The public at large needs a much clearer and more tangible concept, before they can develop a sense of belonging, of loyalty and personal identification.

Amongst committed Europeans it is the vision of a united Europe which brings them together, and European union is the goal to which they would like to commit public interest and allegiance. The trouble is that committed Europeans don't often agree amongst themselves about the nature or objectives of union. Some believe that in the age of super powers, Europe will only be able to count if it itself becomes a super power. To others, European unity is little more than an institutionalised system of inter-governmental negotiations between friendly sovereign states to help commerce, promote cultural contacts and reduce differences which could lead to friction amongst them.

A Super State?

An intriguing case in favour of a super-state sustained by European nationalism was recently put forward by Mr Richard Spicer in an article 'An argument for a European nation' published in the Spring 1976 issue of *New Europe*. Mr Spicer, who is secretary of 'Communists for Europe', bases his argument on a Marxist analysis of historical precedents. He points to the Soviet Union which alone amongst pre 1914 Empires has managed to keep within its boundaries many nations of different races, cultures and languages. By building socialism in one country, the Soviet Union made an appeal to a wider nationalism, which overcame separatist tendencies. He points out that American nationhood and allegiance to the flag similarly transcends loyalties to the states within the union. He ends his argument by claiming that without the bonding of nationhood, the European Community will remain liable to splinter into its constituent parts when it comes under pressure.

Mr Spicer is close in his views to those on the right wing of the political spectrum, who see in a powerful united Europe, with its own nuclear deterrent, a nostalgic re-creation of their countries' imperial past. Both views furthermore coincide in favouring national centralism with those socialists to whom centralised state power is an essential instrument of control and of the reform of capitalism.

Intergovernmental Cooperation?

Then there are those who oppose European integration much beyond the present process of inter-governmental cooperation. They see in the construction of a centralised European federation the dangers of creating another nuclear super-power, one further competing block which would increase the risk of war. They point to the growing alienation between citizens and central government, and argue that concentration of power further away at European level must inevitably increase dissatisfaction and create conflict between government and governed, leading to the weakening of democracy. To them the trend is in the opposite direction of devolution of central power and the promotion of greater local autonomy. A European super-power is anathema to those protagonists of 'small is beautiful'.

That is why many genuine Europeans see great merit in friendship and close cooperation beween governments and peoples across national frontiers, but view with grave suspicion a European union with its own independent institutions and with powers to override national governments and parliaments. They fear a drive for uniformity, which some believe a centralised European government is bound to impose, and of which the mythical Euro-bread and Euro-beer are symptoms. Underlying it all is an anxiety of the loss of identity, best expressed in a plaintive question 'won't we all become foreigners?'

The Present Reality

The introductory paper on the new federalism, printed in the Summer 1976 issue of *New Europe*, argues that neither of the above models of European unity is likely to cope with the present needs or the reality of a rapidly changing technological world of today. The analysis points towards a new multi-tier and flexible system of federal government, which would combine European union with the maximum devolution and autonomy to those components of the federal system closest to the citizen. Whatever the ultimate shape and nature of European union, the present European Community is the only concrete entity with which Europeans could identify now, and towards which they could develop a sense of loyalty and belonging. Indeed without such an attachment, it is difficult to see how public opinion could play an active role in influencing governments to move towards greater European unity.

Existing Attitudes

How does the public view Europe today? The European Commission has, since 1970, conducted a series of attitude surveys, which illustrate the state of public knowledge and opinion on European Community issues. In 1973 the level of British interest was very similar to that of the other member countries. To the question 'are you personally very interested, a little interested, or not at all interested in the problems of the European Community', of respondents in the six original member states, 24% declared themselves very interested, 40% showed a little interest, and 27% none. In Britain the equivalent percentages were 23%, 43% and 31%. By May 1975, in the midst of the referendum campaign, Britain came top with 77% showing greater or lesser interest, against 72% in the original six member states.

With regard to the unification of Europe, attitudes in Britain diverged considerably from those in the original six member states. To the question posed in 1975 'are you in favour of unification of Europe, against it, or indifferent?' 76% of the Six expressed themselves in favour, with only 4% against. There was moreover little change in their attitudes to this question between 1970 and 1975. In Britain opinion fluctuated much more. In October 1972, 37% of respondents favoured unification with 22% against. A year later those against unification rose to 30%, whereas in May 1975 those in favour of unification rose to 50% whilst opponents dropped back to 22%.

Promoting Knowledge

What emerges from the above figures is that there is need, in Britain in particular, to intensify the spread of knowledge about the European Community and its evolution, if public opinion is to play an effective role in influencing decision makers to make progress towards union. The problem is one however of communication. Dr Roy Pryce, Director of Information in the European Commission, described the difficulties in a speech addressed to the International Political Science Association in August 1976 as follows:

'The basic problem in this context can best be illustrated by considering briefly the ways in which national and sub-national political systems make their presence felt among their citizens. Essentially they do this by offering services to and making demands on, the individual citizen in a way that establishes a direct and continuing link between them. This link is forged virtually at the moment of birth and continues to the grave—and even beyond. During the lifespan of each individual there are constant reminders of the demands made, and services offered, by national and regional or local authorities. As the range of tasks entrusted to governmental bodies has increased, so the individual has become increasingly enveloped in a dense nexus of rights and obligations with regard to these authorities.

In taking advantage of these services, and in fulfilling the obligations imposed on him, the individual is constantly brought into contact with the agents of national and local authorities. The policeman, the tax-gatherer, the postman, the social worker, the education officer—all these, and many more, are part of the daily experience of the citizen.

Moreover, this same individual is also surrounded at every moment of his life by the symbols of the existence of state or local authority. Banknotes and coins, stamps, identity cards and passports, car licences and number plates: all these are constant reminders of a certain political reality, as are more formal symbols such as flags, anthems, national ceremonies and the like'.

European Symbols

There is at present no parallel public identification with the European Community. The lack of a flag or other symbols makes it difficult to project an image with which the public could identify Europe. The adoption of an emblem, trade mark or logo is now the accepted system of making a company, industry or local authority familiar to the public. It is surprising therefore that the European Community has still not evolved a flag and symbol with which it could be properly. identified. The adoption of European colours and a distinctive emblem should precede for instance the design of a proposed Community passport, about which the only agreement reached hitherto is the colour of its cover.

Although the idea of having a Community passport has been adopted by the Council of Ministers, it might be preferable if the need for a passport were totally dispensed with for travel within the Community. A single Community identity card with a photograph might well be acceptable in Britain, if its object were to dispense with passports, whereas it would be objected to, if it were seen as a return to the identity card of the last war. On the other hand it would conform with practices of many other Community countries. Apart from in fluencing its holders, the use of a common passport for travel outside the Community would aid in the projection of a Community identity upon the outside world.

The most significant symbolic development would however be the adoption of a common European currency. It is not within the scope of this paper to argue the case for monetary union. If however a European currency were created *in parallel* with national currencies, well in advance of full union, the impact upon public imagination would be quite dramatic. Even if the Europa were not to go further initially, than perform some of the functions which the dollar performs in Europe at present, including denomination for travellers cheques, the contribution towards public identification with Europe would be considerable.

Another area where the Community could make a visual impact would be by the required use of a European Community symbol, as part of the description or labelling of consumer goods complying with common standards laid down by the European Community.

Information

However important a role symbols might play in stimulating an awareness, they cannot replace knowledge consciously acquired and used. In spite of referenda or occasional periods of European activity, reported by the media, the public remains largely ignorant of the European Community, its responsibilities, actions and achievements. People might feel a stronger sense of identity if the Community acted in a way which would generate a sense of pride in belonging to it, or security in being protected by it, from potential adversaries. By and large however people will be resistant to absorbing such information, unless it has some direct relationship with their own lives and activities. The spread of information about the Community needs thus to be geared to the audiences to be addressed, rather than showered indiscriminately upon a public, already incapable of absorbing the mass of information fed to it daily by the press and media. Apart from news of general interest about the Community, which is normally disseminated by the media, specialised information, directed to individual interest groups, ought to be transmitted through the publicity organs of the interest groups themselves. Thus information about Community agriculture should reach farmers through their own press and through their union. Other industrial information should spread via the trade press, trade associations and their appropriate trade unions. In particular Community grants or loans for social, industrial or agricultural projects should get full publicity in the localities which receive such benefits. As the Community extends its responsibilities and activities, the role of an effective Community information policy is becoming increasingly important. Already there is hardly any individual producer or consumer, who is not in some way affected by Community policies and actions. Yet very few people are aware of it.

Communication

In spite of the media having a world wide role they largely retain local or national attitudes to events reported. This goes as much for radio and television as for the press. Eurovision programmes, whether concerned with song contests, jeux sans frontieres or European football games, retain their flavour of competition between nationalities, even if the contestants represent towns rather than countries.

Is there a case then for creating specifically European media of information? As far as the press is concerned efforts to create multilingual newspapers have never met with commercial success. The *Europa* supplement of *The Times, Die Zeit, Le Monde* and *La Stampa,* published in four separate language editions would not sell on its own and is unlikely to interest more than a small proportion of the readers of the newspapers distributing it. There is the *International*

Herald Tribune, which is widely read throughout Europe, but this paper is geared primarily towards English speaking expatriates.

What might be more successful is the syndication of articles by prominent personalities or journalists, and published in translation where appropriate. In the United States syndication is quite familiar, but it may not be generally known that some of the syndicated American material is translated and published both in the ethnic American press and in some European countries. Mr Art Buchwald's syndicated articles appear, for instance, in Dutch newspapers in Holland.

There is furthermore a need for the production and distribution of distinctly European material for use by the existing national organs of the press, radio and television. This would involve a special effort by the European Community, beyond their existing information services. A European Commissioner with appropriate qualifications and with no other responsibility should be placed in charge of specialist staff concerned with European information, not merely about the activities of Community institutions, but also with European developments in the fields of the arts, sports, cultural and social affairs. The Commission should actively encourage the organisation of European festivals, the granting of European prizes for books, music, painting, sculpture as well as for sports and other activities within a distinctly European context. All such activities and publicity about them are bound to promote a much greater recognition of the European dimension in our lives.

Serious consideration ought also to be given to Mr Tindemans' proposal to create a European Foundation with the aims of promoting understanding between European peoples. His proposal envisages an independent body, financed from both public and private sources, which would itself organise or assist other bodies to promote human contacts through youth activities, university exchanges, scientific debates, meetings between socio-professional categories, as well as general cultural and information activities. The Foundation would furthermore play a role in presenting the image of a united Europe abroad. It should not however be considered as a panacea. In this field, multiplicity of activity, even when it overlaps, is preferable to excessive coordination and centralisation.

Education

Major strides have already been made in creating a European awareness in schools on the continent. Curricula are no longer confined to a narrow nationalist view of events. As a result, the younger generation on the continent is much less conscious of national divisions and most of the young take it for granted that alongside their own nationality they are Europeans. In Britain we are lagging behind. Too many history books, written from a strictly national viewpoint before or immediately after the war, are still in general use. The trouble has been Britain's ambivalence over membership of the European Community. With the referendum having settled the issue, there is no further justification for delaying a major effort in our schools to promote a European consciousness and, given financial resources, increase substantially existing European exchange schemes amongst school children.

We need to back efforts for the progressive harmonisation of standards in higher education and speed up discussion and negotiation leading to the mutual recognition of diplomas and professional qualifications. Agreement on recognition of qualifications has up to now been reached only in respect of medical practitioners and specialists. Work is also proceeding in the case of pharmacists, dentists, opticians, veterinary surgeons, nurses, lawyers, architects, accountants and financial advisers. None of these appear however to be close to agreement.

The expansion of existing facilities and improvement in language teaching techniques is also much needed. The Community is unlikely in the foreseeable future to adopt its own lingua franca, and therefore reasonable knowledge of at least two or three languages by all school leavers should be our aim. Once this is achieved a multi-lingual European press, radio and television might well become a practical possibility.

Involvement

Europe's gravest internal problem today is unemployment. It affects practically the whole Community. The tripartite conference of governments, management, trade unions, organised by the European Commission in the summer of 1976, agreed that it was not possible in the future to solve problems of unemployment and inflation at national level in isolation. It was now a Community problem which had to be tackled by the Community as a whole. Particular concern was expressed about unemployment amongst young people of whom more than 1½ million were out of work in the summer of 1976. This is an obvious area for Community action, particularly with the help of voluntary organisations. These can act outside the existing responsibilities of national and local governments and could ensure citizen involvement. New avenues of contact need however to be created between the field of voluntary work and the European Community.

Most citizens are involved in some form of voluntary work, either actively or merely by making financial contributions to voluntary organisations or causes of their own choice. Most of these bodies supplement public services, provided by national and local authorities, or deal with problems which are outside the responsibility of government. Practically every local voluntary effort, whether concerned with peoples' social problems, their environment or leisure pursuits, has a wider than local dimension. That is why most voluntary associations, like councils of social service, environment protection bodies, or sports clubs, have regional and national bodies with the aim of propagating their common cause more widely. One should ensure that every national voluntary body links up with its parallel organisation in other Community countries and creates a European association. European voluntary associations will be in a better position to establish contact, secure action and get help in their field from governmental institutions at European level.

If all appropriate voluntary associations were grouped under a broad European Voluntary Service umbrella, grant aided by the European Community, a major European pressure group would be created for action to improve the living conditions of European citizens. Rapid help with qualified people and resources could be provided under the European Voluntary Service auspices in the case of major national disasters such as the recent Italian earthquakes.

Young European volunteers, paid out of Community grants, might be used to help local communities in improving their living conditions and their local environment, by tackling work which would otherwise not be done. There is no shortage of projects which would engage the interest of the public and recruit their active help, provided information about them is communicated and an organisation exists to channel all help offered. Thus public concern for Europe's problems would grow and active involvement of Europeans in solving them would make a real contribution to creating a European consciousness. At the same time the Community would be seen to be tackling unemployment and making a direct contribution to the improvement of local living conditions.

Twinnings

Many motorists, especially on the continent, are struck by the Council of Europe sign-posts at the entry to towns and villages which, alongside the name of the locality, announce its twinning with some other European municipality. Although twinnings of municipalities have often been confined to bi-lateral junketings of respective Mayors and Town Clerks, many local authorities have developed such links well beyond the municipal exchange of visits and information. These have led to parallel twinning arrangements between local schools, trades councils, and voluntary bodies concerned with sport and leisure activities. Exchange visits, joint events and holidays, involving people between twinned localities, particularly if well covered in the local press, can contribute effectively to mutual understanding and the reduction of narrow minded parochialism.

Participation

Nothing however is likely to do more in promoting a European consciousness and identity than public participation in decisions affecting the government and policies of the European Community. Britain's referendum campaign in 1975 had a dramatic effect on peoples' knowledge and interest in Community affairs. Quite apart from the heightened interest, illustrated by the attitude surveys quoted earlier in this paper, the high turn out for the vote confirmed this trend. Although the political party machines, operating at national elections to pull out the vote, did not work during the referendum, 65% of the electors voted, which was only 5% less than at the previous general election. The next most important single step in this area will be the direct elections to the European Parliament. For the first time the full attention of the electorate will be focused on European policies and how they affect citizens'; ordinary lives. The campaign will not merely consider European issues but offer choices between them, forcing a critical judgement upon a public which has hitherto been largely a passive recipient of European news.

The first elections are likely to excite major interest, because of their novelty and their new dimension beyond previous national experience. They are bound to heighten European consciousness and help the public to identify with the European Community and its government.

This boost to Europe's identity might well however be dissipated if it is not followed up. Responsibility for this will lie with the elected members of the European Parliament. They must realise that seeking a vote once every four or five years will not maintain the European interest of the public. Continuous direct and indirect contact between the Parliament and the European electorate needs to be developed. In the first instance this should include the filming and the recording of parliamentary debates by the information services of the Parliament. This should furthermore be extended to include committee meetings, which ought to be open to the public and the press. The material thus filmed and recorded should be made freely available to the various national and regional broadcasting authorities, with the right of suitable editing to make the broadcasts intelligible and interesting to their local audiences.

Secondly, the Parliament or its fact finding committees should hold sessions in other Community countries. These should offer opportunities for public sessions at which submissions and representations can be made by citizens or their appropriate local representatives. Similarly, public joint sessions should be organised between parallel subject committees of the European Parliament and national parliaments in the capitals of member countries.

Finally, individual MPs must recognise that they have to relate their European work to their electors' interests. Contact needs to be maintained with the public through the regular and intensive use of the local news media including both direct interviews and reports of public meetings between MPs and their electors. This is the missing link between the present nominated European Parliament and the public, which the directly elected MPs need to establish in the future.

Conclusion

Promoting a European identity is a long term task. Its growth will depend on many factors, but above all on a political identification with an emerging European Union, of which an elected European Parliament is the first step. A European consciousness or allegiance must not however be exclusive and conflict with existing national or local loyalties, or it will be rejected by a majority of the public, whose sense of belonging to their local community, or their nation is equally non exclusive. Identification with a multiplicity of interests and dimensions is inevitable in our complex society, provided its organisation responds to present needs. Thus a European identity and allegiance is quite feasible if the European Union is organised on federal lines, which gives due weight and also commands loyalty to national, regional and local interests. By analogy an allegiance to such a federal Europe will not militate against a wider loyalty to the whole world and the rest of humanity.

6 The European Social Partners

GHIŢA IONESCU

The sobering tone of the new leadership of the European Community at the beginning of 1977 was explicitly compensated for by their assurances that, precisely because the prospects were so austere, there would be much less policy-postulating and much more concentration on the ways and means of policy-making, indeed on the feasibility of policies.

The co-ordination of economic policies is put forward as the prerequisite to any anti-inflationary European action, let alone any new hopes of a medium-term European policy. One of the principal aims of such a co-ordination is to stimulate the economies of the 'weak' states of the Community by the more dynamic domestic economic policies of the 'strong' ones, or one. This is only to the good. But a concentration on policy-making requires the Community to examine its own method for making socio-economic policies. There has been a noticeable difference between the open international debate, which accompanied the formation and enlargement of the Community, and the closed inter-governmental way in which socio-economic policies have been made or, more often than not, just discussed. The entrance of all member-states into the Community had been preceded by wide and sometimes stormy consultations of the peoples themselves. If one compares this with the exclusive government-to-government, communist party-to-communist party, approach of the Committee for Mutual Economic Assistance (CMEA), one can understand why, in the West, some privileges of the old national 'sovereignty' have been and are being relinquished, while in the East all proposals for supra-national integration produce a further stiffening of the peoples in defence of their national 'sovereignty'. The direct election of the European Parliament will considerably strengthen the popular legitimacy of the policy-making of the Community, and will accentuate even more sharply the difference with the CMEA; for while the Western European peoples can elect a supra-national parliament precisely because they have freely elected national parliaments, the East European peoples do not even have free elections for their own parliaments.

Because the Community is composed of democracies, the major issues of integration have been accompanied by a constant process of informing the peoples involved. Moreover, the Community was at first formed exclusively from highly industrial and therefore trans-national societies. European industries had achieved a great deal of supra-national unification, before most political parties, parliaments and governments engaged in any public activity aiming at European integration. At the other end of the spectrum, and with obvious functional logic, the trade unions of the Six also realised the advantages of common action at the supra-national European level. Their political counter-part, the continental socialist parties, were among the earliest political advocates of European Union, as behoves parties whose ideology should be essentially internationalist; the concept of the working-class is nothing if not international.

Yet policy-making in the field of the economic and social policies of the Community has not achieved at Community, supra-national, levels the 'concertation' style which has been achieved at national levels. This is because, since 1966, the Council has expanded its policy-making role as laid down in the Treaty of Rome; and, secondly, the Economic and Social Committee has proved until now the most insignificant and the dullest organ of the Community.

The common agricultural policy was in some ways an exception. Unlike other policies, the CAP was not only proposed by the Treaty but in part, at least, was actually implemented. Secondly, this implementation was based on a supra-national concertation of all the interests concerned. The other social and economic policies are still mostly discussed, internationally, between the national governments, and the financial, monetary and social authorities. That governments should in this way limit the processes of community policy-making in the social and economic fields to exchanges of official national views is not only contrary to the idea of supra-national policy-making; it is also out of tune with the modern methods of socio-economic policy-making at the national level in the member-states themselves.

Socio-economic Policy in the Member States

Every student of political science knows by now that in most Western European states economic and social policies are made through processes in which the representative institutions 'share' with the corporate institution in the making of decisions.

In West Germany, to start with a strong country, and a member of the Community which upholds the most 'liberal' and anti-planning doctrine, incomes and wages policy is made by 'Konzertierte Action'. Institutionally this takes the form of regular official deliberations between the Ministries of Economy, Finance, Interior, Social Affairs and Agriculture, the Federal Bank, the Council of Economic Experts and the Federal Service for Cartels, on the one hand; and the Employers' Association, the German Federation of Industries, the German Federation of Trade Unions, the unions of 'white collar' employees and of the civil servants and the Farmers' Association on the other.

In France, the original system of national planning envisaged by the Constitution of the Fifth Republic, has been considerably diluted and adapted to changed circumstances. But the institutional procedures and channels for preliminary concertation with the major interest groups in society, which were the original model for concerted action in Germany and other countries, have remained in full use. By now these procedures involve an avowed broadening of the centre of socio-economic decision-making from the exclusively political to the joint political-corporatist spheres. Many conservative critics still see this Gaullist innovation of so-called 'liberal corporatism' as opening the way, under a future government of the Left, to a kind of corporate state in which the role and power of representative institutions will be much reduced. In a sense the 'Barre experiment' represented a supreme effort to solve the grave socio-economic problems through functional approaches, as against the ideological and political approaches of either M. Chirac or M. Mitterand. Called in more as an expert than as a politician to try to solve the problem of inflation, it is significant that M. Barre had formerly been a supra-national economic expert in the Community. He has openly argued that the problems of the economy of any individual European country transcend the realm of party politics and can be solved, if at all, only by a consensus of the major interests with the government. Both M. Chirac and M. Mitterand oppose this view. The former claims that the mobilisation of political will was the essential condition; the latter asserts that since the consensus of the workers is the prerequisite of concertation, it could not be obtained without the political confidence which the workers would give only to a Left-wing government.

The same argument was put forward in Britain where a compromise between the ideological and the functional methods of policy-making had been reached in the form of the 'social contract'. Here the social and political preference shown by the trade unions for the Labour Party and the Labour Government facilitates the 'bargaining' between the two institutions qua functional institutions. There is thus a double bridge. When appeals to reason fail, appeals to sentiment may still succeed. On the other hand, there may be breaking points beyond which no understanding, rational or sentimental, can prevail: the divorce between the Labour Government and the Trade Unions in 1969-70 provides a traumatic example. The double, ideological-functional quality of the social contract is also a drawback, in the sense that the contract is bilateral, and not multi-lateral, or at least, tripartite. The Government's 'industrial strategy' stresses the need for tripartite collaboration between government, trade unions and employers. Although the NEDC exists, the main institutional organs of direct policy-making in social and economic matters are the new bi-partite 'Liaison Committee' and the old National Executive Committee of the Labour Movement. The Callaghan government has tried to enlarge the processes of socio-economy policy-making in 1977 by calling more actively on the enterprises and the employers, as well as by introducing important legislation for the devolution of some of the powers of central government to the regions.

In Italy, the non-communist trade unions have recently asserted their independence from the political parties. Even the relations between the communist trade unions and the Communist Party may soon be put under some stress. The Communist Party plays an important role in the Parliament, and it is pledged to support, through an ingenious procedure of abstaining from voting in Parliament, the anti-inflation policy of the minority Christian Democratic government. The acute economic problems of the inter-dependent industrial society may yet force the sectional organisation of the trade unions, and the national organisation of the Communist Party, to take different ways. The Italian regions add to the difficulty of producing a coherent economic policy, by trying to impose their own local interests. Likewise the enterprises, both multi-nationals and state holding companies in Italy, have long asserted their independence from constitutional accountability and seem to dominate the political parties with which they are associated. Thus, the policy-making processes in social and economic matters have not yet been able to transform the centrifugal demands of the major groups in this unevenly developed industrial society into an institutionalised pattern of concertation.

The Netherlands is at the other end of the spectrum of concertation in EC member states. Here the Social Economic Council, a tripartite board composed of an equal number of representatives from the labour and employer organisations as well as from the government, is the legal organ empowered to supervise the particularly strict national system of wage and income control.

In all the member states, a second trend emerges, in favour of bi-lateral concertation of the social partners alone, without the intervention of the government as a third member. In the enterprises themselves, as well as in the special agencies to which governments have delegated the responsibility of decision in matters of employment, social security or other such matters, the trade unions and the employers sometimes show a preference for discussion between themselves, without legal or governmental intervention.

Generally speaking therefore, and especially since inflation has played havoc with the economic policies of most West European states, the practice of involving the social partners in concertation has become the established technique for making socio-economic policies in each of the nine member states.

Role of the Social Partners in the Community
In the European Community the processes of direct concertation with supra-national social partners called to consider supra-national policies have developed only very slowly, for three good reasons. The first, which would be sufficient in itself, is that the European Community has failed to produce supra-national economic policies (except for agricultural policy) sufficiently concrete to interest directly the European social partners. Unlike political parties, interest groups tend not to participate in speculative or abstract debates. As their name indicates they react only when and where their direct interests are touched upon, or are clearly at stake. The speed of institutionalisation of interest groups is proportionate to the speed of formulation of issues affecting their interests in given centres of power. The slowness and looseness of the activity of the supra-national European social partners can be regarded as a good test of the failure of the Community to formulate European social and economic policies.

The second reason is that the Treaty of Rome itself was considered by the Community as a doctrine for market-liberalism especially during its first 'legalistic' decade. The primary aim was above all to eliminate tariff barriers. In so far as any significant form of decision-making by the Community with the social partners implies intervention by the national or supra-national authority itself it was regarded by some member states, notably West Germany, as undesirable.

The relative insignificance of the Economic and Social Committee as an institution of the Community can be explained by these two reasons. On the one hand the lack of European socio-economic policies resulted in a lack of interest in the European socio-economic groups; on the other hand, the past hesitation of the major institutions of the Community (with perhaps the partial exception of the Commission) to involve the Economic and Social Committee has helped to broaden the gap opened by a mutual lack of interest between the supra-national policy-makers and the supra-national interest groups.

The third reason why the process of concertation with social partners has developed so slowly is that medium-term economic programmes, including an active social policy, have foundered on the divisions between liberal and dirigiste members of the Commission.

The Economic and Social Committee

The Economic and Social Committee is itself only an advisory body, initially consulted only on a designated range of issues, and composed of national delegations representing various national interest groups rather than European groups representing European skills and professions. It has been further weakened by the lack of attention paid to it, especially by the Council and the Committee of Permanent Representatives. Relations with the European Parliament have in the past also been somewhat ambivalent, in part because of duplication of effort. This inferior position was widely acknowledged, not least by the Committee itself. After efforts to improve relations, especially with the Council, the Heads of Government meeting in Paris in 1972 granted the Committee a right to issue opinions on its own initiative. The increase in the number of opinions has been impressive, rising from 9 in 1959 to 109 in 1975, and the range has been extensive, including for example, its unsolicited 'Proposals on European Union' during the Tindemans exercise. But the reform was of limited effect. Subsequent developments such as the resuscitation of the Standing Committee on Employment in 1974, and the Tripartite Conferences, have tended to draw the attention of both sides of industry away from the Committee.

The aim of the Committee remains the establishment of a more satisfactory procedure entailing a two stage consultation, changes in the drafting of opinions and a more effective arrangement for presentation to the other institutions of the Community. The contribution of the Committee is problematic, especially when its opinions coincide with those of the European Parliament. A systematic information procedure would certainly be necessary for any clearer assessment of its impact. The Committe's own conception of what its role should be is stated in its 'Proposals on European Union' (CES 363/75). There should be formed 'a European Economic and Social Council, which would not be a mere consultative body, but rather an assembly representing organised economic and social interests at European level . . . Its members would be proposed by the representative European Organisations . . . Proposals of an economic or social nature would have to be submitted to the

75

Economic and Social Council by the Commission at the same time as they were sent to the European Assembly . . . The opinions would be mandatory'. Such proposals raise significant questions, not least the relationship between such a Council and a directly elected European Parliament, and the identification of the 'constituency' of the various other interests, in addition to employers and trade unions, which are brought together in Group III of the present Committee.

In spite of the institutional and procedural shortcomings of the Committee, the social partners themselves bear much responsibility through failing to make the Committee a more influential popular and innovative organ of the Community. While enterprises and employers found means of organising effective, centralised, but at the same time diversified representation at the European level, the trade unions have been less successful both in organising their European representation and in proposing original and coherent policies or programmes. The European Trade Union Confederation (ETUC) was until 1975 weakened by the fact that it did not represent all European trade unions. The responsibility of the British trade unions for this sad course of events is particularly evident, but some of the ETUC's constituent or affiliated bodies remain based upon ideological exclusiveness. The ETUC remains very much a confederation of confederations, with sectoral union federations, such as the European Metalworkers Federation, affiliated to it. Although the bulk of its work has been concerned with the Community it continues to include unions from non-Member countries.

Hampered perhaps by their unrepresentative character, and aware from the beginning that they might always find themselves in a minority in the Committee because the employers could out-vote them with the help of the other interests in Group III, the performance of the trade unions in the Committee has often been timorous, indifferent and altogether uninspiring. While national socio-economic policies may have suffered from the militancy of the unions, no future coherent European socio-economic policies can be elaborated without directly involving European representation of organised labour. There is also a danger that the Community's popular image could become that of a 'businessman's Europe', thus risking the loss of interest of the young European generation in the fate and progress of European integration.

Agricultural and other committees

The Community has not failed in all respects to reproduce at its level the concerted processes by which socio-economic policies are being made now at the national level. The case of the Common Agricultural Policy confirms that when a European policy is being supra-nationally applied, the supra-national groups duly appear; and secondly, that once they appear they have no difficulty in securing recognition by the European institutions, and especially by the Commission, as contributors to the making of the policy. No fewer than 133 European interest groups crystallised around the Common Agricultural Policy; and one major supra-national agricultural interest-group, the Committee of Agricultural Trade Organizations of the EEC (COPA) which assumed the role of the European umbrella organisation, was in turn diversified into thirty specialised sections. The European agricultural interest

76

groups have been constantly and closely associated with the implementation of the Common Agricultural Policy, and as such involved in quadripartite discussions with the Commission the national governments and the national agricultural interest groups. The harmonisation of the supra-national and the national points of view is the main duty of the management committees of which there is one for each major agricultural product. These expert Committees act as supervisory bodies over the decisions taken by the Commission, which is obliged to take their advice. The Commission's decisions are sent to the Council for examination only if these Committees give negative responses. In practice this has never happened, which suggests that the collaboration between the Directorate-General for Agricultural Policy and the Management Committees is effective.

The fact that in the composition of the Management Committees the 'experts' are representatives of the national governments, and not of the European interest groups, makes these Management Committees very different from the kind of supervisory bodies which European interest groups would like to establish within the policy-making machinery of the Community. Even so they are already useful models for such future groups. There are now innumerable consultative committees attached to the Commission. Some were established under the aegis of the Treaty of Rome, for example, the Social Fund Committee, composed of national representatives as well as representatives from both sides of industry. Others were set up by the Commission itself in response to demands, as for example, in 1975 when the Consumers Consultative Committee was established. There is now a special division of the Directorate-General for Social Affairs to service these committees. In addition, there has been since 1973 a Social Partners Bureau attached to the Office of the President of the Commission. This encouragement to the establishment of interest groups at the European level has, however, tended to undermine still further the position of the Economic and Social Committee, particularly as the consultative committees are involved in the formulation of policy at an earlier stage.

Two other relevant activities of the Community should also be mentioned. First, the Community has proposed within the framework of the harmonisation of company law that companies in all Member States should have worker participation on their boards. While some West European industrial societies like Sweden and the Federal Republic of Germany have experimented successfully with worker participation on the boards of enterprises, others, including the UK, have only begun to consider the possibility of introducing this element into their company structures. Despite controversy about methods, there is a wide consensus that worker participation at all levels within the firm is a necessary basis for good industrial relations. The Community significantly took the lead in its Draft Directive on Company Structure in 1972, and in its Green Paper: *Employee Participation and Company Structure* in 1975 in pressing its member states to consider in earnest this essential reform.

Another innovation of the Community was to create and finance two independent organisations. One is a European Trade Union Institute, the special purpose of which is to extend the training of trade unionists in European affairs. The second is the European Foundation for the Improvement of the Environment and Living and Working Conditions. The Community followed the example of some of its member states by hiving off large parts of the social problem to the social and professional groups, financing their establishments, and keeping for itself the role of referee. The Community derives several advantages from the use of this method. It does not have to stretch its own administrative services. It de-centralises, thus answering the growing criticisms of the accumulation of powers in the hands of the 'faceless Eurocrats'. Hopefully, it can also stimulate interest in European affairs and ways of thinking of the social and professional groups which have remained until now almost exclusively national.

The resuscitation of the Standing Committee on Employment originally set up in 1970 was an intriguing development. It is formed by representatives of both sides of industry: 18 representatives of the employers organisations (the Union of Industries of the European Communities (UNICE), the Committee of Commercial Organisations in the countries of the EEC (COCCEE), the Union of Mastercraftsmen of the EEC (UACEE), the European Insurance Committee (CEA), the Committee of Agricultural Trade Organisations (COPA)); and the European Trade Union Confederation, now grouping representatives from all nine member states.

Since employment problems are only the end product of economic, financial, and social problems they cannot be solved until the basic economic problems are gradually solved 'by dialogue, concertation or consultation'. But the social partners, and especially the reluctant trade unions, participated with genuine interest in this new venture, possibly because here they were on a par with the employers. They were also meeting directly with the Commission and the Council, and could conceivably decide together on a common course of action. Their national experiences, in Germany, Britain, France and the Netherlands had shown both the employers and organised labour that only common efforts from both sides could alleviate unemployment. In all nine countries direct collaboration between the social partners in matters of employment, or manpower policies, has been genuine and fruitful. If, as some statesmen surmised, the problem of unemployment could be solved only at the Community level, the social partners should try to project their good work at the national level on to this complex, but possibly more effective level.

Two 'Tripartite' Conferences, in November 1975 and June 1976 produced a crystallisation of a European point of view, as distinct from the nine national points of view. The commitment by the social partners 'to adapt trends in incomes of every kind to objective economic criteria' was in principle accepted at the Community level, whereas most national trade unions would refuse it at the national level. No doubt this more amenable attitude was partly to be explained by the fact that such a Community declaration is entirely exhortatory. However, another explanation should not be totally excluded; the possibility that problems may be seen in a different light, and solutions appear more feasible at the European level.

Promising as some of the initiatives have been, developments have been constrained by both the jealous desire of all governments of the member-states to be the sole sources of power, and by the limited character of the Community's policies and its information policy. The Community has not, therefore, attracted around it the multiple layers of the European society for which it was created and by which it could be made viable.

The dialectics of integration

The very terminology of federalism is characterised by a revealing ambiguity. The verb federalise is used to describe the unification of separate states into a federal polity and also the permanent diffusion of authority and power within a nation. In this ambiguity lies the essence of the federal principle . . . the perpetration of both union and non-centralization. Federalism is a special mode of political and social behaviour involving a commitment to partnership on the part of the individuals and institutions that at the same time take pride in preserving their own integrities.

British Encyclopedia

Nous ne coalisons pas des états, nous unissons des hommes.

Jean Monnet

Integration, even of the pluralistic kind, requires a very high degree of integration of the social fabric.

Karl Deutsch

European socio-economic problems cannot be comprehended, let alone solved, unless and until they are visualised in a complete and relevant European perspective and terms of reference. Given the complexity of socio-economic problems in modern industrial societies, most Western European governments have long since involved all the affected interest groups at national level. Therefore, European socio-economic problems must be comprehended, and solved, by all the European interest groups affected by such decisions.

The three factors which make up this syllogism, the European socio-economic problems, the European interest groups and the European decision-makers, are at present in limbo. Their existence can be detected, but they have not fully materialised. They may even never fully take shape: European integration, or federalisation, may not crystallise. It may even happen that, due to adverse internal and external developments, the pace of disintegration of what has already been achieved may be more rapid than the pace required for the completion of integration in Europe. But if integration were to continue its course and the three factors were to manifest themselves fully, then, inevitably, the relationship between them would be articulated at the European level in a similar way as at the national level.

It cannot be assumed that the solution of the socio-economic problems will be easier to achieve at the European level than it has been at the national level. The large structural blocs formed by the interest-groups across the nine countries may become overwhelmingly conscious of their own importance in decision-taking, and therefore more intractable in negotiation. Huge trans-national blocs of companies, trade unions, farmers, merchants, and, last but not least, consumers, may 'confront' each other, and the European authorities, with the imperative demands of their international rank-and-files, uprooted from the familiarity of their national environments, and therefore even more fixed in their functional interests. This vision is frequently projected in the speculations of futurologists.

But there are at least three reasons why European socio-economic problems may be easier to solve than the socio-economic problems of the separate states. The larger the resources and means which can be drawn together, the easier their global and rational adjustment across the board; this is one of the basic motives behind integration and federalisation.

A second reason is that the resources and the means of control provided by integration may give participants in decision-making at the European level a sense of higher effectiveness than they have at the national level, where decisions jointly made may afterwards be nullified by adverse international developments. This renewed confidence would, by itself, enhance the sense of responsibility and the positive disposition of all participants in the making of decisions. For example, European trade unions could be progressively convinced that the elusive multi-national companies, and the elusive transnational investment funds, could be more easily co-ordinated and oriented towards public purposes. In turn, European companies could obtain a better and more unified response to their plans from the European trade unions and the tripartite agencies than they are receiving now in, say, Italy or the UK. Trade unions, firms and national authorities may all feel increasingly that progressive integration is bringing with it a real stabilisation in the international position of the European economy, thus allowing more realistic long- and medium-term forecasts and orientations.

If such developments were actually to occur, the participants in European decision-making could derive a much more objective sense of commitment from their participation than they get out of the precariousness and unpredictability of the outcome of the decisions which they have been taking at the national level. There is, of course, no way of saying at this stage whether events will take this course. Integration and federalisation are a kind of spiral in which the more one advances, the more the results can be perceived; and, conversely, the more one hesitates (let alone cheats at the game) the less the entire action can be judged in itself. Perhaps the only firm judgment that one can make on the present course of the evolution of European integration is contained in the third reason why European socio-economic problems may more easily be solved than national ones.

The third is the so-called negative reason, the reason why the national governments of the nine member-states have joined and have remained in the Community. They realise the impossiblity of their own country finding solutions for national socio-economic policies without sharing and co-ordinating these solutions with the other eight countries. It is true that the national governments and political circles around them have played and are playing an important part in bringing about European integration. But it is also true that everything they have done in this direction had the ambivalent aim of ensuring that their sovereignty should be affected as little as possible by trans- and supranational power sharing. Moreover, and the point is crucial, the official circles of each of the member states have visualised European problems only through the perspective of their own national problems, and have proposed to solve them only so far as their interests were concerned. But, it is precisely this ambivalence which is the acid test: for much as they may dislike sharing the attributes of their sovereignty with the Community, they pay this price because none of them can renounce its commitment to the Community without dramatically endangering its own viability.

Foreign relations

It is clear that while some policies can be made by international, or particularly by inter-governmental decision-making processes, other policies can not be treated in the same way. The external policy (officially called foreign relations) of the nine members of the Community has made such great strides that it is one of the few policies which has gone further than the Treaty of Rome allowed for. It is the best example of a policy which can be made inter-governmentally, indeed by what is institutionally defined now as 'political co-operation'. This is natural because, on the one hand, decision-making in diplomatic matters needs to be protected by a veil of confidentiality and, on the other hand, because the objectives of a contemporary 'European policy', peace, security and detente, are obviously shared by all the nine peoples of the Community. There may be different ideological and political interpretations by the various political groups within the Community which may be expressed at the European level, as, for example, in the European Parliament. But these groups do not play the *direct* part which interest-groups play in the making of socio-economic policies. We have seen that the existing Common Agricultural Policy had the effect of bringing to the fore European agricultural groups; their participation was unavoidable. Even more predictable therefore will be the emergence and participation of European industrial groups, because in industrial matters the result of withdrawing direct participation, either by organised labour or by employers, is incomparably more effective than in agriculture.

But, is there a solution to the chicken-and-egg problem of how to formulate European socio-economic policies without European socio-economic groups and, how to form European socio-economic groups without the catalyst of concrete European socio-economic policies? The only possible solution is a full and intensive discussion of the possibilities of European socio-economic policies with all the representatives of socio-economic groups, who would thus learn to leave behind their strictly national interests and concentrate exclusively on the new and unexplored European perspectives. An example of what can be done from this point of view was given by President Ford, who, as the new President of the United States of America was faced with the anguishing problems of inflation. He called a mammoth conference of all the interests, officials of the Federation and of the States and experts of all kinds to discuss the problems from all viewpoints. The 'consultation' was also extensively televised, broadcast and publicised to the American Federation at large. One of the significant parts of the exercise was that the people who took part in it were thinking in 'American' terms, not as, say, Texans or Californians, trade-unionists or farmers.

The authorities of the European Community, which should act as proto-federal institutions (their obligation will be even clearer once direct elections have legitimised fully the European Parliament) have failed until now to interest

81

the people at large in what *could* or *should* be the socio-economic policies of the European Community. Information Policy has tended to concentrate on explaining how the institutions work, on how many and what kind of funds are available (with apologies for their inadequacy), and on the uncertainties of achieving 'European Union'. Brochures have been produced in large quantities with the purpose of explaining each 'policy', although most of those 'policies' are still only in embryo.

There should be less emphasis on the abstract question of whether to unite for reasons which may seem esoteric and which certainly do not affect directly each individual or group. If European public opinion can be shown that European integration consists of an innumerable range of direct European policies which are fresh and powerful alternatives to obsolete national policies, it will have been encouraged to 'think European'. Only then can it, and the multitude of vertical and horizontal, latent and manifest, interest or value groups which form the European society, begin to formulate and apply policies at the new level. The Information Policy of the Community should in reality be from now on a debate and a consultation by the Community with all European groups about the feasibility of European policies.

Three mottos head the final section of this essay which, with different modulations, state the principle that integration cannot be achieved if it does not entail from its very inception a *concentration of power* for the purpose of resourcefulness and effectiveness, as well as a *diffusion of power* for the purpose of participation. Take for instance Monnet's short dictum: 'Our purpose is not a coalition of states, but the union of peoples'. One of the ways in which the dictum can be taken is that in so far as the 'people' are sovereign, the legitimacy of integration is proportional to the degree of the adhesion of the people to the European conception. To be sure direct elections of the European Parliament will be the great threshold toward this new legitimacy. The representatives will carry a European mandate; their duties and loyalties will be to Europe, they will think and speak 'European'.

But, 'people' in modern industrial society wear not only the political hat achieved in the 19th century; they also wear a second, functional, hat. The modern industrial society is best visualised as an enormous functional grid. Each of us has a set of values, a political orientation and, possibly, a party; but each of us has also a function, a job of work by which we become yet another link in the great chain of interdendence which is the activity of a modern industrial society. Moreover so imperious is the functional inter-dependence that, on the one hand, is can no longer be contained within the various national limits but transmutes itself into the trans-national European chain. And, on the other hand, it reverberates so strongly on the political institutions and processes that by now, it becomes increasingly difficult to know whether the political factor conditions the corporate factor, or the corporate factor conditions the political factor. The major phenomenon of contemporary politics is the emancipation of the socio-economic groups from the tutelage, or chaperonage, of the political parties. This is one reason why it would have been so stimulating if, from the beginning, the European parliament could have been multi-cameral, comprising at least one Chamber of Social and Economic groups, producers and consumers, and one Chamber of the Regions, as auxiliaries to the main Political Chamber. Be that as it may, the fact is that in their roles as the political centre of a potential Community composed of industrial societies, the European Commission and European Parliament will now have to find the means of rallying around them the various categories of people who will be operative in the preparation, making and implementation of the decisions in European social and economic matters.

PART B
ECONOMIC AND
SOCIAL POLICIES

7 European Monetary Unification: Problems and Perspectives

GIOVANNI MAGNIFICO *

The Analytical Framework

The official approach to monetary unification, as it has been pursued since the end of the 1960s on the basis of the Werner Report was unbalanced in that it hinged too much on monetary measures, and too little on the economic elements of integration. It aimed to create in the first place *de facto* an exchange-rate union. The attempt to freeze intra -EEC exchange rates among the members of the European Community was made at the very time when the whole monetary order based on the Bretton Woods system of fixed exchange rates, was crumbling. The intention was to create in Europe an 'island of stability' as a defence against instability in world monetary relations and the threat which that instability implied for the achievements of the Common Market. But the objective was ill-founded since it ignored the fact that within the Community itself there were, as indeed there are, substantial monetary tensions. Exchange rates, the prices at which currencies are bought and sold against one another, can be kept fixed only if the ratios of the average price levels in different countries, expressed in the respective national currencies, are kept broadly in line, in other words, if prices in different countries rise at roughly the same speed or, to put it still another way, if the purchasing power of different currencies changes over time by approximately equal percentage amounts.

The 'purchasing-power-parity' theory is a useful if crude explanation of changes in exchange rates over the medium and long term especially with reference to major industrial countries selling competing goods in international markets. It assumes also a broadly parallel evolution for costs. Only

* Dr. Magnifico wishes to express his gratitude to Dr. Rainer Masera for many helpful discussions, and especially to acknowledge the large contribution made to the second part of the paper.

for a short while can exporters, by cutting profits, preserve their competitiveness when unit costs rise faster than in competing countries. Fairly soon prices and the exchange rate will have to be adjusted in order again to make room for a 'normal' margin of profit. Equilibrium implies both that prices are kept in the right relationship to exchange rates, and that costs maintain the right relationship to prices.

If unit costs tend to rise faster than in competing countries, prices will also soon rise faster. Price movements cannot be curbed in a manner consistent with fixed exchange rates without correspondingly curbing cost movements. But it is highly unlikely that costs, the prices of inputs, can be curbed when the price of the main input, labour, is determined in national markets each dominated to a different degree by oligopolistic or monopolistic labour organisations. Within the Community there have been large labour migrations, but there is no Community-wide labour market. Labour is still organised in national trade unions and contacts between the unions of different countries, though increasing, are still scanty. National unions have different aims, different strategies, different tools. Institutional mechanisms for regulating wage and salary claims have developed along separate lines, and hardly any efforts have been made by member countries, or by the Community itself, to bring them closer together. In some member countries there is no automatic link between earnings and the cost-of-living index; in others, wages, salaries and pensions are nearly fully indexed. In the latter group of countries, increases in indirect taxation or in import prices are reflected in the cost-of-living index in some cases, but excluded in others. Therefore, the development of earnings of workers with comparable skills differs from country to country. Forces can be detected already at work for the integration of the national labour markets, but for the time being they have a perverse effect. A sort of income demonstration effect causes unions to push parity of real earnings throughout the Community at a time when labour productivity is still widely unequal, and in fact has tended to diverge further. This only widens further the divergence of cost and price trends between the member countries.

A stabilisation of the monetarist type would have prevented the mismanagement of demand and the inflationary peaks which occurred, but no stabilisation policy could have equated completely the rates of inflation at the low levels of the least inflationary countries, without raising the costs in terms of loss of growth and unemployment to an unbearable level in the more inflationary countries. Discrepancies in cost and price trends, in so far as they are due to differences in the national propensities to inflation, cannot be eliminated in the short term and therefore have to be *offset* through limited exchange flexibility.

The argument to the contrary made by the supporters of the Werner approach, that the setting up of a common monetary framework would bring with it the harmonisation of both policies and economic trends required for a system of fixed exchange rates, has been proved wrong by the experience of the European monetary snake between 1972 and 1977.

The snake could have a truly European meaning only in so far as it succeeded in maintaining a stable, if not fixed, relationship among the four major currencies: the British Pound, the Deutschemark, the French Franc and the Italian Lira. It could achieve that end in two inter-related ways, first, by encouraging policy coordinations; and secondly, by discouraging currency speculation at a time of disorderly conditions on world money and exchange markets. In fact it achieved neither. Sterling had to quit the arrangement in June 1972 only a few weeks after joining because of massive speculation, which suggests that foreign exchange markets were not confident that the arrangement could produce the promised harmonisation of economic policies and trends. The Lira followed suit a few months later, also as a result of speculation. Earnest though discontinuous attempts have been made by France to harmonise its policies with those of the Federal Republic of Germany. Even so, the Franc has on various occasions been vulnerable to currency speculation. Having joined and left the snake twice, France is now, understandably, reluctant to consider even mildly constraining exchange-rate arrangements. Thus, only one of the four main currencies is now in the snake: the Deutschemark. If the role of the snake was, as indeed it had to be, to stabilise exchange rates among those currencies, the snake has failed and does not exist any longer as the European exchange rate system it was intended to be.

The fact that the currencies of some smaller countries, within the Community and outside it, float with the Deutschemark does not change the substance of this conclusion. Smaller countries, with a very high degree of economic integration and openness, can hardly envisage floating in a truly independent way. Usually they peg their currency to a major one, normally the currency of the country with which they happen to be most closely integrated for trade and other transactions. The countries which are now in the snake have pegged their currencies to the Deutschemark in what has become a one-way monetary arrangement. Germany does not normally negotiate with its smaller partners, or anybody else, about its exchange-rate policy vis-a-vis third currencies, which would mean agreeing mainly on the relationship of the snake to the US dollar. Thus, from an economic point of view, the Deutschemark exchange rate is not on a different footing from that of the other three major currencies; it too floats independently.

Pooling the Reserves

The official approach was in fact doubly unbalanced. Within the overall monetary approach, the requirements of an exchange-rate union were emphasised to the detriment of other ingredients of monetary union. No progress was made towards pooling the reserves, even before the explosion of the oil crisis made reserve pooling appear unrealistic. It is worth noting, however, how little logic there was in a position which claimed that membership of the snake would help to harmonise member countries' policies, but at the same time declined to accept the consequence for reserves of the common exchange-rate policy implied by the snake. Gains or losses of reserves, arising out of the defence of the agreed margins, were and are gains or losses for each country, not for the Community. If it was felt that coordination of economic, monetary and fiscal policies was not pushed far enough to justify pooling of changes in the reserves, then the obvious conclusion should have been that lack of policy coordination could not preserve the snake either. As it was, exchange-rate policy was elevated to the rank of a Community objective, but there was no creation of an immediate instrument for pursuing it, such as the pooling of reserve losses and gains or, to put it another way, of interventions on exchange markets.

The failure of the Werner approach has meant that the Community has had to face the most serious ordeal since its inception, the oil crisis and price increases of the mid 1970s, with a common monetary armoury which, if not altogether non-existent, certainly was and is utterly inadequate. Moreover, the failure of the official attempt at monetary unification has created political disenchantment and underlined divergence at a time when cohesion was more than ever needed.

The succession of monetary crises and the failure to coordinate policies at Community level have shaken the confidence of businessmen in the soundness and resilience of the Community. Doubts have arisen as to the ability of the hardest hit member countries to abide fully by their liberalisation obligations under the treaty of Rome. The profitability of investments intended to cater for the whole Community area has appeared doubtful in view of the danger that some national markets might no longer be good outlets for the goods produced, because demand could be restricted through a sharp reversal of previous expansionary policies and/or through administrative controls.

This change of mood could not fail to reduce the rate of economic growth and to create more instability, whereas the Common Market was supposed to make a positive contribution to both. The reduction of growth and stability over recent years, rather than the vicissitudes of the snake, indicates the real failure of the endeavours to improve economic welfare in the Community.

Future Prospects

While a balance sheet of achievements so far in the field of monetary union is overwhelmed by liabilities, looking to the future there are one or two positive features. One is the disenchantment of governments and public opinion in member countries with the supposed effectiveness of floating exchange rates and monetary demand management as policy instruments. In the context of vanishing money illusion, largely due to the link between wages and salaries and the cost-of-living index, and the strong dependence of the latter on changes in import prices, exchange rate changes seem to have lost their usefulness except in the very short term. Thus, there is a growing realisation that in the long term the exchange rate can do little to cure disequilibria which are caused by real maladjustments in the economy.

This train of thought has recently become popular mainly in academic quarters. The argument can be regarded as an extension to the exchange rate of the monetarist argument about the loss of autonomy in domestic monetary policy. The monetarist proposal is that the authorities give a pledge to make the money supply, or another relevant monetary aggregate, grow each year at a given rate, kept steady over the years and close to the potential rate of increase of GNP in real terms. In the monetarist view, as is well known, there is no point in pursuing an expansive, inflationary, monetary policy since in the long run there is no trade-off between inflation and unemployment; actual unemployment tends to equate to the 'natural' rate of unemployment and the latter is compatible with any rate of price rises, even including a zero rate of inflation. But if that is so, then by joining a monetary union countries risk little or nothing in terms of employment and growth. In the words of the 'All Saints' Day Manifesto': 'since the rate of unemployment is not, in the long-run, related to changes in the price level, a monetary union cannot be regarded as a cause of unemployment.'[1]

While the experience over the last few years with floating exchange rates and monetary demand management has produced a more realistic appraisal of the usefulness of these two policy instruments, it would clearly be far-fetched to conclude tht governments are now ready to surrender the right to use them. It would be politically unrealistic to pretend that governments are now prepared to give up their autonomous use of policy instruments, either out of fear that the tool is too powerful to run the risk of misuse implicit in the present state of knowledge in the case of the monetary aggregates; or because it is essentially irrelevant, since it can hardly affect real variables (as in the case of exchange rates). It must not be overlooked that governments resort to exchange depreciation usually in order to *undo* an existing distortion, that is, they use depreciation as a (necessary) instrument of adjustment after failing to control inflation.

If the increase in money wage rates tends to exceed the rate warranted in an open economy by the evolution of productivity and prices relatively to the average for competing countries, exchange rate flexibility will help to correct the distortions, which would appear if the rates of exchange were fixed. To correct existing maladjustments arising from a higher national propensity to inflation by means of credit restriction would not be without consequences for long-term growth prospects, since a credit squeeze hits at investment. With an over-valued exchange rate there is a danger that the economy may come to rest around an equilibrium of sluggish growth or outright stagnation with a high level of unemployment. This is why exchange rates have in the end been unpegged even in countries where, because of widespread indexation of incomes, there is a real danger that exchange flexibility will start a circular process, in which faster inflation leads to currency depreciation, and the latter, often reinforced by capital movements triggered by expectations, in turn feeds inflation.

Early in 1973 governments abandoned the system of fixed exchange rates in order to use the rate of exchange as a policy instrument. They still attach paramount importance to the exchange rate; they have their own notions of what in relation to any given set of objectives the equilibrium rate should be, and, subject to the constraints of any particular situation, they strive for it. Governments are unwilling to relinquish whatever degree of autonomy they still enjoy in the use of external and domestic monetary instruments, because it has still to be demonstrated that monetary policy does not affect in a permanent fashion the overriding policy goal: economic growth. The monetary criticism of the Keynesians' trade-off theory is developed in terms of inflation

(1) The Economist, *1 November 1975.*

and unemployment, or monetary stability and employment. But employment and growth are not synonymous, and indeed not even always complementary. In particular, a low level of unemployment is not necessarily conducive to growth.

To assume that governments have pursued what in the end turned out to be an inflationary expansion of money and credit in order to reduce unemployment, is perhaps to misread post-war experience. It is probably more accurate to argue that the main goal of economic policy in the post-war period has actually been the maximisation of the rate of growth, despite appearances to the contrary. Governments are under a compulsion to give priority to growth. People have grown accustomed to expect, year by year, increases in private and public affluence. This helps to explain why it has proved so difficult to adjust to the increase in oil prices, although for some countries this implied surrendering to the oil exporters only a one-year normal increase of the gross domestic product.

Growth being a compulsory goal, and one to be regarded more as a constraint on governmental action than a policy variant, the Phillips curve relationship between inflation and unemployment, and its monetarist critics, miss the real point which is the relationship of inflation to economic growth. If that is so, it is not enough to argue that monetary policy makes no difference to the rate of unemployment in the long run, and therefore to suggest that autonomous monetary management has lost significance is a *non sequitur*. Autonomous monetary management may still be relevant for growth.

The main implication of the foregoing is that any arrangement in the exchange rate field must for the time being allow room for a (limited) measure of flexibility. Past failures have given rise to an urgent need for new initiatives, for full floating is clearly not synonymous with progress towards monetary union. The present situation is fraught with dangers. If weak currency countries do not make the needed adjustments in their domestic economy, a bias towards depreciation will definitely be built into their exchange rates, with instability for all currencies. On the side of the strong currencies the snake may develop into a fully fledged Deutschemark area. The only important element of a currency area which is missing in the present situation is a true reserve role for the Deutschemark; but this would develop over time, since the reasons for West Germany's lack of enthusiasm about allowing such a role to develop for the Deutschemark would not apply if that role were restricted to a few small countries.

The benefit to Germany is the broad trade preference which is implicit in being the leading member of a monetary area. An agglomeration of smaller currencies and countries is building up around the Deutschemark and the German economy. But it does not represent Europe now, and it holds little hope that it might do so at a later stage if the German Federal Republic was thought, rightly or wrongly, to wish to 'go it alone'.

While arrangements such as the snake are not incompatible with a Community approach, to be truly Communitarian the arrangement should not be divisive; it should be such that *all* member countries could adhere to it. The degree of economic interdependence already achieved, though not sufficient to make a fixed-rate system possible, implies that no meaningful and lasting stabilisation of exchange rates can be achieved by each member country in isolation. Moreover, the present discrimination between members and non-members of the snake, and their identification in the public mind with a 'good European' and a 'bad European' image respectively, has political connotations. However, these are unwarranted because there is no economic foundation to such judgements; as pointed out earlier, all four major currencies float freely.

A Blueprint for Action

The need for effective coordination of economic policies among member countries of the Community should be reiterated at the outset; this must be regarded as a necessary condition for entering a new decisive phase of integration. The operational content of this message is to be found in the invitation to agree on some degree of symmetry in the adjustment process.

While the gold standard implied a symmetrical sharing of the adjustment process between surplus and deficit countries, the dollar-exchange standard which gradually evolved in practice from the original Bretton Woods mechanisms shifted the burden of adjustment to surplus countries. The workings of the present system imply a significant turn-round, in that the onus of adjustment now falls mainly on deficit countries.

The concept of symmetry propounded here is based on the previously explained distinction between those factors of inflation which are the result of mismanagement of demand and monetary policies, and those, more deeply rooted, that can be considered of a structural nature. This approach has a definite practical content precisely in the field of exchange-rate policies.

Target Zones

An arrangement which might unite, rather than divide, member countries is the *target zones* scheme for exchange rates.[2] It would comprise all Community countries, and would be compatible with the continued existence of the snake which only links some of them. To be symmetrical, that is, to put an end to the present discrimination, a target zone would be agreed upon also for the snake. This means that the snake countries should be willing to discuss their policy vis-a-vis the dollar and other third currencies.

The virtue of the target zone scheme lies in its evolutionary nature. At the outset its implementation would impose on member countries a minimum of constraints. These might be of the negative type: such as a pledge not to take policy measures which would push the exchange rate outside the target zone

---

(2) *The suggestion of 'target zones' was formally proposed to the EEC Council of Ministers in July 1976 by the Netherlands Minister of Finance, Mr Duisenberg. For each member country of the Community a target zone defining upper and lower limits for its exchange rate would be set. Each country would undertake to refrain from policies and interventions that could have the effect of causing the exchange rate to move outside the target zone. In return for this undertaking, each member country would be supported by the other member countries in implementing policies that would help to keep their exchange rate within the target. The proposal of target zones is thus essentially one of the rules for the managed floating of currencies, and for cooperation in stabilising, changing them only in agreed situations and after consultation.*

(or farther from it, if already outside), and not to change the zone without prior discussion with the Community Partners. A positive obligation to intervene could be fitted into the arrangement at a later stage, when sufficient progress had been made in the harmonisation of economic and financial trends. In brief, it would be a semi-flexible arrangement, which at the outset would have much more flexibility than rigidity.

However, governments appear at present rather reluctant to engage even in the semi-flexible exercise which is implied by the target zone proposal. Disillusionment with flexible exchange rates has not made them more willing to take chances. France is now disinclined to consider anything that might bear resemblance to the snake. Because of its unsettled domestic conditions, Italy does not feel in a position to accept an undertaking in this field. The United Kingdom finds itself in much the same plight as Italy, except that it has recently succeeded in bolstering its foreign-exchange position and that North Sea oil holds a promise of further relief in the future.

Yet the time must soon come when governments will realise that there is a strong interaction between domestic and external monetary stability and will try to orient their policies in ways that would gradually produce more stability in intra-European exchange rates. Greater exchange-rate stability of a weak currency can at a given stage make a distinct contribution to internal price stability. Conversely, as progress is made towards domestic stability it will be easier to gain and to keep control of the exchange rate.

The search for and study of exchange rate arrangements to help us out of the present impasse must therefore continue. The target zone scheme is only one of the possible arrangements; it has been discussed here because it is now under consideration by the competent Community bodies.

The Europa

A more ambitious approach also needs further study. Its implementation would no doubt pose difficulties and would require a coordinated effort of all Community countries. However, the scheme has a great potential for setting in motion a dynamic process leading towards European monetary integration.

The philosophy behind this approach is that real and monetary aspects of integration should be covered simultaneously in the adjustment period, and that the introduction of a European parallel currency, the 'Europa', in the early stages of the integration process, if carefully planned, would act as a powerful catalyst.[3] The exchange-rate part of the overall scheme which will be outlined should not, therefore, be considered in-isolation, but should always be regarded as only one component of the whole plan.

---

(3) *The proposal for a parallel currency, usually called the 'Europa', has been one of the major alternatives to the 'snake' as a transitional step towards monetary unification. The proposal has many variants, some of which are discussed here, but the central idea is the creation of a new currency under the control of a common institution. This would circulate in parallel with the existing national currencies. Initially its use could be restricted to official transactions, but later it could gradually be extended to progressively wider transactions, and smaller denominations. Finally it would replace the national currencies, as a result of the greater convenience of a currency which would come to be freely accepted throughout the Community. An earlier statement of the Europa concept was made by Giovanni Magnifico and John Williamson in* European Monetary Integration, *the Report of a Federal Trust Study Group, published in 1972.*

The snake approach, by restricting itself to nominal exchange rates, could well lead to disequilibrium values of effective, trade-weighted, rates. On the other hand, a disadvantage of the target-zone system is that, by focussing on movements in effective rates, it neglects variation in nominal rates; an implicit bias is thus introduced in favour of the evolution of the customs union character of the community, and against monetary and financial integration.

An alternative and arguably more promising line would consist in introducing a scheme whereby the launching of the Europa is linked to an agreement on the evolution of nominal exchange rates of the various Community currencies in terms of the Europa itself. The definition of the Europa could well be the same as that of the basket European unit of account (EUA), already officially adopted in the Community. A link with the EUA would raise some technical questions concerning the ex ante intervention process which would be required to implement the agreements. But these difficulties would by no means prove insurmountable.

This unit-of-account role of the Europa should be accompanied by the creation of a primary reserve asset function. To this end, in the initial stage, member countries would be credited with Europas at the European Monetary Cooperation Fund (EMCF), possibly against the deposit of gold, valued at market-related prices. This would be the first step towards the creation of a Community counterpart of the SDR, which should gradually fulfil the functions of both reserve and intervention asset.

The introduction and evolution of the Europa at the official level would be paralleled by its acclimatisation in private credit markets, in order to foster the process of financial integration. The establishment of the Europa in the Community markets should not however be left free and unguided, in the way the Eurocurrency market evolved. Rather, the credit creation process should be submitted to the surveillance of the EMCF itself, with regard to the build-up of asset and liability positions held by non-residents. As to residents' holdings of Europas, the principle should be accepted by all member countries that, even in the initial stages where the Europa represents a purely 'parallel' currency, its use should generally be subjected to regulations implemented by each individual country, but agreed at Community level. To this purpose, it would seem desirable to lay down some broad guide-lines to the process of determination of yields in the market for interest-bearing assets denominated in Europas. Two specific suggestions are offered here, which should not be viewed as mutually exclusive, in fact they might well co-exist, as options for market operators.

In the first place, semi-indexation clauses could be introduced to provide *partial* cover for inflation in terms of each of the nine currencies, in proportion to their weight in the basket. The aim here would be to ensure that Europa assets and liabilities were protected from inflation, but not 100 per cent as in the All Saints Day Manifesto proposal. A 100 per cent guarantee would make the Europa the strongest currency by definition, and would therefore imply insoluble problems for the idealistic monetary system in which the Europa should initially co-exist with the nine national currencies.

Alternatively, a mechanism could be envisaged whereby interest rates on Europa deposits and Europa loans would be linked to a weighted average, with

95

weights based on the initial values of the individual currencies in the basket, of (say) inter-bank deposit rates in the various countries. The analogy would be with the variable-interest credits and bonds already issued in international capital markets.

The introduction of the Europa in private financial markets should, as we have seen, be submitted to the guide-lines and the overall surveillance of the EMCF, which would thus add a new dimension to its activity, consonant with its eventual role as a true Community Reserve Bank. The dynamic interaction of market and official forces should be extended to the use of Europa by the already existing financial institutions of the Community.

A key role in this process would be played by the European Investment Bank (EIB). Here again the stress should be laid on the need for a sustained and coordinated effort to finance the capital accumulation process inside the Community, with a view to narrowing and gradually eliminating the structural differences and the regional imbalances existing at present. Within this framework, it seems desirable to shift today's emphasis on credit policies to finance balance-of-payment deficits as such, towards policies aimed at the financing of specific investment projects. In terms of this approach the EIB could well play a major role in the process of European integration, simultaneously attacking the real and financial sides of the problem, by the use of the Europa to assist in financing key investment plans in relatively underdeveloped regions and areas.

This many-sided process of establishment of the Europa as a parallel currency should be accompanied by a cohesive set of actions in respect of monetary, fiscal and incomes policies. As to the latter, its adoption might well represent a short-term instrument to help reduce the centrifugal forces which are to be reckoned with at present.

More generally, however, to buttress and implement the overall approach outlined so far, it appears desirable to envisage the adoption on the part of the member countries of quantitative targets with respect to the evolution of monetary aggregates and, on the fiscal side, on such key variables as the overall deficit of the public sector and the share that may be financed by methods that expand the credit base (creation of high powered money). The novelty of the scheme presented here lies in the suggestion that the undertakings to formulate and to adhere to the targets should be linked to regular meetings at Community level of representatives of economic ministries, central banks, trade unions and industrialists' associations; what might be called a Community Economic Development Council. The purpose of these conferences would be to confront the national objectives, to ascertain their mutual consistency at the Community level, and to ensure a common undertaking of the national and social partners to adhere to the programmes. In this way, in particular, the national initiatives for incomes policies would evolve towards a concept of a 'socially responsible Community wages policy'. This crucial aim should indeed be fostered by the Community itself, by actions designed to create a truly unified European labour market.

Should this comprehensive approach be adopted, the present tensions in intra-Community monetary exchange relations would be substantially reduced. In this perspective, it is conceivable that over a relatively short period the Europa could enhance its contribution to economic and monetary union by acquiring the additional dimension of a domestic currency in at least some smaller European countries.

The benefits of an independent exchange-rate policy are necessarily limited for relatively small countries, as already discussed. In a Community perspective, these countries would no doubt benefit from linking their currencies to the Europa. As a result, their currencies would display an average trend with respect to those with which their international trade is bound to increase and diversify further. Growing economic integration of a given area implies a profound rearrangement of commercial flows, following a multilateral scheme whereby each economic region is integrated with the rest of the area taken as a whole and with every single region of the area itself. The link to the Europa would confer new impetus to this process, and thus foster the pace of integration.

In view of these externalities implicit in the adoption of the Europa by the smaller members of the Community, an active support policy by the Community itself might be envisaged. For instance, if the small country which undertakes to peg its currency to the Europa is characterised by problems of relative underdevelopment, the Community might devise a set of special financial support measures, which would allow the country in question to pursue an active investment policy.

Among the direct benefits to be obtained from an early link to the Europa, mention should be made of the comparative advantage which would accrue to a country such as the UK, which has already established itself as a major international money and financial centre, from the early centralisation and coordination of credit flows in Europas.

The set of proposals presented here, while concerning mainly monetary and financial issues, should, however, prove capable of directing Community action along a path where economic and social factors would play a much more significant role than has been the case so far. A broadly based process of dynamic interaction between all these elements would thus be set in motion, leading, hopefully, to a truly unified European economy.

8 A Federal Budget for the Community?

DOUGLAS DOSSER

The budget of the Community is a key measure of European economic integration, since it reflects those joint economic policies that member-states currently operate: the Common Agricultural Policy, the Social and Regional Funds, and Community Development Aid.

If and as progress is made on the various parts of economic and monetary union,[1] these would immediately be reflected in the budget. On its expenditure side, an expanded Community Policy on unemployment and the other social dislocations of growth would require expanded Social and Regional Funds, while new and more positive industrial policies assisting advanced technological sectors would, if the existing methods of the member states are followed, be financed through current and capital accounts of the Community budget. Capital expenditure, and perhaps even some current expenditure, would be expected to be financed by borrowing. This would pre-suppose monetary union and integration of the capital market, so Community short- and long-term bills could be sold to the private sector or other public authorities. Finally, as the budget became significant in size and of an appearance resembling modern member-state budgets, its role in the management of the economy: stabilisation, growth, redistribution, would become important. It would become the chief instrument in control over the integrated Community economy, which would be the culmination of economic and monetary union.

Further, the budget will fill a crucial role in the progress of political union. Already, a leading concern of the European Assembly is their lack of power over the budget. Extending such control will be the principal test of the increase in the power of the Parliament following direct elections to a European Parliament, and its adoption of a role corresponding to Parliaments in member-states.

Its potential role is great, but the budget starts today from a small and primitive base. This article dicusses some of the problems likely to be found in the enormous transition that has to be made.

---

(1) See E.E.C., European Economic Integration and Monetary Unification, *Brussels 1973.*

Present Size and Structure of the Community Budget

In 1976 the budget was 7576 m units of account, or approximately £4,500 m. This represented under 1 per cent of the combined GNP of the Nine, that is, less than 1 per cent of the Gross Community Product. The budget is balanced, so this figure represented total expenditure and total current income received, there being no current/capital, 'above the line'/'below the line' distinctions. Some 98 per cent of expenditure was on account of the Commission, and only miniscule amounts for the operation of the European Parliament, Council and Court of Justice.

The percentage distribution of budgetary income and expenditure over principal items was as follows.

Revenue (%)		*Expenditure (%)*	
Customs Duties	46.9	Administration	7.6
Agricultural levies	9.7	Re-Imbursement to Member-States	5.7
Contributions based on GNP	42.6	Research and Development	1.8
		Social Fund	5.8
		Regional Fund	4.0
		Agriculture : Guarantee	68.1
		: Guidance	4.3
		Development Assistance	2.7
	100.0		100.0

The revenue side of the budget represents a transitional phase between the old system of direct contributions by member states, and the new system of 'own resources' agreed for the Community in 1970 by the Six, and accepted by the acceding Three on entry in 1973. When fully realised, the new system will grant the Community its own revenues from three sources; customs duties, agricultural levies, and an additional sum to meet the balance of agreed expenditures from the VAT revenues of member states, but not to exceed the equivalent of a 1.0 per cent VAT rate in those member states. In 1976, the Six were on the 'own resources' system as regards agricultural levies and tariffs, but not VAT; the Three will phase into the system by 1980.

The expenditure side was dominated by the European Agricultural Guidance and Guarantee Fund (commonly known as, and hereafter referred to under the French initials, FEOGA) to the extent of 72.4 per cent. Industrial, social and regional policies account together for only 11.6 per cent of expenditure. Re-imbursement to member states is a provision to repay 10 per cent of 'own resources' to cover the costs of collection.

A potentially important distinction exists on the expenditure side between 'obligatory' and 'non-obligatory' expenditures. The former consists of items necessarily resulting from implementation of the Treaty of Rome and subsequent treaties, and includes the FEOGA and development aid. 'Non-obligatory' expenditure, over which the European Assembly has more power, includes the Social Fund, research and development, and administration; the category of the Regional Fund is in dispute. The Commission has to calculate each year a permissible rate of increase in 'non-obligatory' expenditure, as a check on the Assembly's power to expand expenditure. For 1976, the limit was put at a 15.3 per cent increase over 1975, though the apparent figure was over 16.0 per cent. The confusion lies in a dispute between Commission, Council and Assembly about the proper definition of 'non-obligatory' expenditure.

The Financing System for the Budget and its Impact on Member States

The 'own resources' system, whereby the Community has access to tax revenues arising in the Community as of right, was agreed in 1970 on the basis of certain reasoning about what constituted Community resources, and accepted by the Three on accession. Proceeds from the common external tariff and levies on agricultural produce from third countries have been said to be logically Community finance since they arise from Community policies, and it is only by chance, for example, that much of the revenue accrues territorially to Belgium and the Netherlands due to goods entering the great ports of Antwerp and Rotterdam for onward journey to Germany. The same argument cannot, however, be made of the other great 'collector', the UK, where the cause of relatively high duties and levies is greater dependence on imports from non-Community sources.

The third source, the VAT, has a different rationale. It is intended to be the start of a Community tax system, a tax levied on the same base (the same goods taxed, the same exempt) throughout all member states and, according to earlier hopes, at an identical rate. Progress toward this ideal has been extremely slow and difficult. When it is reached, the contribution of each member state will be roughly proportional to its share in the GCP and, strictly speaking, proportional to its share of Community consumption expenditure. At present this is not so, which gave rise to the excessive contribution 'overpayment' problem which was the central issue in the UK re-negotiation of the terms of membership.

The relative significance at present of customs duties and agricultural levies in each member state, reflecting differences in the levels of imports from non-EEC sources, creates this problem. 'Overpayment' is said to occur where the proportional share in financing the budget exceeds the proportional share of a member state in the Community gross product. The 'overpayment ratio' (Gross contribution divided by GNP share × 100) was greatest for the UK at 142 per cent, and also exceeded 100 per cent for the Netherlands (130 per cent) and Belgium (118 per cent).

A clawback of excess contributions is permitted under a complex scheme agreed at the Dublin Summit meeting in March 1975. First, the GNP per head has to be below 85 per cent of the Community average, the rate of growth of this below 120 per cent of the Community average, and the member has to be in balance-of-payments deficit. Then, a sliding scale comes into operation according to the degree of 'overpayment'. Finally, the ceiling for the clawback is £125m, *or* 3 per cent of the budget, *or* the size of a country's VAT contribution. Only the UK, Italy and Ireland satisfied the first condition, but the latter two countries had little or no 'overpayment'. The UK was the only member which fell into both the 'overpayment' and 'below-average income' categories.

This complicated controversy would be removed, of course, if and when the VAT contribution becomes the sole source of 'own resources'. But this could lead to a further dispute about the 'equity of the arrangements'. The VAT falls on consumption expenditure, not on investment, exports or government expenditure. It penalises countries with relatively high private consumption expenditure.

The re-negotiation of budget contributions, instigated by the UK, was in any case argued and concluded on a rather simplistic level. The UK was seemingly put to a disadvantage by the 'own resources' system agreed by the Six before British membership. However, some of the 'excess' payment was in fact borne by foreign producers because they bear some of the burden of tariffs and levies in reduced receipts for their exports to us. Further, the substitution of net receipts from the budget rather than gross contributions as a basis for calculating any 'overpayment' would have weakened Britain's case. It might be said that the UK did well to substantiate 'overpayment' and gain a relief.

But one further sophistication in the equity argument would have strengthened the UK case whether on a gross or net basis. The implied principle throughout is one of proportional taxation. If the progressive principle that is accepted in all member countries for internal direct taxation were to be applied in inter-state taxation, the UK, as third-poorest of the Nine, would be entitled to a much reduced contribution on a gross basis or a larger net receipt on a net basis.

The Community Budget in the next few years

A vital distinction exists between short-term and long-term perspectives for the Community budget. The distinction is a double one, involving not only a quantitative issue of financial resources, but also a qualitative one of the functional role of the Community budget in the European Community economy. The longer-term aspects are discussed later; here the position up to the early 1980s is examined.

Estimates are recently available of forecast expenditures and 'own resource' revenues for 1978 (at 1975 prices[2]), when the 'own resource' system should be fully operational for the Six, with the Three still in transition to it.

These estimates show a potential revenue, of 11,235 m units of account in excess of expected expenditure of 8,420 m units of account. In this situation, the VAT source of revenue need only be taken up to the extent of Member-states paying over to Brussels the yield of a 0.55 per cent VAT. This projected surplus revenue may prove to be over optimistic. It assumes a reduced real rate of expenditure on the CAP, and may not fully anticipate the steady erosion of 'own resources' from the Common External Tariff and the Agricultural Levies, which diminish as more and more trade pacts are concluded with third countries and as Community agriculture is re-structured. The appetite for further discretionary expenditure may also grow rapidly after the European Parliament becomes a directly-elected assembly. Certainly, it would seem that the budget will run into a crisis as regards continued expansion after 1978 because

---

(2) *EEC Com 75/330.*

of the limitations on the sources of finances in the 'own resources' system. The budget can only grow if substantial new tax revenues can be found or deficit financing introduced. The latter seems unlikely in view of lack of progress towards monetary union, which would permit the issue of Community bills of various kinds, and in view of the distaste of some powerful member states for budgetary financing of this kind.

Thus the only dynamic sources of revenue will have to be new taxes. The established Community tax is, of course, the VAT, which represents a departure from the precedent of the US federal income tax. Other sources of taxation have been discussed from time to time, principally a federal corporation tax. This remains of long-term interest, but is hardly likely to be implemented soon, since it requires a harmonisation of the law and administration of company taxation in the nine member states, a mammoth task not yet begun. It also presupposes abandonment of the notion of 'equity' between national contributions, since the size of the incorporated business sector relative to GNP varies greatly from state to state. It therefore requires acceptance of the difficult concept of a European tax levied irrespective of the location of taxable units.

Role of VAT

The only prospect for increased tax revenues therefore remains the VAT, plus earmarked taxes or levies or charges associated with newly agreed programmes.

The advantages of the VAT as a federal Community tax lie in its wide tax base, on the whole of private consumption expenditure, so that a small percentage rate brings in massive revenues. It is also commonly regarded as a 'neutral' or non-distorting tax, though this claim appears rather bogus since government current and capital expenditure, and investment, are all exempt, exports are taxed by the country of destination, and multi-rate systems (different rates of VAT on different goods) influence expenditure and production between one sector and another. It was also claimed that VAT could improve general tax administration and enforcement by the complex and detailed accounting it imposed on all traders, but different member states appear in practice to have persisted in their pre-existing traditions of high tax compliance and severe legal enforcement, or the opposite!

The disadvantages of the VAT, a virtually unknown tax before the emergence of the Community,[3] consist of the aspects just referred to: discriminatory effects, and the costly and onerous administration arising from trying to collect a tax from so many tax points. Of more interest here is the disadvantage, at least from the point of view of achieving expanding budgetary revenues, that VAT revenues may barely increase in step with the Community gross product. VAT is levied on private consumption expenditure, and, as already mentioned, penalises those member states with high ratios of private consumption to GNP. The rate of growth of private consumption, moreover, seems unlikely to keep up with member states' growth rate of GNP, if investment expenditure

---

(3) *The VAT was recommended as the harmonised form of sales taxation for the Community by the Neumark Committee, which reported in 1963.*

is encouraged, and particularly if recent trends continue for the transfer of resources from the private to the public sector.

This so-called 'unitary tax elasticity' of revenues from a fixed VAT rate contrasts with the positive effect on revenue for the UK budget, where tax revenues increase at a faster rate than real or money GNP (an overall tax elasticity of about 1.2, and 1.4 for the personal income tax alone).

Not only does this imply a rate of growth of VAT revenues for the Community budget less than proportional to Community gross product, it also poses a structural problem for the federal relation between member state and Community budgets. Parity between the Community and member state budgets, in the sense of equal growth rates of each, or each remaining a constant proportion of gross product, can only be achieved by agreement on ever-increasing VAT percentage rates for the Community budget, or steadily decreasing VAT rates in member state tax schedules, both of which raise political difficulties.

Beyond this parity problem there are the more straightforward issues of the VAT rate and the VAT base for an expanded Community budget.

The present size of the Community budget is less than 1 per cent of GCP and would be roughly 1 per cent if the full permissible VAT revenues yielded by a 1 per cent rate were taken up. It is fairly easy to estimate broadly the VAT revenue requirements of an expanded budget. A doubling of the budget to 2 per cent of GCP would add another 1½ per cent to make a Community VAT rate 2½ per cent (bearing in mind that the first *tranche* of finance includes the common external tariff and agricultural levies and the second *tranche* consists only of VAT). A Community budget of 5 per cent of GCP would require a Community VAT rate of 8 per cent, equal to the current UK standard rate.

This poses the most critical problem in a stark way; is the Community VAT to be a substitute for or an addition to member state VAT rates? It surely has to be a substitute, and this implies the *transfer* of revenue and expenditure functions from member state to Community public authorities. Such an outcome certainly requires parallel development of the European Parliament if it is to be politically credible by the early 1980s.

In preparation for a Community VAT, even the currently agreed 1 per cent provision, the member states have to agree on a common tax base for the VAT. This is necessary to preserve equity between member states, in the sense that no one member may diminish its liability by drawing the base narrower than other states.

The Sixth Directive, for harmonising the VAT base, was held up for 2 to 3 years, by different states' insistence on excluding sensitive sectors, but was finally agreed late in 1976. The UK wanted to exempt food sales from the tax base, the Italians and Belgians wanted much wider exemption for small business than the extremely low turnover limit proposed by the Commission. Germany was interested in differentiation of the tax treatment of land. The Sixth Directive was agreed only with derogations allowed to different member states to cover these various special requirements. Members will nevertheless have to pay revenues to Brussels 'as if' the given sectors were included, and not derogated from the VAT base.

This represents a break in the concept of a Community tax raised on a uniform basis on all citizens of the Community. For example, UK consumers of food will be exempt from payment of a tax which other Community consumers have to pay. That the member state has to make a compensatory payment is a step back toward direct contributions: the private consumption (including imports) part of GNP is being used as a key to determine the size of contributions. There seems no reason in logic why other national political and social considerations should not lead to further adaptations of a tax supposedly imposed equally on all citizens of the Community, thus reducing the original idea of a Community tax to a mere accounting formula. This tendency is likely to be accentuated if much higher rates of 'Community' VAT are eventually used to finance an expanded Community budget. The blame for this blighting of an ideal may seem to rest with the obstinacy of member-state governments. However, the opposite argument can be made; that the Commission should never have chosen such a novel, complex and 'bureaucratic' tax as the vehicle of tax harmonisation and Community finance. A tax with far fewer tax points, and simpler in administration, would have been easier for many member states to conform to.

In view of the obvious difficulties of raising more finance for the Community budget via the corporation tax and VAT, programmes with an integral tax element have been canvassed.

For example, expanded Social or Regional Fund ventures, aimed at retraining redundant workers in relatively depressed sectors or regions, could be financed from payroll taxes on firms in prosperous sectors or regions, on the argument that their prosperity had been enhanced by the existence of the EEC, just as that of others had been disadvantaged.

Such schemes again run into the 'augmentation' objection of higher Community VAT rates. At a time when higher business investment is the objective in many member states, higher business taxation over the next few years appears a non-starter. The alternative, Community schemes replacing national regional and unemployment policies, again runs into the equally difficult obstacle of the surrender of member-state sovereignty.

The obstacles to any substantial expansion of the Community budget, allowing development of non-agricultural policies, thus appear to be formidable in the next few years. Corporation tax, increased VAT, integral expenditure-tax programmes, are all difficult to implement. A fundamental political shift would appear to be required to allow the necessary transfer of powers. This may begin with an increase in the authority of the European Parliament after direct elections, but a shift of power to that body and its executive would be a substantial and time-consuming political development.

The Long-Term Role of the Community Budget

The Community budget can be looked at either as a book-keeping operation, accounting for the agreed expenditure programmes and their finance, or as an instrument of management of the Community economy. At present, in both size and concept, it can only be regarded as the former. It may indeed be premature to consider it in the latter aspect, except in one important respect. The lines of expansion are still an open question; what expenditure role it should play or take over from Member-states; what tax or other means of finance it should command. A consideration of the instrumental role of the budget in a more developed federal fiscal structure may illuminate the incipient lines of extension of Community expenditure and taxes.

In public finance literature public rather than private provision of a good or service is explained either by the unavoidable 'social' nature of some types of goods such as the provision of military defence, requiring tax 'pricing' rather than voluntary purcahse; or that a society ethically demands more or less of a 'merit' good than people would voluntarily consume, for example, compulsory schooling to a given age. The question arises: is there a Community public good? That is, do the above concepts imply public provision on a Community scale rather than a member state scale?

The classic case is defence, particularly a 'nuclear umbrella'. The multinational character of defence provision is already met through NATO. The classic public goods of the US, Canadian and Australian federations (transcontinental railways, highways and postal services) are already highly developed and co-ordinated in Europe. More scope may eventually be generated by the other type of public goods, 'merit' goods. Common norms regarding education, health, and environment may emerge, and demand common public provision throughout the Community. Other possibilities include large-scale advanced technological developments, for example aerospace or nuclear power, where capital provision and risk-taking is necessary on a scale impossible for private firms acting autonomously. These are not public goods in the classic sense, but depend on sheer magnitude for the justification for public provision.

There are two further functions of a budget, to redistribute real incomes between groups in the Community, and to assist in the achievement of macroeconomic goals for the Community and its constituent parts. These roles depend on both the expenditures and the taxes in the budget.

A redistributive role cannot be envisaged at present, especially since member states are insisting on *juste retour,* receiving as much from the budget as they pay in. The European Regional Development Fund is a tentative step towards redistribution between regions, but it is hamstrung by lack of resources, constraints imposed by national quotas, and a prejudice against poor regions by those who have to pay.

More scope may exist for an economic management role for the budget. As economic integration develops between member states, in the sense of increased imports and exports, increases capital mobility and the flow of technical ideas, often though corporate integration, abnormal behaviour (higher than average inflation, higher than average unemployment) increasingly spreads into other member-state economies. Floating exchange-rates, which will not exist after monetary union anyway, do not succeed in correcting the situation, and large deficits or surpluses continue to exist in the balances between member states. Adjustment through Community policy instruments could become increasingly necessary.

What instruments would there be? After monetary union, there are no national monetary instruments. The Community may control changes in member-state fiscal instruments, or exercise control through those in the Community budget. A flat-rate VAT is hardly useful for the purpose. Even a rate which can be varied by member states is an instrument mostly abandoned due to its direct effects in increasing prices and leading to increased wage claims. creased wage claims.

The longer-run perspective of the Community budget by no means confirms the present form of VAT as the most suitable Community tax, since it is weak as a redistributive tool, and rather outmoded as a stabilisation instrument.

In conclusion, the problems of the Community budget are more serious on the revenue side. On the expenditure side, the CAP spending should steadily decline, but social, regional, and industrial programmes will be under pressure, given European parliamentary development, to grow at a faster rate than resources released from agricultural support. At the same time, non-tax revenues are likely to weaken. The pressure for increased tax revenue for the Community budget will be great, and as it grows, the budget will be evaluated for its macro-economic impact on the economy.

Concluding Remarks

The VAT was conceived as the Community federal tax in the first five years of the EEC, 1958-63. During this time, the prevailing philosophy, as exemplified in the Treaty of Rome, was to finance state economic activity, such as it was with minimum disturbance to equal competitive conditions for all production units throughout the Common Market. The low priority given to state intervention in the economy was seen in the lack of a Regional Fund in the Rome Treaty, the small Social Fund, prejudice against subsidies, and lack of discussion of macro-economic management. A low percentage flat-rate VAT fitted into this scheme of neutral financing of a non-interventionist budget. The 1963 agreement on the VAT as a harmonised tax, and the associated 1970 settlement on 'own resources' were taken by and for the founding Six. Even those states have substantially changed, for example, in the relative size of their own public sectors. They have been joined by the three new members, one of whom, the UK, had the greatest modern tradition of macro-economic management by fiscal means. Now several further states are on the brink of membership, Greece, Portugal, Spain, and eventually Turkey. Is the VAT, indeed the whole 'own resources' system, still going to be appropriate in the new circumstances?

There will be no shortage of expenditure projects in an enlarged Community, as regional and industrial problems proliferate in new Member-states. But to finance these, the present VAT seems an inept means from the point of view of both equity and efficiency. Greece is about to institute a VAT, but the problems can be well imagined. Any harmonisation of base or rates is likely to remain inequitable due to the enormous difficulties of an even tax administration throughout all nine or even thirteen member states. And the tax is, as explained above, inefficient as a macro-economic management instrument.

What improvements might be made? The situation would be improved initially by drawing the harmonised tax on a much narrower base. If the retail sector were excluded, as indeed it was in the original Neumark proposals, and all businesses up to some 25 employees, the UK, Belgium and the Netherlands would immediately get most of their exemptions without impugning the original concept of a uniform Community tax. The never accounted-for cost of VAT to the private sector would be drastically reduced. The prospective member states would find it much easier to introduce the VAT. The concept of a single rate could and should be restored. This would provide a more economical and a more equitable Community VAT. It may even provide a vehicle for macro-economic management, by use of temporary surcharges on the basic Community rate, since its impact on retail prices, and on food in particular, would be much less direct. If not, a supplementary Community tax should be sought, for example a payroll tax for direct instrumental use rather than as a major source of revenue.

The Community will need substantial tax revenues in the future, and new and revised forms of tax from the present conception of VAT, are required to raise this in an economical, equitable and efficient way.

9 Industrial Policy for a Federal Europe

GEOFFREY DENTON

A small, overcrowded peninsula on the edge of Asia can hardly survive, let alone increase or even maintain the standards of material well-being now enjoyed by its people, if it cannot create and maintain an efficient and competitive industrial structure. Over the three decades since the second world war the industrial performance of western Europe has been formidable. But the success was not shared by all the countries, there has been much soul-searching about what constituted a sound national industrial policy, and almost complete failure to create a common industrial policy for the European Community. Moreover, the world climate has in the last few years become much harsher, and the need for effective national and Community industrial policies has become both more urgent and at the same time more difficult than ever before. To discuss the political and institutional structures and the social and external policies of an emerging federal Europe without examining its industrial policy would therefore be an empty endeavour.

All the countries of western Europe have had industrial policies, in the sense that all have employed a range of fiscal, monetary, environmental, trade, regional, social and educational policies, all of which were intended, among other purposes, to contribute to the successful development of industry. But 'an industrial policy' means not so much an array of policies affecting industry, as an industrial strategy, a clear long-term view of what should be the structures of industry, how they should be adapted in the light of already apparent needs and made flexible in the face of future requirements. Such an industrial strategy clearly has many components, including policies for the internal structures of individual sectors, for encouraging the development of science and technology, for the regional distribution of industry, and for manpower and employment. But the central issue, on which this discussion will be focussed, is the sectoral structure of industry. Which industries have a long-term future in Western Europe? Which industries have good prospects for growth and should be developed rapidly? Which have no prospects of survival, and should be phased out? The central question then is the strategy for developing new competitive industries, and running down older uncompetitive industries.

Since much of industry is owned and controlled by private interests, subject only to certain overall regulation by company law, etc., and since even publicly owned industry is deliberately given a good deal of freedom to make its own decisions within fairly loose overall guidelines, industrial policy implies operating in the area of relations between government and industry.

Two views have become polarised in much of the discussion of these relations: the first, a negative or market-oreinted view, is that government should on the whole leave industry alone to get on with the job. The second, positive or interventionist view is that government needs to involve itself directly in many aspects of industrial decisions, and to operate a wide range of powers, incentives and interventions. National industrial policies have differed widely among the members of the Community, and have evolved considerably in the different countries over time, in response to the wide variety of institutions, historical experiences, attitudes, political differences, etc., and it has never been possible to categorise each national industrial policy clearly as falling into either the 'liberal' or the 'dirigiste' camp. For example, to categorise German industrial policy simply as 'liberal' is to ignore the structures of industrial financing through the large banks, which coordinate industrial structures that otherwise might have had to be coordinated by government intervention. In France, though attention has been concentrated for many years on the planning system, as a tightly organised structure for decision-making on industrial policies, the reality has been rather that close links, educational, professional and social, between leaders in industry, the civil service and government, enabled a large degree of cohesion to be achieved. In Italy large state-owned holding companies, a form of public enterprise quite unlike national-ised industries in the UK, played a large part in developing the industrial structure, but alongside a vigorous development of independent firms that responded to opportunities in a flexible way. In the UK, there has been considerable confusion about industrial policy, and a failure to achieve a satisfactory basis for industrial strategy, arising out of the isolation of the financial community, the low regard in which industry is held in educational, professional and political circles, and a sterile controversy about the use of state intervention versus private enterprise.

So far as the European Community is concerned, given the wide disparity in methods and achievements of the national states, and the jealous guarding of national prerogatives to make policy, which applied to the industrial as much as to other fields of economic policies, there has been much talk but little action. Consideration of what a European industrial policy might look like began with the second Medium-term Policy Programme in 1968. This examined certain sectors of industry, both declining and with potential for development, and commented on their prospects, the policies that would be needed for orderly run-down or for exploiting opportunities for expansion, and on the contribution that common policies could make. The Colonna Memorandum in 1970 carried further and deeper the analysis of Community industrial problems and policies, and set out in more detail a programme for the Community itself. This consisted in the establishment of common actions in certain key areas for industrial development, where the individual member states on their own were less likely to succeed. An important motivation for these discussions was the comparison of European with US industry, as examined, for example, by J. J. Servan-Schreiber in 'Le Défi Amèricain'.

However, given the overall prosperity, rapid growth, relatively stable prices and full employment of the 1950s and 1960s, there did not seem to be a great urgency in most countries to improve their industrial policies, though the UK was an exception because its industrial performance compared relatively badly not only with the US but with the other European countries. Though particular sectors, both declining and with potential for expansion, seemed capable of benefitting from common EEC policies, there also seemed no great urgency to develop Community policy, and given the nationalistic inhibitions about doing so it is not surprising that very little happened.

The Impact of the Economic Crisis

The situation has now been changed radically. This has happened partly because the world economic crisis has brought about a realisation of important structural changes that were already going on in the 1960s but were not at that time fully realised. But the economic events of the 1970s have also really made the industrial position of western Europe more insecure. Certainly, the comforting thesis, common among many economists in the early months after the 'oil crisis' and in the first part of the recession in 1974, that the problems were basically cyclical and the world economy would return to the previous pattern after a period of adjustment or 'shake-out' has now been universally abandoned.

Technological trends that were raising labour productivity fast and making it harder to maintain full employment were evident in many European industries from at least the late 1960s. For example, the Sixth Plan in France was formally rejected by the trade unions in 1970, because though growth would be maintained at a high rate, jobs would not be created fast enough to maintain full employment in 1971-5. Competition from developing countries and other new entrants in markets for industrial goods were already threatening jobs in some European industries long before 1973. The Club of Rome produced its controversial projections in 1972 and was rightly criticised for the misleading, even alarmist, results of some of them. But the changing trends in the supply of and demand for oil and other materials were already obvious (for example, the switch from a surplus of production to a surplus of consumption in the US, the growing dependence of western Europe on imported oil, and the concentration of oil producers in the Middle Eastern Arab countries). Monetary instability began to plague western Europe already in the late 1960s. The oil cartel already existed, in a rather ineffective form, from 1960; the organisational basis for the oil crisis was already prepared. The growth of world population and the failure of food supplies to grow rapidly enough to match this growth, at least in years when bad harvests in several parts of the world coincided, was also causing concern well before 1973. Pressure of industrial activity on the environment, also, did not begin suddenly in the mid 1970s, but was already apparent long before. So was the 'alienation' of many workers in European industry in the midst of their new-found prosperity.

The European economy and industry will therefore need substantial restructuring before recovery from the crisis of the mid 1970s is complete. Some necessary structural changes have been made, but many remain to be implemented. Structural changes in the world economy are still proceeding, and the crisis of 1974-76 has ushered in a period of adaptation whose magnitude may still be greater than it is at present possible to foresee. It is necessary to take stock of the process of adaptation to assess how much has already been done; to note where adaptation appears to be inadequate; and to define the further changes that will be needed over coming years until the adjustment is more or less complete.

Divergence of the National Economies

The European national economies reacted in divergent ways in the face of the crisis. Their basic economic structures, resource availability, industrial structures, institutional patterns and behaviour were different. The impact of the oil crisis and other shocks from outside varied, depending on their levels of dependence on imports. Policies in reaction to the crisis were subject to different degrees of flexibility and room for manoeuvre.

In most countries the initial phase of the oil crisis was met by a variety of methods of reducing the consumption of oil. As it became apparent that the problem was one of price, not supply, these restrictions gradually faded, though some vestiges remain and useful economies have been made. But the real reductions in oil consumption, and they have been significant, came about as the recession reduced demand from industry and consumers. The price problem was in general met by borrowing, 'recycling' the oil revenues as it came to be called, pending an increase in the absorption of imports by the newly rich oil-producing countries. It was generally perceived that to insist in the short-term on balancing external payments would be to make the recession much more severe, so national payments accounts began to distinguish the oil from the non-oil balance.

Resources, or potential resources, available within the EEC countries caused considerable differences in the payments experiences of different countries. Germany's efficient manufacturing industry continued to produce massive surpluses on non-oil account, which offset the oil deficit. Some countries had larger indigenous energy sources, such as the natural gas in the Netherlands. The UK, less dependent on oil imports owing to its large coal industry, was also able to borrow against expectations of future oil production from the North Sea. While the exploitation of this oil was costly in terms of investment requirements, and brought no immediate relief to the enormous oil deficit superimposed on an already sizeable non-oil deficit, at least the financing problem was eased since the prospects of import-saving, and even of oil export revenues a few years ahead, made the UK more creditworthy. The situation of a country like Italy, with no major existing or prospective indigenous energy supplies to relieve its dependence on imports, was much worse. The position of France, with its considerable natural resources, especially in agricultural production, was never so serious as those of the UK and of Italy.

The development of the crisis was very different in the European countries, reflecting not only these differences in vulnerability to the oil price increases, but different economic structures and policy. In Germany, inflation never rose above about 7 per cent per annum; in the UK it went above 20 per cent. These countries also diverged sharply in the experience of the recovery phase.

111

While inflation in Germany was brought down below 4 per cent, in Britain it is persisting above 15 per cent. Not only did the recession widen dramatically the differences between the best and the worst managed economies, it also left a residue of wider divergences in this respect than existed before 1973. The task of integration and monetary cooperation in Europe has therefore been made more difficult.

The European countries have not brought about the necessary structural change, and have indeed not even succeeded entirely in stabilising their economies. Inflation and unemployment, and payments deficits, remain in most EEC countries at unacceptable levels. So do public sector deficits. Not only have the member countries failed to achieve either adequate structural change or stability, but there are few signs that public authorities are sufficiently in control of the situation to be able to implement a meaningful policy to resolve their numerous economic and social problems. Many adaptations have, of course, taken place in response to price changes and other economic indicators, where these have been allowed to function; but all too often governments cannot accept the social or political consequences of such adaptations, and intervene to prevent, rather than to encourage them. Overall, the European economies have become more rigid, less responsive to the need for change, as the necessity of change has become more pressing. Expectations of economic growth may have moderated since 1970, but expectations in other areas have not. Especially in respect of job security, social benefits, and education, expectations are higher than the capacity of any government to perform.

The society that emerges when what now seems likely to be a long-drawn-out process of adaptation is finally over, may be more balanced, have a better pattern of demand, and a greater appreciation of the quality of life, than the consumer society of the 1950s and 1960s. There are many positive aspects of the adjustment that will take place. But the prospectus for change still facing the EEC countries is alarming in its sheer scope, and in the possibilities of renewed instability and deeper social crisis that could arise before it is fully implemented.

The Rise of Structural Unemployment

Throughout the European Community one of the most worrying aspects of the crisis was the rise in unemployment to levels not experienced since the 1930s. It was accepted that the post-war period was one in which inflation was endemic, but it was assumed that at least the forces making for continuous growth and the new policies of economic management would ensure that the economic downswings would be recessions, not depressions. The crisis shattered that illusion. In most of the EEC countries the worst appeared to be over by mid-1976. The rise in unemployment had slowed down and even begun to fall in some countries.

However, despite plans and expectations of a resumption of rapid growth, unemployment is expected to persist at high levels through the 1970s and into the 1980s in all member countries. There are numerous reasons for this. Rigidities in the labour market, the failure to educate and train new recruits to industry in the skills that industry needs, are an important cause of persistent unemployment in addition to the macro-economic forces. Technology is advancing so fast that output can grow rapidly in many industries without the need for increasing labour supply. Indeed, in many industries there are plans to reduce manpower substantially. Competition in world markets of manufactured exports from developing countries is more severe, with pressure in many industries, especially the more labour-intensive, from motors to footwear, electronics to plastics, from Japan, Taiwan, Brazil, Eastern Europe, Southern Europe.

At the same time that unemployment has become so much more serious a problem for the European countries, it is becoming in most of them also a more sensitive political issue. The prolonged period of prosperity raised expectations, and shifted attitudes towards job security. Many industries, under pressure from trade unions, have already been providing jobs for more workers than they know what to do with. Governments, impressed by the social and financial costs (in terms of social security benefits) of unemployment, have intervened to subsidise jobs through industrial and regional aids and direct subsidies to employment. Firms that get into financial difficulties are rescued, with the result of further burdens on public expenditure, because governments cannot accept the political consequence of major redundancies. If governments are reluctant to intervene, workers occupy the factories. These are natural responses to a problem that has become more acute and raises powerful political and social emotions. But the danger in this type of response is that it undermines the economic incentives and disciplines on which the largely market economies of western Europe have so far relied.

Many anomalies already exist in labour markets, and more will be created by some of the current policies of alleviating symptoms. Youth unemployment has become massive and socially destructive. It is closely related to the job security offered to older workers. In a free labour market, there would be more redundancies of old workers, and less unemployment among the young. It is therefore urgent to find other ways of dealing with the difficulties for older workers, so as to avoid this re-shuffling of unemployment from one category to another. Does retirement have to stay around 60 or even 65? Do hours of work have to be fixed around 40 hours per week? If both income and the opportunity to work are to be shared more equitably, but at the same time with some respect for efficiency, it will be necessary to develop more fundamental changes in working practices and in remuneration than have so far been considered.

It should be borne in mind always that these are problems of affluent societies. The capacity to produce so much with so little labour should not really be a problem, but an opportunity. But the 'work ethic', and the sheer immobility of the structures through which work is organised, appears to be preventing Europeans from seizing the opportunity.

Unless more imaginative solutions to the unemployment problem can be found, it will put such strains on the political and social fabric that many other issues will become harder to handle. In particular, there is an intimate connection between unemployment and inflation. It is by now very apparent in the UK, and in other countries, that the public expenditure deficit must be brought under control as an urgent priority. There are also worries that taxation has finally reached such levels as to be a major disincentive to effort and investment. The combination of high penalties reducing the rewards from work, with fairly generous benefits to a large proportion of the population for not working, make it extremely difficult to control the public sector deficit and therefore to stabilise prices.

In the context of structural unemployment, there are many dangers to liberal trading arrangements, as European producers put pressure on their governments to impose import quotas, negotiate voluntary export limitations, or take other measures to curtail the flood of imports. Such policies, the pressure for which could become irresistible, would undermine many of the external policies of the European nations and of the Community. To continue to aid the industrial development of the poorer countries, while refusing to allow European consumers to benefit from buying the products of their new industries, would seem a particularly sick joke. Such a policy would also conflict with that of accepting the enlargement of the EEC to the South, by admitting Greece, Spain, Portugal, and later even Turkey. Tariff free access for their industrial goods to the markets of existing Community members must imply acceptance of the implications for employment in the relevant industries. In the labour market, any policy of cutting off the inflow of migrant workers from Southern Europe would be a serious blow to these economies, removing their best chance of relieving their own high levels of unemployment and under-employment and the payments problems they must face during their industrialisation process.[1]

An Industrial Strategy?

In the face of trends that are already creating major redundancies of labour and idle machines in factories, it appears necessary to continue and to strengthen polices for the orderly reduction of the human and physical assets engaged in some industries, and to ease their transfer into other industries enjoying greater comparative advantage. How much direct intervention will be needed is a matter for detailed investigation and decision in each sector. But these interventions require that a clear long-term picture should be established of the potentially viable industrial structures given the trends in trade and technology, so that both government and those involved in industry can take the decisions about investment, education and training, commercial policy, etc. in the light of a coherent industrial strategy.

This strategy cannot be easy to establish. The method of the 'industrial strategy' exercise presently under way in the National Economic Development Office appears unlikely to be adequate. It consists of examining with each industry what it considers to be the future prospects, where investment should be concentrated and where resources should be withdrawn. But this method of planning allows too much scope for defensive responses by existing firms, too much clinging to established structures. These exercises therefore smack far too much of making out cases for government assistance, rather than

---

[1] *These problems of external policy of the Community have been examined at greater length by John Pinder in* A Federal Community in an Ungoverned World Economy (*Chapter 17, below*).

defining in as objective a manner as possible what structures will be viable and only later passing to the question of what policies should be used for bringing about what has been mapped out. In other words, it is not easy to devise a sensible strategy in the midst of pressures to intervene on behalf of this or the other vested interest. The industrial strategy needs therefore to be worked out in a more independent way, and thereafter used as a basis for particular decisions. But it will also be essential to recognise the limits to the value of this kind of exercise. One reason for the present disarray of governments with respect to industrial policy is that they find it so difficult to predict the speed and the magnitude of the changes in world production and trading patterns. With the best will and the best planning in the world, it is not going to be easy to forecast changing structures of world production and trade and shifting comparative advantage accurately enough to enable industry to adapt smoothly and swiftly. Exercises carried out by economists in attempts to predict the impact on employment in European countries of competition from imports, especially from developing countries, are based on extrapolations of past trends in world trade, and face the usual uncertainty as to how rapidly these trends may change. Certainly the predicted loss of jobs from import competition in the 1980s, assuming existing commercial policies, is much higher than it was in the 1960s. But it is not clear how fast the loss of jobs will be, again assuming present policies, in each industrial sector. Policy changes that might slow down the adaptations are also hard to predict. In any case the loss of jobs through technological change appears to have been faster than through import competition.

If it is difficult through an industrial planning exercise to work out a convincing long-term strategy, it seems impossible to ensure that a meaningful industrial policy package can emerge from the political and administrative system. The pressure on governments from workers, unions and private capitalists alike is for the negative, defensive retention of existing structures and not for the promotion of the industries that have the best long-term prospects. Immense efforts go into the elaboration of justifications for subsidies, protection or other forms of intervention, on the grounds of orderly run-down of plant and labour force, as for example in textiles, or of the social importance of the industry, as for example in agriculture and railways. The aid given to individual industries tends to be given, for similar reasons, to the firms that are least efficient, have the poorest prospects, are on the verge of bankruptcy, rather than to the firms that have prospects of future successful operation. Within the UK shipbuilding industry, for example, the bulk of the subsidies have been concentrated on three firms that have teetered on the verge of bankruptcy for years, while firms with a more successful record and better prospects have been left with only minimal aid. Whatever the intentions of legislation to promote investment, for example, it is exceedingly difficult in administrative practice to prevent subsidies being used to cover operating costs in the short term, so that they make little or no contribution to the longer-term viability of firms. Moreover, it must always be borne in mind that if some industries and some firms are aided, other firms and industries are being burdened, directly through taxation of their profits, or indirectly through the loading of their costs. Given the uncertainties, the difficulty of devising and

115

implementing a satisfactory policy, and the awkward problem of assessing what has been the overall result of an interventionist policy, economists often conclude that the best policy for the governments to pursue would be one that minimised specific interventions, and emphasised the creation of an economic environment in which individual firms will adapt successfully to changing economic trends.

A New Approach to Industrial Policy

The environment within which industry operates must certainly be restored and maintained so as to provide the incentives and sanctions which will bring the right flexible responses from both private and public industry. This must be in part a matter of dealing more successfully than in the recent past with questions such as the rate of return on investments, and levels of taxation, both on companies and on the incomes of skilled workers, executives and professional people. This will have implications for other policies, such as social expenditure financed out of the revenues raised from industry. There is no way of avoiding this kind of choice; if encouragement of industry is to be given priority, other forms of expenditure must be down-graded, at least for some time.

In addition it will be necessary to take new measures to make and keep the industrial system more flexible. This must be partly a matter of dismantling some of the structures that have been causing increasing rigidity, and partly a matter of deliberately introducing policies that will facilitate flexible response to changing trends in world production and trade and technological progress. With demands on all sides for security, which usually take forms synonymous with rigidity, and the large scale of the transfers of resources that will be needed, it is unlikely that an environmental policy of the traditional kind could make industry flexible enough. It is all very well to talk in theoretical terms about flexible labour markets, but it must be remembered that what that means is more uncertainty for workers at all levels, and this is what, in our affluent society, they are not willing to accept. But in many ways the natural human aversion to excessive disruption of established locations of job and home is reinforced by artificial constraints on mobility. One example, of great importance in the UK, though not so much in other European countries, is the method of allocation and financing of local authority housing, which has produced for half the population an enormous financial penalty on moving house, and therefore, in many cases, on finding a new job.

A third and newer part of the new industrial policy must therefore be a more fundamental restructuring of our institutions and attitudes to combine greater security of employment with greater flexibility in the response to change, while maintaining economic incentives. This will be no easy task, but it is essential to start to consider what it might consist in. What is so tragic at the moment is that no substantial consideration has been given to anything beyond the conventional solutions.

Naturally, given the very different economic structures and performances of the Members of the European Community, it is not possible to generalise about the policies. The emphases would have to vary depending on the different situations and needs. For example, the UK is probably an over-populated

116

country while France, with twice the land area and a smaller population, is still in some respects a developing country. Or again, while the UK has suffered in recent years a process that has been described as 'de-industrialisation', West German industry, measured in terms of the proportion of the working population employed in industry, continued to expand up to the early 1970s. Policies must be tailored to meet the specific needs of each country. Nevertheless, the earlier comments about industrial strategy and environmental policy have a broad application in all countries, though the gaps between the existing and the desired situation are greater in some countries than in others.

Why a Common European Policy?

If these are the tasks of a new industrial policy, and if policies must be tailored to the needs of each country, what is the role of the European Community? Why can we not rely on a set of national policies to bring about the transformations of industry that are called for? There are a number of important reasons why the policies must have a Community dimension and not be merely national.

First, if the policies are purely national they will inevitably take forms that could disrupt and even destroy the common market. National governments, unconstrained by operating within a common framework, would resort to competitive subsidisation, nationalistic public-procurement policies, even direct barriers to trade. So far the existing rules have held reasonably well, and trade free of tariffs, and with at least a modicum of control over non-tariff distortions, has been maintained. But at present western Europe is only in the early phase of realising how profound are the changes that have taken place, and how drastic the further adaptations that will be needed. The persistence of unemployment at present levels into the 1980s would subject the existing structures of the Community to a pressure under which they could break. A common approach to industrial policy, in which measures would be taken together, and any unequal burdens of adjustment on one country or another shared either through the overall balance of industrial policy, or in the last resort through a larger Community budget, is therefore essential to the survival of the Community.

Another reason why policy must be common and not national is that many of the most important enterprises in European industry are now multinational firms. The industrial policies of individual countries therefore tend to be disrupted and made ineffectual by the mobility of these firms, which can escape from the controls or taxes of one country by shifting their investments and operations to other countries. Many of the problems raised by the multinationals have, of course, already been the subject of discussion in the Community, and in other international organisations.

The need to influence the decisions of the multinationals is all the greater because labour mobility across the national frontiers within the EEC is, and must be expected for many years to remain, rather low. There are many obvious reasons for this, including language and cultural differences, density of populatiom, still unharmonised professional and social institutions, etc. Thus one important adjustment mechanism which could have assisted in the adaptation of industrial structures, and alleviation of unemployment, is not so effective in the EEC as it is, for example, in the US. It will therefore continue to be necessary to operate rather more interventionist regional and labour-market policies, and these must include a degree of influence on the decisions of multinationals.

The EEC has developed policies towards some aspects of the problems, for example providing for more effective mutual cooperation of the national revenue authorities. But many other difficulties arise that already need, and will in future require more and more common policies. It is certainly not possible to operate a common policy for industrial re-structuring without discussion with the large multinationals involved in a particular sector. Shifts in the location of industry within the Community are already in many cases shifts internal to the structure of a multinational, as for example, when Ford, or ICI, locate new investments in Germany rather than in the UK. If there is to be a common policy influencing industrial location, it must also be a common policy towards multinationals.

There are also more positive reasons for a common policy rather than a set of piecemeal national policies, reasons that were already clear in the late 1960s. The essential point is that the scale of operations in many industries, and especially in those that are most open to international competition, is now so large that in many industries it is only by rationalisation on a Community basis that enterprises can be established that will be able to survive, and prosper, in the face of the competition from the US and Japan, and in future from other rapidly developing exporters of manufactured goods. Numerous reports have outlined the detailed evidence in support of this contention, for computers, telecommunications, nuclear power, aircraft, etc., and despite the foundering on the nationalistic attitudes of the governments of virtually all the proposals for common policies, nothing that has happened in the 1970s has reduced the persuasiveness of that case. Concorde may be a ghastly monument to the commercial unrealism of some of the attempts at common industrial development, but the European Airbus is a better example.

To these 'traditional' cases for common action can now be added less technologically advanced industries such as motors and domestic electrical goods. Much of the re-structuring can and should take place as a result of market forces (as, for example, Italian refrigerators took over the markets of other EEC countries in the 1960s). But when there is a defensive reaction at national level that obstructs the necessary redeployment of resources, there is an important role for the Community to help the Member countries to arrive at fairly balanced agreements. It is unlikely that this could mean equity in the distribution of industry as between one country and another in each industrial sector taken separately. The problem of the large scale of efficient plants may require that production at least of some types of some products should cease altogether in some member countries, if a competitive European industrial structure is to be established. Hence the importance of a comprehensive policy covering many sectors, within which it would be easier to devise a package of decisions on industrial re-structuring providing each country with its fair share of the industrial capacity of the Community.

The budget of the Community will undoubtedly have to play a vital part in relation to this industrial policy. It will be necessary to use it to finance some of the actions that will be needed, such as compensation to workers who have to move, or incentives to scrapping of industrial plant. Decisions in the area of industrial policy will also be one component of the overall economic policy of the Community, covering also agriculture, regional policy, etc., within which equitable contributions and any re-distributory financing will have to be worked out. Industrial policy will thus operate within a federal system of economic policy-making and financing.

Beyond these well known arguments for action at Community level, there are new important reasons for a Community policy given the need for more radical transformations of industrial and labour market structures. If we are to transform our industrial society in ways that will increase the amount and the enjoyment of leisure, diminish the alienation of workers from their work, widen participation in the control and ownership of industry, guarantee employment to young people, and provide a healthily smooth transition out of working life into retirement for older people, it will be necessary to overcome one important obstacle which so far inhibits progress, and even discussion, on these issues. This is the fear that such measures will, at least in the short-term, increase unit costs of production, and therefore drive into bankruptcy any firm that tries to lead the way, and into economic collapse any national economy that tries to advance over the whole front faster than other competing countries. The solution to this kind of inhibition is to adopt policies in common for the whole European Community.

It will be objected that while this could, in principle, resolve the difficulty so far as the Community is concerned, it cannot moderate the impact of wider international competition, which is an important cause of the adaptations under discussion. This is indeed correct. But the Community has a common-commercial policy, which can be applied to help create the international frame work within which these policies could be successfully pursued in Europe. This is emphatically not a question of using a blatantly restrictive policy to create a wall of protection against imports behind which the EEC countries could indulge in costly experiments in shorter hours, worker participation, etc. Rather, it is a matter of regulating in some degree the growth of trade so as to avoid the disruption that occurs when particular interests are put under a too sudden pressure to adjust, and thus create a climate in which more basic structures and practices can be altered.

For other countries also have an interest in pursuing these economic transformations. In Japan there is grave concern especially about the natural environment, and energy supplies. In the US the pressure on resources may not be so great, but it exists, and there is an awareness that the US cannot continue to pre-empt so much of the world's scarce energy and materials without serious damage to others and repercussions on its own objectives in foreign policy. So others have an interest in regulating world trade and production in ways similar to those outlined above for the EEC, and a common position by the Community would enable world trading arrangements to be adapted to allow for them. As experience has shown, a common position by the EEC is a pre-requisite for successful negotiations among the industrial countries as a whole.

119

The Tasks of a Common Policy

A new industrial policy for the Community must therefore go a good deal further than the targets, let alone the achievements, of the common policies of the 1960s. Then the common environmental policy consisted in the policing of private cartels and abuse of the position of monopolies, plus attempts to curtail beggar-my-neighbour interventions falling under the category of 'state aids', and measures to open up public procurement for firms in all member countries. Given the deterioration in the economic environment in the 1970s, to continue only with these measures would be inadequate. On the side of interventionist policies, most of the attempts at common programmes for industrial re-structuring have been abortive, while further industries have been added to the list of those for which a common structural policy appears to be essential. Not only are the targets moving further away in these two traditional areas of industrial policy, but further needs have been added in the form of the adaptations to meet the problems of finite resources of energy, materials and natural environment that have become apparent in place of the world of limitless growth that used to be assumed.

To spell out a detailed blueprint for a common industrial policy is beyond the scope of a short paper aimed at opening up discussion about the future of industrial policy in a federal Community. What can be done is to set out the fundamental objectives. They can be enumerated under three broad headings.

First, to release human energies in industry and in the economy as a whole. The economic upheavals of recent years, coming on top of gradual changes that have worn out the positive impulses creating continuous growth in the 1950s and 1960s, have created industrial stagnation and pessimistic expectations in some countries of the Community. This must be overcome by policies, many of which will have to operate at national level, for reviving the incentives to individual effort, raising industrial profits to levels that will again attract investments, and encouraging innovation and initiative throughout the economy. The Community can assist this process, especially by providing, through monetary integration and the coordination of economic policies, a more stable economy within which national governments will be able better to manage their own fiscal and budgetary policies, and firms, large and small, to exploit the potential of the whole Community market.

Secondly, to conserve physical energy while exploring new sources. The problem of physical energy and other resources is one that is still not recognised as urgent. Yet the warning signs are there, and it will certainly become apparent to the governments in the 1980s that they have to devise energy policies more effective than those they have toyed with so far. A Europe that will remain dependent for many decades on importing large proportions of its energy needs will be in a better position to secure its supplies if it can enjoy joint management of its indigenous resources, and a common policy to procure, in negotiation with OPEC and others, its imports.

Thirdly, the European countries must change the nature of growth, emphasising all aspects of the 'quality of life' and abandoning the naive concentration on the growth of the gross national product, as conventionally measured, which has characterised the whole period since the second world war. The increase of leisure, intelligently used; the increase of participation in the control and ownership of industry, and the enrichment of individual satisfactions in work; the improvement of the urban environment; could all increase the gross *social* product even though they may reduce the growth of the material output that enters into the measurement of gross national product with which policy-makers and electorates have been mesmerised for too long. The Community could play a most important part in promoting these kinds of changes in the underlying industrial structure. It has already made proposals in the field of industrial democracy and company structure, which, though not yet adopted by the Council, have had considerable influence in promoting changes in member countries. So far as the labour market is concerned, the Community could have a vital role to play in encouraging solutions to the ludicrous inequity of a society in which some work too hard too long, while others suffer the indignity of being entirely unwanted. The instrument of a Community Directive, which lays down a fairly broad requirement which is then implemented in detailed legislation by all member states within a stipulated time, appears to be well adapted to this kind of policy. Details could differ, in accordance with the many differences in labour market institutions and practices in the different countries, but the overall aim would be established, and the fulfilment by each country of the agreed objective could be checked by established Community procedures. Similar methods could enable the Community to help the national governments and administrations to break loose from established structures and modes of thought in other areas of policy, and a federal Community could thus be a dynamic force in the rebuilding of European industry.

10 The New European Enterprise*

MICHAEL FOGARTY

Europe today is creating a new type of enterprise, a new pattern of industrial relations and management very different from the classic patterns of both capitalism and socialism in the past. What is it? What are its importance and prospects? And what contribution to its emergence can be expected from the European Community? This paper begins by describing the elements of this change, comments on their significance and stage of development, and comes finally to the question of the special contribution of the Community.

The elements of change

Until a few years ago there were in Europe well-established patterns of industrial relations and management. In industrial relations there was the UK and Irish pattern, based on collective bargaining, and in the case of the UK especially on the shop steward. There was the pattern common to the original six EEC countries, centred around the statutory works council, with the trade unions backing and controlling works councils but themselves for the most part bargaining at district, regional, or national level. In particular there was the highly developed German model, with works councils in the form not of joint bodies but of works committees exclusively representing employees, equivalent in British terms to unusually strong shop stewards' committees. Germany also had the unique feature of effective employee representation on company boards: minority representation on the supervisory boards of all companies since 1920, except for the Nazi period, and parity with shareholders in the coal and steel industries since 1951. There was also the intermediate Swedish system, based like that of the UK on collective bargaining, but with far more central control through the national employers' and trade union organisations.

Management for its part retained everywhere a high degree of what has traditionally been known as 'management prerogative'. The central role of the manager in all economies is that of a promoter or entrepreneur. If one looks at company law, or the practice of collective bargaining, or the law and practice

* This paper is based on a lecture originally presented at a Conference of the Irish Association for European Studies, Galway on 15 January 1977.

of contracts between a firm and its customers and suppliers, it is clear that managers are never expected to have the last word on a firm's policies. They are in principle free to do only what owners, whether private or public, or customers, or suppliers, or trade unions and their members acting through collective bargaining or politics, will approve; to say nothing of controls by the Government or pressure groups in matters such as the environment and pollution. The manager's job is to negotiate with all the parties concerned in the enterprise terms profitable enough to persuade them to continue to make their money, work, supplies or legal authority available to the enterprise; and to see that the terms agreed with the various parties are mutually consistent, and that effective action follows from them, so that the enterprise remains viable in the interest of all concerned. But until recently managers could also in practice if not in theory expect to do much more than this. Collective bargaining traditionally covered only a small range of issues about pay and working conditions. Shareholders' control over private firms has often been weak. State control of nationalised industries has sometimes, as the National Economic Development Office has recently shown,[1] been simply chaotic. Legal controls in the interests of consumers and the environment have often been patchy. As a result managers have in the past had, not only their permanent function as promoters and negotiators, but effectively the last word on a wide range of their firms' policies. This is what has traditionally been meant by management prerogative.

These old-established patterns of management and industrial relations might work well or badly. Often, as in Britain and Ireland, they worked a good deal better than the public and the media have given them credit for.[2] But in any case they were there, they existed, and everyone understood them. However, since the 1960s they have been breaking up throughout western Europe, in the course of what for convenience may be called the 'participation revolution'; though that title does not convey the full extent of what is happening. This revolution has five elements.

Job and career control

The first element is the movement for 'do-it-yourself': the rising tide of interest everywhere in greater control by workers at all levels, including managers, over their own jobs and careers and over the distribution of their time between work and the rest of their life.

One aspect of this is the movement to re-design jobs and work groups for greater autonomy. Action on this has originated mainly from social scientists and from certain far-sighted managements or employers' organisations particularly but not only in Scandinavia, interested in such things as work satisfaction, reducing labour turnover, and the long-term development of initiative and adaptability in the work force. Trade unions are now increasingly taking up this movement as well.

---

(1) National Economic Development Office, A Study of UK Nationalised Industries, HMSO 1976.

(2) For Britain see in particular S. Parker, Workplace Industrial Relations 1972 and Workplace Industrial Relations 1973, OPCS for the Department of Employment, HMSO 1974 and 1975. For Ireland B. Hillery, A. Kelly, and A. Marsh, Trade Union Organisation in Ireland, Irish Productivity Centre 1975.

There is also a movement to ensure continuing opportunity in careers, for example through laws against race, or sex, or age discrimination; through establishing in one country after another—France, Germany, Belgium, Sweden, —the right to paid educational leave for mature as well as younger workers; or through new thinking about career opportunities and personal development within organisations, particularly in the case of managers. Initiatives in this area have come not only from the usual parties to industrial relations but from outside pressure groups such as women's organisations.

A third aspect is the new interest in ways of making the margin between working and non-working time more flexible, through such things as flex-time or flexible retirement, backed by pre-retirement counselling. Another, of a more traditional kind but pressed much more strongly by trade unions in the last few years, is the movement to give workers greater security in the jobs which they already hold and to tighten up provisions about dismissals, redundancy payments, and unemployment compensation; and in countries such as Sweden, Germany, Britain and Ireland to overhaul labour market services and to improve arrangements for training and new placements.

The extension of joint control

The second element in the 'participation revolution' is the steady pressure to extend and strengthen joint control over the policies under which work at all levels is done. The strongest and most obvious pressure of this kind comes from trade unions, including white-collar and management unions; but shareholders, environmental or consumer groups, and above all governments, are also getting into the act.

At plant and office level trade union pressure is naturally most important. Different countries choose different routes. The British and Italians prefer collective bargaining. The Germans and the Dutch have strengthened their works councils. The Swedes have simply legislated management prerogative out of existence. But the net result everywhere is, in the terms of a statement to which the Confederation of British Industries signed its name four years ago,[3] that 'literally anything' from the traditional issues of pay and working conditions to the recruitment and deployment of labour and the closure or re-location of plants is becoming a matter for joint decision.

At enterprise level there is the famous question of employee representation on boards. Until recently most trade union movements were at best hesitant about this, and radical and especially Marxist movements, notably in France, continue to prefer an arm's-length relationship through collective bargaining. But in most European trade union movements, since the middle 1960s, the penny has dropped. Many decisions normally taken at board level are very important for workers, and are hard to influence strongly enough or in good time unless from the inside; about long-term investment policy, the location or closing of plants, mergers and takeovers, or major decisions about markets and production policy. One trade union movement after another has accordingly come forward with proposals for board representation, usually on the

---

(3) M. Cobb and K. Graham, *UK National Report to OECD's Regional Joint Seminar on Prospects for Labour-Management Cooperation in the Enterprise, OECD 1972.*

basis of parity with shareholders. Again there are many formulae; representation on supervisory boards, as in Germany, the Netherlands, and now pro-proposed in France;[4] or on single boards, as in Sweden and Ireland and as now proposed by the majority of the Bullock Committee in Britain; with or without the co-option of a neutral third party, as proposed in the Draft Statute for the European Company; representation through company assemblies, as in Norway; standard rules, as in Germany or Holland, or formulae leaving several options open, as in the European Community's draft Fifth Directive on Company Law. Employers, though unenthusiastic about board representation for employees (German employers' enthusiasm for minority representation on supervisory boards, such as they have known and come to appreciate since 1920, is exceptional), are at least in a number of countries learning to accept it.

But it would be a mistake to think of the movement for joint control at enterprise level simply as a matter of relations between shareholders and employees or their unions. In Britain there is a current and much needed debate over the failure of banks, insurance companies, pension funds, and other financial institutions to play a strong enough part in monitoring the efficiency of management. The National Economic Development Organisation's devastating report already referred to has reminded British governments of the need to develop a more coherent policy in their capacity as owners of State enterprises. The Italians are also considering this problem. There has been a movement in several countries towards 'concertation' and planning agreements between governments and large enterprises. And of course there are new pressures from consumer or environmental groups.

At national level the problems of incomes policy, with related issues of taxation, social security, and economic development have given rise in the last few years to a wave of more or less formal social contracts between governments, unions, and employers. Finally, it is important not to forget the part which tripartite arrangements are now playing in the work of the European Community; or the relevance of this to issues such as that of regulating multinational corporations.

The new role of management and government: the collapse of prerogative and the rise of leadership

The two previous developments, and especially the movement for joint control, are in turn bringing about a major change in the role of management. Directors and managers are increasingly made aware that they have responsibilities towards other groups besides owners, and surveys in the United States as well as in Europe show that they increasingly accept them.[5] But it is not simply a matter of responsibility towards or for these interests; managers are also increasingly held *accountable* to the interest-groups behind them. Old-style management prerogative is on its way out. Less and less do managers have the last word on what their organisation's policy is to be, and more and

---

(4)   La Réforme de L'Enterprise *(Sudreau Report), 1975: Union Générale d'Editions, Paris.*

(5)   *S. Webley,* British Businessmen's Behaviour, *Industrial Educational and Research Foundation, 1971, and* British Policy and Business Ethics, *J. of Business Policy, Spring 1973: D. W. Ewing,* Who Wants Corporate Democracy?, *Harvard Business Review, September-October 1971.*

more they are thrown back on what was always their central role as leaders, not dictators; as promoters, entrepreneurs, and above all negotiators who stand in the middle and lead the way in negotiating coherent policies, without having the final power to determine them. The key word for management is ceasing to be prerogative and coming to be social responsibility; or better, social leadership, which brings out the continued need for forceful initiative in managers' role as well as the wider range of the interests they have to take into account.

But of course this is not only happening to management. Governments in advanced democracies are going the same way as well. Stalinist governments in Eastern Europe can and do still dictate economic and industrial policies. That, among other reasons, is why they are so much more effective than Western democracies or a socialist market economy like that of Yugoslavia in enforcing incomes policies. Government direction can also be effective in the simple economies of developing countries. But once an economy is both advanced and democratic, governments increasingly find, in the face of the complexity and interdependence of their economies, and the power of pressure groups, that they, like managers, must be promoters and negotiators, with the force and initiative as well as the breadth of view which this requires, rather than the final arbiters of what is to be done.

The distribution of incomes and wealth

On a rather different wave-length, the participation revolution has led to new thinking about such things as pay differentials, fringe benefits, the social wage, and the ownership of wealth. Incomes policy has been a powerful factor. Rising expectations, relatively full employment, and strong and often unco-ordinated trade union pressure have led in country after country to a tendency for wages and salaries, much more than other incomes, to rise faster than production, so increasing inflation and leading eventually to a situation where expectations of inflation begin to take over. But if any kind of overall restraint is attempted two problems emerge.

Simple and crude restraints interfere with the normal and continuing process of rationalising pay systems and adapting them to new circumstances, and thus reduce economic efficiency.

Subtler forms of control are extraordinarily difficult to devise and operate. Once one ceases simply to leave the labour market to look after itself, there is no clear standard of fairness or efficiency at which to aim. Labour markets and the determination of pay structures operate on the basis not only of market pressures but of customarily accepted assumptions about what pay relationships ought to be. Once people are forced to think about pay structures a whole series of issues and anomalies creep out from under the stones, and spill over into questions about taxation and social expenditure. What level of pay differentials is really needed for efficiency and justice? Would it be true to say that the squeeze of differentials under recent pay policies is consistent with efficiency in the long run, as younger people grow up with it and take it for granted, but needs to be mitigated in the short run because of disgruntlement among older managers or craftsmen who are used to higher differentials? Are existing differences between manual and white collar workers and between the

126

public and private sectors necessary or desirable, or should we aim for single status all round? What is the right relationship between current pay, fringe benefits, and the social wage; especially in the light of how widely this relationship at present differs from one country and occupational group to another?

The prospect of a revolution in ownership, the movement for what the Swedes call economic democracy, also arises. All over Europe the emphasis is moving from the old debate about public versus private ownership to the very different question of the distribution of personal capital, and particularly the more equal distribution of shares and the power as well as the wealth which goes with them. Pressure for action on this is coming from both Right and Left. Trade union movements and their related socialist parties, one after another, German, Danish, Swedish, Dutch, British, have come forward with proposals to transfer to national or regional funds largely under trade union control the title to a proportion either of companies' equity shares or of their re-invested capital, on a scale big enough to give the funds within a generation a substantial minority interest in well established firms, if not full control. Workers would hold certificates in these funds and draw a return on them, but ultimate control of the investments and of the voting rights arising from them would remain with the trade unions. The British Labour Government proposes to legislate for 50 per cent trade union participation in the managing bodies of pension funds, which directly or indirectly control perhaps 30 per cent of the quoted shares of British companies.

On the side of employers and of conservative and liberal parties there has always been an interest in profit-sharing plans, employee shareholding, and generally in the idea of a property-owning democracy. Their aim is of course different from that of the trade unions; to enable individuals or small savings and investment groups to acquire capital assets, and therefore a better understanding of investment, profits, and the problems and responsibilities that go with them. But whereas in the past this aim was pursued piecemeal, and on a scale too small to make much difference to the overall pattern of company ownership, today the scale of proposals has changed. In a number of countries the Right as well as the Left is now interested in what amounts to a fundamental change in patterns of ownership. Some employers' organisations, as in Germany, are interested in a massive but still voluntary extension of workers' ownership through subsidised saving and collective bargaining. But it was a French conservative government in the time of General de Gaulle which set up in 1967 the first nation-wide compulsory capital-sharing plan for companies, and so far the only one actually operating. The British Conservative Party has announced that it is now working on a similar scheme.

The economic backlash

Finally, however, the economic difficulties of the last few years have written a new footnote to all the proposals mentioned so far. Proposals for participation have always been recommended as likely to increase economic efficiency as well as to contribute to work satisfaction and a sense of fairness and social justice. The events of the last few years have underlined that these proposals *must* pass the test of increasing efficiency or at least not diminishing it. This change of accent is particularly obvious in a country like Britain whose relative economic performance has been declining for several decades; the disturbances since 1973 have simply been the final shock which brought it home that this trend must be reversed. But it is not confined to Britain. American managers still treat participation proposals with respect, but are also insisting much more strongly than a few years ago on the question of their economic payoff.

These are the five elements of change in European industrial relations and management, defined as the 'participation revolution'. What are we to say of them?

A system change: Europe's new type of enterprise

When de Tocqueville wrote his history of the *Ancien Régime* in France, he read through the endless series of *cahiers* of complaints submitted to the States-General from all over the country in the last days before the Revolution. He records how when he completed this task he realised 'with a certain terror' that when taken all together, and without most of those who submitted them having intended anything of the kind, what the *cahiers* amounted to was no less than a proposal for the demolition of the entire established order. The developments and proposals which make up what has been called the participation revolution are a matter of building on and developing the established order rather then demolishing it. Yet in several ways the analogy with what de Tocqueville found is a good one. What these developments and proposals amount to, taken together, can quite fairly be described as a revolution in the enterprise, a revolution which has crept up on us piecemeal, without most of those who put forward proposals or initiated changes in particular fields having any clear picture in their minds of what the total result was likely to be. Capitalists and socialists, trade unionists and employers, hard-headed technologists and business men, and humanists interested in social justice or work satisfaction have all made their contribution. But the new type of enterprise which Europe is in the process of forging is most unlikely, once all their contributions have been taken into account and current trends have been pushed to their conclusion, to resemble either the Western capitalist or the East European socialist enterprises of the past, or even the newer model of market socialism practised in Yugoslavia.

It will not be a classic capitalist enterprise. The role of management will be altered, from old-style management prerogative and responsibility essentially to shareholders, to social responsibility and leadership in a framework of joint control. The ownership pattern will be different; working people or their representatives, not only a limited class of shareholders, will sit on the owners' side of the table. The role of workers will be different. The work-force will increasingly be part of a firm's overhead rather than an easily disposable element of marginal cost; remunerated on the basis of 'single status' for manual and 'white-collar' workers rather than of class; with a new accent on adapting work and training to use workers' initiative, give scope for their careers, and permit the easy dovetailing of work with non-working life, rather than on forcing workers into a pre-determined framework of jobs, careers, and hours.

Neither will the new European enterprise be socialist in the forms so far experienced. It will certainly not be a State capitalist enterprise such as has been usual both in nationalised industries in the West and in the socialist economies of most of Eastern Europe. What has been said about the changing role of workers in the private sector applies equally to State or semi-state enterprises. Managers in the public as in the private sector are losing and will continue to lose their old-style management prerogative. More and more they too have to lead from within a framework of responsibility towards many groups and of joint control. The role of government both in relation to enterprises and in the economy generally is coming to be different from what classic socialist practice has assumed, a matter of bargaining and concertation rather than that of direction. For example, interesting proposals for policy councils for State enterprises were put forward in the National Economic Development Organisation's report on nationalised industries in Britain. With reservations for the case of wars and other catastrophes, Europe will continue to have a mixed economy relying strongly on the market, rather than one which is centrally planned on the classic model of the Soviet Union. This is partly because a market economy is the most effective way of managing an advanced and complex industrial society, as the socialist countries of Eastern Europe have been finding out. But it is also because it is only in a market economy that participation can be fully effective; only in market conditions can management, unions, and ordinary workers have the autonomy and the final responsibility for their own destiny which the participation revolution requires.

A socialist market economy can, of course, exist with autonomous enterprises, as in Yugoslavia. But the indications so far are that the new European enterprise, though the ownership of its capital will be more 'socially' distributed than now, will still not be a Yugoslav-type co-operative. There are signs in some countries, including Britain, that the number of worker-controlled co-operatives may increase. But there is as yet no sufficiently widespread movement in that direction to suggest that co-operatives will set the tone of European economies in the foreseeable future. Shareholders will remain, though in a new guise, and may well be more active and effective as a pressure group on management and speak with greater authority, thanks to a more popular distribution of ownership, than has been usual in large firms up to now.

This will be true whether the ownership revolution takes the centralised, union-controlled form so many trade union movements are pressing for, or the more de-centralised pattern preferred by employers' organisations and the political Centre and Right. It is probably also desirable. *Some* co-operatives have a useful part to play in a market economy both in providing opportunities for participation, and as alternative channels of competition and enterprise. But Yugoslav experience suggests that in a predominantly co-operative economy investment may become too exclusively concerned with improving the position of the workers who are already inside each enterprise's magic circle. External finance and external scrutiny of the use of finance by enterprises are needed to ensure that investment is spread and used so as to maximise employment, equalise its conditions, and ensure the best service to consumers.

For three reasons the prospects of achieving the new type of enterprise now developing in Europe are solid and real. First, the trends described here are not a one-off development confined to particular sectors or countries. It is true that countries will continue to choose rather different routes and put the emphasis in different places. But the trends are general right across Europe, and countries are learning from each other all the time. One of the important achievements of the European Community has been to promote these developments.

Secondly, these trends are not one-sided nor, so to speak, class-based. There is something in them for everyone. Employers and managers prefer to emphasise 'do-it-yourself', and especially direct participation through job re-design and the re-structuring of work groups; a dispersed rather than a concentrated pattern for re-distribution of ownership; and of course economic efficiency, adequate differentials, and a clear and effective role for managers. Unions are more interested in joint control, equality, and new patterns of ownership which strengthen union power. There are deep suspicions on both sides, which will have to be overcome. But the pressures for the new trends have come from all directions, and from outside industry as well as from within it. It is clear that there is a growing degree of consensus at least on the questions which are important, the general direction which development needs to take, and therefore on the framework in which differences have to be argued out.

Thirdly, what is happening in the enterprise is not isolated from what is happening in the rest of society; it is simply one example of trends which are visible in many other places as well. 'Pressure-group democracy' or the 'bargaining society' are not only or even primarily a matter of joint control-in industry or of what is happening to the relation between governments, firms and trade unions. These phrases refer to a general change which runs right through the political and social system. The movement towards more autonomy and initiative for individuals, 'do-it-yourself', is not confined to industrial relations. It shows itself equally in consumption and leisure activities, in education, and even in sex roles and relationships in the family. The significant point about the change in sex roles is not simply that old stereotypes have broken down; rather, that what has replaced them is not any single stereotype but a whole range of socially acceptable relationships between which individuals and couples have to choose. The movement for 'economic democracy' in the ownership of company capital runs parallel to, for example, the owner-occupation revolution in urban housing in the UK. New thinking about differentials, fringe benefits and 'single status' reflects a concern for equity and equality which runs right through social policy.

Unfinished business

But it is devastatingly clear that all this is unfinished business, and business which is unlikely to be finished for a very long time. It is clear that there is still an immense amount of work to be done before definitive policies can be agreed, in any of the areas discussed.

On the 'do-it-yourself' side of industrial relations there are now many interesting experiments and new beginnings, from the five hundred examples of work re-structuring in a recent report by the Swedish Employers' Federation[6] to British legislation against race or sex discrimination, or the general

(6)   Summary in European Industrial Relations Review, September 1975.

130

movement now developing towards flexible retirement. But naming measures such as these shows how patchy and unfinished the performance of European countries in these areas has been.

On joint control and the role of management an endless series of arguments has still to be worked through. An obvious example is the history of the European Community's Draft Fifth Directive on Company Law, dealing with employee representation on company boards. In its original form the Draft Fifth Directive of 1972 offered a simple choice; representation on the established German or Dutch patterns, or, if employees so chose, no board representation at all. The more recent Community Green Paper on *Employee Participation and Company Structures* in 1975 had on the contrary to accept that because of differences in national traditions and current interests, and not least, of divisions in the trade unions, no single or simple pattern of representation will be acceptable for many years to come, and the way must therefore be left open for countries and enterprises to experiment in their own way. In Britain the Bullock Committee's debate on board representation highlights not only the divisions which remain but the fact that many of the opinions presented to the committee had simply not been thought through. For example, on the question of single or two-tier boards the TUC and the employers' representatives on the Committee ended by supporting precisely the opposite views from those from which the TUC and CBI respectively had originally stated.

The role of management in the new type of enterprise is clearly understood in some countries but not in others; well in Germany, less well in Britain. German company law says clearly, in the words of the Companies Act of 1965, that the managing directors (usually, in a large German company, a group and not an individual) 'shall lead the company on their own responsibility'; for top executive managers, and only they, stand sufficiently close to and in the centre of all the business of a firm to provide leadership of the kind which is required. In providing it they must come to terms not only with customers but with owners, workers, and unions. They must account for their stewardship to their supervisory boards and may if they fail in it to be dismissed by them. But German law is clear that they and they alone have the right and duty to decide how to go about providing leadership and to act accordingly. They cannot shuffle off this responsibility on to others or shelter behind superior orders, for the supervisory board has no legal right to give them any. British company law recognises that this is the right relationship as between the board of directors and the shareholders' meeting, but corresponding recognition of the full and independent role of the managing director or directors, as in effect a third organ of the company alongside the full board and the shareholders' meeting, has emerged only slowly. Recent British proposals on industrial democracy still show strong traces of the original concept of the chief executive as the servant of the board; not a managing director but a general manager carrying out 'day-to-day management'.

There is also the question of the collective representation of managers at board or other levels. There has been a particularly fierce debate in Germany about their right, in their capacity as employees, to a seat on the employees' side of supervisory boards, which has in fact been granted to them under the Co-Determination Law of 1976. The debate rested on the assumption, by both

131

employers' organisations and trade unions, that a management representative could be expected to act on the board as in effect the shareholders' or the chief executives' man. Employers, therefore, tended to like the idea of management representation and unions to oppose it. But in fact the basic assumption of both sides was wrong. There is evidence from Germany itself[7] that managers acting in their collective capacity are neither the bosses' nor the trade unions' men but a separate group with distinctive interests of their own. Managers are not only a group with distinctive interests but also one with a distinctive point of view, a capacity from their place in the middle for seeing and judging what goes on at both the top and the bottom of the enterprise, and so one which can make a major contribution to any system of participation and which no other group's contribution can replace.[8]

Trade unions' role

Clarity about the role of the trade unions is also often lacking. British trade unions have saddled themselves with a quite unnecessary back-lash from public opinion, including, judging from opinion polls, that of a large proportion of their own members, by insisting not merely on the reality of power under systems of joint control or 'economic democracy' but on its canonisation in what many find a highly offensive form; that of denying voting rights to workers, including members of dissident minority unions, who do not carry a recognised union's card. Where unions are even moderately effective, experience shows that they will and do in fact dominate systems of joint control. German workers are free to elect whom they like to works committees, but in fact at the last elections in 1975 filled 81 per cent of the seats with union members; and the unions take all the key posts as works committee chairman and their deputies and as board representatives. These trade unionists in turn are expected to and do work within the terms of national collective agreements to an extent which many British shop-stewards would find startling. It is not a question of sacrificing national union policies to the autonomy of what the Germans call 'factory kings'.

This reality of union control is both inevitable and desirable, for again the experience of all countries shows that without strong union backing what appears to be a system of joint control is liable to be no more than a hollow shell. But it is another thing altogether to deny formally the equivalent in industrial democracy of the right of every citizen to vote, particularly in a case like that of pension funds where it is a question of managing members' own money. Political democracy cannot manage without parties any more than industrial democracy can manage without trade unions; but not even the keenest Labour canvasser would care to face an elector on the doorstep with the proposition that he can enter the polling booth only on production of a paid-up card from a 'recognised' political party.

The question of national union policy and local autonomy, and of how to combine them in systems of representation, is of course real, and far from

(7) H. Hartmann, Managerial Employees—New Participants in Industrial Relations, British J. of Industrial Relations, July 1974.

(8) M. P. Fogarty, The Place of Managers in Industrial Democracy, British J. of Industrial Relations, July 1976.

settled. Regarding the balance of national and internal representation of employees on boards one country alone, Germany, at present operates no fewer than three systems at once for companies in different categories. The majority report of the Bullock Committee shows that in this respect the imagination of industrial constitution-makers is still not exhausted.

How much standardisation of procedures should there be? Tactically, the answer depends on the history and traditions of each country, but even at the level of principles there remains room for dispute. The Germans like standardisation and compulsory arbitration in their machinery for works representation, and make them work well. But not only the British and the Americans think that there is also something to be said for the more loosely structured Anglo-Saxon pattern of plant or enterprise bargaining, and when necessary confrontation. Even German trade unions look with interest at the British shop steward, and the Italians in the last few years have moved far in that direction. What sort of balance is it best to strike?

And so on through the rest of the list. The movement for 'single status' for manual and white-collar workers goes steadily forward across Europe, but still tends to stick at certain points. Standardisation of holiday entitlements or pension rights is one thing; standardisation of payment systems is another. In the case of the ownership revolution, debate is only just getting off the ground, and the state of the debate on differentials, incomes policy, and inflation remains chaotic.

It is also important not to forget the connection between many of these issues about industrial relations and management and some of the problems which have still to be solved about the management of whole economies.

One of these is the question of how to recover full employment and growth and to reconcile them with other requirements such as price stability and a sound balance of payments. There is a real risk in conditions of less than full employment of developing a dual labour market, in which the established employees in established firms benefit in full from the new trends; but for young entrants to the labour market, or the elderly, or married women, or those who need to switch careers in mid-life, the idea of greater career opportunity or freedom for personal development through work becomes a mockery. Arguments about differentials or about the right balance between current pay and pension rights inevitably become bitter when it is a question, not of giving a bigger share of current growth in the national income to one group rather than another, but of cutting back one group to help another because there is no growth to share.

Another of these general problems is what is now called the issue of the 'corporate state'. It is a fact that we have moved far towards pressure-group democracy and a bargaining society, and that governments, like managements, have increasingly to rely not on their prerogative to impose final decisions but on their capacity to lead the way towards effective and coherent policies through consensus within a framework of joint control. But have they in fact the organisation, the authority, and the backing from public understanding and consent which will allow them to do this? Or will it be necessary, in order to escape from an anarchy of pressure-groups, to fall back on the concept common to Mussolini and Lenin of a government which keeps or recovers its dictatorial prerogative, and treats trade unions and other industrial and social organisations not as negotiating partners but as transmission belts to enforce policies which it alone finally determines?

Government by prerogative is in the long run not viable in politically and economically developed societies, but governments in countries such as Britain may not have yet the capacity to govern in a different style. In particular there are immense deficiencies of civic education and discussion, and a great need to work harder at building understanding and agreement on how political and managerial processes today should work, and what contribution people and social organisations of all kinds can make towards this new ideology.

At the moment there exists on these matters only what may be called an agenda, in which people have seen the inadequacy of old concepts, many new ideas and experiments have been laid on the table, but the hard work of turning these into finished, mutually consistent, and generally acceptable policies has still to be done. Decisions take time, and the time required for major social changes such as those in the enterprise discussed here is fairly well established. It tends to take twenty to thirty years for a new set of ideas to make its way fully into public discussion; twenty years, say for the new ideas to register substantially with the public, and thirty to establish them as the accepted base for a new social agenda. A similar length of time, another generation, is needed to convert this agenda into finished or at least semi-finished policies for general application. For the biggest changes of all even two generations may be too short, and the whole process may have to be run through again before a definitive consensus is reached. In the participation revolution and the movement to create a new type of European enterprise the agenda stage has been reached, but it will be at least another twenty to thirty years before the problems now placed on the agenda receive generally accepted answers.

The contribution of the European Community

What, in the light of this discussion, is the contribution to be expected from the European Community?

The first contribution is advertisement. Some people can recognise a revolution only when it marches in with banners, guns, and blood on the streets. But revolutions do not only happen that way, and it is better that they should not. What is happening in Europe, quietly, is a revolution in the structure of enterprises, in the economy, and in the conditions of working life. That is a genuine revolution, and capable if handled rightly of bringing great advantages to workers and managers, consumers, and the community at large. But it is also one whose importance and progress are not obvious to those who see only part of the game. It must be advertised, and with it the fact that Europe is achieving something which others may wish to take up in their turn. Whereas a few years ago those who were looking for the next steps in the development of management and industrial relations in capitalist economies made their pilgrimage to America, and socialists still looked for models in what used to be known as the socialist sixth of the world, today eyes are turned primarily to internal trends in the European Community and its neighbours. The task of developing a new European type of enterprise is not finished, but a change worth working for is on the way.

Secondly, and more important, what the emergence of the new European type of enterprise most needs is understanding. It is not a question of imposing on any one European country the formulae developed in others. But though different countries will continue to follow different paths in the light of their particular problems and histories, what is developing now is a broad similarity of approaches to the next steps in management and industrial relations, based on experience in all our countries together. For this purpose those who are pushing development forward in each country need not only to be aware of what might be relevant in experience elsewhere in Europe but to understand that experience correctly. The different aspects of new developments in the enterprise in Europe need to be put in their right perspective and relation to one another; the stage they have reached and the time-scale of their further development need to be understood; and misunderstandings about what particular measures actually mean have to be removed.

Sometimes removing misunderstandings is a quite simple matter of finding the correct terminology. British trade unionists are liable to interpret German works councils as joint bodies with the employer in the chair, as in Britain, and are accordingly not enthusiastic about them. But the whole atmosphere of discussion changes when it is pointed out that German works councils are actually committees of shop-stewards. Another classic case is the widespread misunderstanding in Britain of what the respective roles of a German supervisory and executive board actually are; which happens, as the debate on the Bullock Committee's proposals is showing, to be a point particularly important for a correct definition of the role of management in future systems of joint control.

It is in this sort of mutual information and clarification, of helping people in all parts of Europe to see issues in their full and correct focus, that the institutions of the European Community have done much of their most useful work.[9] The preparation of directives and regulations on job security and access, or on company law and participation; or of direct European legislation as in the case of the Draft Statute for the European Company, has been a focus for discussion and mutual education even where final agreement has been deferred. The new European Foundation for the Improvement of Living and Working Conditions provides a further focus for the exchange of ideas on participation and, in particular, on job and career control; and one of the direct services which the Community has set out to develop is the exchange of information on developments in collective bargaining. The existence of the Community has led trade unions and employers to come together in European-level federations, the European Trade Union Confederation (ETUC) and, for the employers, the Union des Industries de la Communauté Européenne (UNICE). Joint working by both with the Community and its institutions provides another focus for exchanges. An immediate task is to develop these means of mutual information and discussion more fully under the Community's second Social Action Programme.

---

(9) M. P. Fogarty, Work and Industrial Relations in the European Community, *Chatham House and PEP, 1975.*

11 European Social Policy: the Next Stage

MICHAEL SHANKS

1976 was supposed to be the year of the big 're-think' on social policy for the European Community. In January 1974 the Council of Ministers approved the Community's first-ever social action programme, covering the years 1974–76. In so doing they stipulated that before the end of 1976 the Commission should come up with a fresh set of measures in the social field, broadly understood to cover the period to 1980. Also during 1976 the Commission was committed to preparing proposals for the reform of the European Social Fund, by far its biggest social budgetary item, running at around £300 million a year. By mid-summer 1977 the Commission's very modest proposals for reforming the Social Fund had been discussed by the Council of Ministers, and the Fund's resources further increased. But the Commission had still not formulated its proposals for the next stage of the Social Action Programme, for reasons which remain elusive.

The 1974–76 social action programme was based on three policy objectives: the achievement of full and better employment, improved living and working conditions, and greater participation. Within this broad framework it listed some three dozen measures—some of which, like the proposals for the migrant workers and for greater opportunities for women in the employment field, were themselves 'mini-programmes' grouping together further specific measures. During the first two of its three years most of the largest and most contentious measures in the programme were steered through the Council of Ministers, but in 1976 progress slowed down considerably, and by the end of the year the programme was still not completed. The same period saw a very substantial increase in the size of the Social Fund[1] and a marked extension in its coverage. All in all, therefore, the years 1973–75 can be regarded as relatively successful ones in the social policy of the European Community,

---

[1] *In 1972 the Social Fund budget was around £40 million.*

justifying the description by a distinguished and impartial UK observer as 'the time when the Community not only acquired a wide-ranging social policy but made it visible and felt.'[2]

During 1975, as director-general for social affairs, I set up working groups to consider both the next stage of the social action programme and the possible reform of the Social Fund. By the time I left Brussels in January 1976 a great deal of work had been done in both fields. In view of the ensuing silence from the Commission, it would probably be helpful to set out publicly the principles which in my view (which needless to say in no way commits or implicates any one of my former colleagues) should guide the Commission in considering the next stage of social policy and of the Social Fund. That is what this paper seeks to do.

The first question which arises is of course whether the postulated 'second social action programme, 1976–1980' needs to be radically different from the first. After all, at the end of 1976 there was still a lot of 'unfinished business' from the first programme: follow-up measures in for example the migrants and women's programmes, measures which the Commission proposed for the programme but which the Council refused to include in it at the beginning of 1974, areas in which the Commission's proposals were watered down by the Council, and so on. Do we want, in short, another 'shopping list' of good and useful measures on the lines of the first social action programme, or do we need something radically different—and if so what?

To resolve this question we need to look briefly at the genesis of the first programme, and the circumstances in which it came to birth. The programme in fact represented a compilation and distillation of a series of measures which had been discussed fairly exhaustively over a period of about three years prior to 1974, a period during which the Community was groping for a 'human face', for a programme which would render it more meaningful to the ordinary man and woman in the street, the field and the factory. It was a period when Europe was still enjoying overall full employment and rapid economic growth, but was also experiencing growing dissatisfaction with the fruits of growth and growing resistance to some of its costs. The opening sentences of the social action programme expressed the prevailing mood very clearly: 'Since its inception the European Community has achieved a substantial increase in the rate of economic growth, which has literally transformed the life and face of Europe and brought to the great majority of its people higher living standards and wider horizons. But greater prosperity has not resolved the social problems of the Community, and indeed in some cases it has exacerbated them'. The preamble went on to specify the unequal pattern of economic development and employment, the problems of uneven distribution of income, wealth and participation, the inadequacies of parts of the infrastructure, and the 'social costs' of growth: environmental pollution, growing dependence on migrant

---

[2] *'Work and Industrial Relations in the European Community' by Michael Fogarty (Chatham House P.E.P. May 1975). For other accounts of the social action programme and the thinking behind it, see my Social Priorities in Europe (London Council of Social Service 1973), Social Planning for Europe (BACIE 1974), Inflation and Social Policy (NEW EUROPE Autumn 1974) and Can Europe Reform Itself? (ENCOUNTER May 1976), and my book European Social Policy, Today and Tomorrow (Pergamon, May 1977).*

workers, value-conflicts between industry and society, and so on. And it concluded: 'Unless the process of growth con be put more fully at the service of society, growth itself may become politically unacceptable'.[3]

It was from this analysis that the three broad principles: full and better (in the sense of better-distributed, better-qualified) employment, improved living and working conditions and greater participation, were derived. Nobody could dispute that these remain priorities. For the next social action programme I would want to add only one other: social justice: for reasons given below. But when one comes to look at the detailed measures prescribed under these headings, it is clear that they were chosen on a somewhat pragmatic, one might say opportunistic, basis; broadly speaking, they were the measures on which a reasonable amount of preparatory work had been done, measures for which the Treaty of Rome provided a clear mandate, measures for which it was reasonable to believe political support could be won.

During the ensuing two years the overall situation changed radically. First, the 'political will', which received its strongest expression in the communiqué of the Heads of State and Government of the nine member-States at the end of 1972, evaporated with alarming suddenness, with the removal from the political stage of virtually all the signatories of that communiqué, and more fundamentally with the growing impact of inflation and balance-of-payments problems (and the shrinking of political horizons and the preoccupation with containing public spending which resulted) in every one of the nine member-States. In this climate concern to give the European Community a 'human face' became overlaid at national level with more urgent preoccupations, and there was a growing tendency in the social field to substitute rhetoric for action.

The other major change was of course in the employment situation. As indicated above, the social action programme was launched against a backdrop of full, if patchy, employment, and continued, if unsatisfactorily patterned, economic growth. Both these perspectives changed radically during 1974. By mid-1975 unemployment had become overwhelmingly the most important social preoccupation for Europe, and present indications are that it is likely to remain a major problem at least up to 1980.

Thus the next social action programme will be launched into a very different Europe from the first. I believe therefore that we need to begin with a radical critique of Europe's social needs, and of the contribution which can be made at Community level to their solution. And we must recognise straight away two unpalatable facts.

The first is that the Treaty of Rome, the basic mandate for all the Community institutions, is far from being a 'social' document. Its orientation, it hardly needs stressing, is essentially *laisser-faire*. A social action programme which based itself strictly on the Rome Treaty would be a somewhat eccentric document, and would not be widely seen as addressing itself to the social preoccupations of the late 1970s.

On what would such a programme concentrate? There are two main

---

[3] *'Social Action Programme'* (*Commission of the European Communities Bulletin Supplement 2/74*). *This document lists all the measures in the programme.*

relevant aspects. First, measures which facilitate or ensure the free movement of labour throughout the Community. Second, measures which would
ensure the equalisation of competitive conditions among enterprises in the
Community. The first principle would embrace, for example, questions of
social security for migrant workers, and measures to make the labour
market more 'transparent' (by improving the information flow on job
offers, removing hidden discriminations against job aspirants from other
Community countries, etc.). The second principle is much more wide-
ranging, and indeed represents an open-ended commitment. A large proportion of social costs fall on enterprises, and one could therefore argue that the
equalisation of competitive conditions requires the harmonisation of all social
benefits and conditions of employment throughout the nine Member States.
A literal interpretation of the Rome Treaty could be argued to require
exactly this.

The second fact is that the different Member States not only base their
internal welfare systems on substantially different principles which would
be hard to reconcile, but that they are at different stages of economic
development and wealth. A poor country like Ireland or Italy cannot afford
to duplicate the welfare system of a rich country like Denmark or West
Germany without outside assistance. But there is no evidence that the richer
members of the Community are prepared to envisage subsidising the welfare
systems of the poorer members, nor is it politically thinkable or desirable that
the richer countries should slow down the development of their own welfare
systems to enable the poorer to catch up. The scope for harmonisation
in the field of social protection and labour law is therefore somewhat limited.
What we have to aim for is rather the establishment of 'minimum standards'
on which individual member-States should improve wherever they can afford
to do so.

So the two basic problems facing the Commission in drawing up a social
action programme are, first, the weak and uncertain guidance given by the
Rome Treaty; and, second, the fact that each of the Member States has
different priorities in the social field, deriving from their degree of economic
strength and their cultural and historical background.[4]

At the same time it is clear that there *are* social problems in Europe which
require a Community approach. It is also clear that the need to broaden the
appeal of the Community, to give it a 'human face', to be seen to be
dealing with the adverse social consequences of economic change and
growth, remains. The Community must have a social programme. But it has
to be selective, to address itself to problems which are not only relevant but
to which there is a Community as well as a national dimension. There is no
magic available in Brussels which will enable the Commission automatically
to find solutions to national problems which national governments themselves
cannot solve.

---

[4] *For example, Catholic countries tend to have a different approach towards family policy
compared to Protestant countries. Germany's welfare system is traditionally oriented towards the
work ethic, while France's has in the past been heavily biased towards the protection of a peasant
community, apparently on the basis that Napoleon thought peasants made the best conscript
soldiers!*

Thus, if one looks at the broad heads of social policy as they appear at national level, in which does a Community dimension appear most evident? In *housing* and *education* the role of the Community would appear to be somewhat marginal. The Commission is at present concerned with housing for migrants and handicapped people, and is interested in the role of housing in regional development; it is also concerned with education for migrants' children in the context of the migrants' action programme. But beyond this, these aspects of social policy do not appear to be priority areas for Community involvement.[5]

Health is a more difficult area. Certainly there seems little scope for attempts to harmonise the organisation of health protection in the different countries. The differences between the British National Health Service and the Continental systems are too broad to reconcile. Even were there a need to do so. But there are emerging problems of social medicine and research, and of environmental health hazards, where (as in the related fields of industrial safety, ergonomics and job humanisation, poverty programmes and rehabilitation of the disabled) the Commission can play a useful role as a coordinator of research, as a catalyst, as a data bank and in appropriate cases as a standard-setter; (the same is true in other areas, for example vocational training). This is indeed one of the more useful, if less spectacular, roles of the Commission in the social policy field; to act, not as a legislator, but as a catalyst, providing a forum in which national ministers or officials or experts can exchange ideas in a way which facilitates a gradual convergence of national thinking and policies within the Community. It would be a great pity if this activity, which developed greatly during the period 1973–75, were allowed to atrophy.

The same applies in large measure to the field of *social protection*. I have already indicated my scepticism with regard to the scope for large-scale harmonisation in this field. But there is a major catalytic role to be played in trying to move towards a convergence of national policies and common treatment of common problems; and in identifying those groups, of whom the migrants are the outstanding category, who for one reason or another are not receiving in all cases the social benefits which appear normal in an advanced industrial society.

This is an important, and I suspect in the long run a growing role, for the institutions of the Community. But it is when we come to issues of *work* and *employment* that we reach what in my view has to be the core of the next social action programme. The prognosis is that Europe will suffer from weak employment at least until 1980 and probably beyond. This fact must condition the Community's approach to social policy, for if the Common Market continues to generate unemployment and lost jobs as well as the inevitable irritants of change and upheaval, not only will the Community fail to project a 'human face' but the Common Market itself may come under threat from increased demands for protection.

---

[5] *This comment relates only to education as an instrument of social policy. There is a Community interest in some other aspects of education policy. It is possible that work on urban deprivation arising out of the poverty programme in the social action programme may lead to further interest in housing studies.*

Inevitably the main thrust towards full employment must come from macro-economic policies, which fall outside the scope of this paper. Nevertheless, there is much that can and should be done at the level of the social action programme. First, the Commission has to see that the instruments at its disposal are making a meaningful contribution. This brings us to the question of the reform of the European Social Fund.[6]

At the present time the Fund is restricted to providing 50% of the funds for approved schemes in the field of training, re-training and re-adaptation of workers affected by redundancy presented to it by the member-States, who themselves have to guarantee the remaining 50%. The Fund is divided into two Articles—Articles 4 and 5; it is a very difficult process to get money transferred from one Article to another. Under Article 4 priority is given to projects concerned with young workers (under 25 years old), migrant workers, handicapped, workers in textiles and clothing, and farm workers leaving the land for industry. Under Article 5 priority is given to projects in areas of regional priority (defined in the same way as for the Regional Fund) and for handicapped workers.

In considering measures for reforming the Fund, it is clear that the present rules are unduly restrictive. The division between Article 4 and Article 5 is outmoded, as is evidenced by the fact that the handicapped appear in both categories. Equally, there is some overlap between the Social and Regional Funds, since more than half the money in the Social Fund goes to the regions; broadly speaking, the Regional Fund operates on the demand for labour, by subsiding capital investment, while the Social Fund operates on the supply of labour. If one considers the two Funds together, one sees relatively small amounts of money being disbursed in a very cumbersome way with duplicated management. A combined Fund, which could be called an Employment Fund, operating under a single management with more flexible terms of reference, would be far more effective. (To put the situation into perspective, at present the Social Fund is thought to account for between 5 and 10% of the total training budgets of the nine Member States).

A second possible subject for reform is the 50% rule. If the Fund's rules prevent the Commission from ever paying more or less than 50% for a project, it means that it can never take the lead and initiate projects; the initiative must always remain with the Member States. It also means that some useful projects, which would require a small injection of Community money to be viable, but do not justify a 50% contribution, cannot be undertaken. I would therefore like to see the Fund having the freedom to vary its contribution to projects submitted to it to anywhere between, say, 10% and 90%. This would enable it in appropriate cases to sponsor projects itself.

One fundamental question which arises, both in the case of the Social Fund and the Regional Fund, is the so-called 'additionality' question: i.e. is the aid provided under these Funds to be regarded as additional to the aid

[6] *The proposals put forward by the Commission in mid-1977 represent only a first step towards the reform of the Fund, introducing a little flexibility but going much less far than the proposals advanced in this article.*

141

provided by the national taxpayer, in which case its priorities in any given country may legitimately differ from those set by the national authorities; or is it to be regarded as substitutional, in which case it must presumably follow national priorities? Linked with this are the two related questions of the size of the Funds, and whether or not there should be national quotas to determine the distribution of aid (as there are in the Regional Fund but not in the Social Fund).

On these points I believe the position can be clearly stated. To the extent that the Social and Regional Fund are seen to be 'non-additional', in other words simply providing substitution at the margin for taxpayers' financing of national training and regional aid programmes, to that extent the Funds will remain small; for the willingness of the German and French governments to subsidise the British, Irish or Italian taxpayer is limited. To the extent that they are seen as making a new, European contribution to common problems, to that extent they will be allowed to expand. And clearly, if they are subject to national quotas, their ability to play this creative 'European' role will be circumscribed. If country A knows that it has an entitlement to £x million out of the Fund in any given year, regardless of the quality of its projects, all it has to do is to present proposals to the Fund for exactly that amount, and the scope for initiative or choice at the level of the Fund disappears totally. It becomes a purely mechanical operation for transferring a certain amount of money from one Community country to another. So in my view it is necessary to preserve the principle of 'additionality' and to avoid the imposition of national quotas. At the same time there must clearly be, as indeed there has been and is, very close coordination between Social Fund officials and those responsible for national training programmes, since the latter clearly are likely to be better informed on the real needs in the different countries, and it would be unhelpful if the Fund were seen to be spending the bulk of its money on projects of marginal utility.

This leads directly to a further point of immense importance to the future functioning of the Social (or, as I would hope, an expanded Employment) Fund. At present the Fund is limited to sponsoring the redeployment of workers from declining into expanding industries or occupations. Its function is not to underwrite national unemployment benefit or redundancy schemes. But in a recession such as we have been recently undergoing it is far from easy to identify those jobs which offer rapid opportunities for expansion. I believe therefore that in such periods the Fund should be employed in appropriate cases to train workers for skills for which there may be no immediate outlet, 'training for stock' in fact. But for this to happen the Community needs a far better system of manpower forecasting, to identify those skills which are going to be in long-term demand, than it has had up to now. We took the first steps along this road in 1974 and 1975, but a lot more needs to be done to create a credible European manpower forecasting system to which the uses of the Social and Regional Funds can be related.

There are other things that need to be done in the employment field. More attention should be given to the special needs of women in the training and re-training fields, especially for married women coming back on to the labour market after years of child-rearing. I regret that virtually no use to date has been made of the Social Fund in this respect by Member States. But more urgent at the present time is the plight of the under-25s, who in every country have borne the brunt of rising unemployment in the recent recession. The evidence suggests that we face a long-term problem of structural unemployment among young people in Europe, and the social implications of this need no under-lining when we see the role that this group is playing in the civic violence in Belfast and Londonderry.

The Community needs to consider, therefore, what measures beyond the use of the Social Fund can be taken to promote youth employment. What is the scope for publicly-sponsored Youth Employment schemes? Is there a case for planned moves to earlier retirement, more flexible working patterns, shorter work-weeks and so on, specifically to create more job opportunities for the young? And what more can be done to improve the liaison between the world of education and training on the one hand, and the world of work on the other?

A framework for the discussion of these and similar questions exists, in the shape of the tripartite Standing Committee on Employment which brings together Ministers of Labour and leaders of trades unions and employers' organisations, together with the Commission, at European level. The reactivation of this Committee, after years of estrangement and non-cooperation on the part of the unions, was one of the achievements of 1974–75. But up to now the Committee has lacked an adequate work programme.

The emergence of unemployment has also radically affected those parts of the social action programme concerned with *migrant workers* and their dependents. When the migrants programme was being prepared in 1974 the Community was still recruiting migrant workers from non-Community countries in large numbers. We estimated at that time that there could be up to 12 million migrant workers and their dependents in the nine Member States, of whom one-third came from within the Community (mainly Italy and Ireland) and two-thirds from outside (mainly from Turkey, Spain, Portugal, Greece, Jugoslavia, the Maghreb countries of North Africa, the Indian sub-continent and the Caribbean). There were two major problems. First, and most important, was the need socially to integrate the migrants, to ensure that they enjoyed reasonable access to social security, education, housing and health protection, and that they were not allowed to become an embittered and exploited sub-proletariat like the Negroes, Puerto Ricans and Chicanos in the United States. The second need was to see that the labour market worked with sufficient 'transparency' to ensure that Community citizens, notably Italians, had a reasonable opportunity to apply for jobs elsewhere in the Community.

With the onset of the recession things changed abruptly. All the major labour-importing countries in the Community imposed a virtual ban on the import of labour from non-Community countries, a ban which is still maintained. This abrupt reversal of a relationship which had been allowed to build up over a number of years has imposed very severe economic and social strains on the Mediterranean countries, who lack the ability to provide jobs for anything like all their people. The situation is complicated by the fact that three of the labour-supplying countries, Greece, Portugal and Spain, have applied for full Community membership. Another, Turkey, is an associate member. These four countries, together with the Maghreb countries all have existing treaty relationships of one kind or another with the Community. It is difficult to envisage the ban on new recruitment from these countries being maintained indefinitely; equally it is difficult to foresee a return to the former 'free-for-all'. What is needed, urgently, is a Community policy on immigration, which will relate the intake of workers to the likely job opportunities in the Community, to the priority needs of the labour-exporting countries themselves, and to the Community's ability and willingness to ensure decent conditions and basic social rights to the migrants and their families. This must surely be one of the priorities for the next social action programme.

Apart from jobs, the other great social problem facing Europe today is *inflation*, and a social programme which has nothing to say on this question and on its social implications is unlikely to carry a high degree of credibility. As with jobs, the main attack on inflation has to come from macro-economic policy rather than from social policy as such; and once again the caveat has to be made that Brussels has no peculiar magic denied to member governments, in finding solutions to intractable problems. Nevertheless, just as the first social action programme was born of the need to humanise the processes of change brought about by the opening of the Common Market and the economic boom which followed, so in the very different situation of today social measures are needed to help to ease the strains caused by continuing inflation, continuing unemployment and the necessary shift of resources into exports and export-supporting investment to meet Europe's increased fuel bills.

What social measures? First, we need to explore the possibilities of ensuring more adequate provision for the victims of the economic system, by developing the concept of the 'social income'. Second, we must explore the scope for extending more broadly what is called in Britain the 'social contract', that is to say, the establishment of consensus policies on the growth of real incomes and the distribution of wealth, embracing where necessary measures of wage and price restraint. Third, as an essential element in this exercise we need to extend the scope of work already launched into aspects of industrial democracy and work humanisation; and we need to intensify our efforts to raise Community standards in the field of industrial health and safety and improvement in the working environment.

I would call this a 'programme for social justice'. It would seek to elicit the cooperation of the powerful interest groups in European society (the so-called 'social partners') in a joint programme to combat inflation while at the same time protecting the vulnerable groups in our society, extending the role of participation and seeing where living and working conditions can be improved without major budgetary costs. In so doing it would be making a contribution towards meeting what is probably the most dangerous trend in European society, the growing signs of a creeping paralysis of 'ungovernability'.

To mount such a programme would pose a major challenge to the institutions of the European Community. Clearly it could not all be done by the

144

Commission alone, still less by the Social Affairs Directorate-general working in isolation. Indeed, one of the gravest weaknesses of the present working methods of the Commission is precisely the tendency for each directorate-general to develop its own separate programmes with the bare minimum of inter-departmental coordination. This has to be changed. The Commission has to be seen to be working to a coherent strategy. And it has also, in my view, to be prepared to work more closely with other institutions—with national governments, with the European Parliament, with OECD, the ILO, the Council of Europe and others, rather than regarding them as in a sense rivals. Only by pooling all our efforts can we combat the challenge of ungovernability now confronting the European Community.

The success of such a programme could not be measured, as the Commission tends to measure its success today, by the number of legal directives pushed through the Council of Ministers. Indeed, the prime role of the Commission would be in the first instance to act as a catalyst, as a generator of ideas, as a conciliator between the different groups; only at a later stage would it become apparent what new directives, institutions or other instruments—in addition to those which already exist or are in the pipeline—would be required to carry out the programme.

Crucially important in this exercise will be the relationship between the Commission and the 'social partners', the representatives of employers and trade unions at European level. During the period 1974–75, after initial difficulties, this relationship at least in the social affairs field developed remarkably well, and it is important that it should be maintained. At the same time, if we are to avoid the evident dangers of 'corporate statism', the ganging-up of big producer interests with the political authorities, we have to broaden the concept of 'social partners' to include some of the other major stakeholders and interest group representatives in our society. For example, there should be a greater convergence between Community social and consumer protection policies. In the social services field the Commission achieved something of a breakthrough in the poverty programme, one of the most exciting elements in the social action programme, by involving voluntary welfare organisations in all the nine countries as equal partners with governments in the programme. This undoubtedly enriched the content of the work and helped to ease the bureaucratic constraints which could otherwise have killed it. In the programmes to promote equality for women the Commission rightly insisted against trade union opposition, in involving women's organisations fully in the dialogue; (but we did not do so—possibly wrongly in my view,—for migrants).

Another major interest group, more strongly represented in Catholic than in Protestant countries, is the Family Organisation. I believe that family policy is going to re-emerge as a major issue of European social policy over the next few years, though whether this side of 1980 is more problematic. But the major changes which are taking place in the role of women in our society, coupled with the general traumas of our time and the manifold implications of the 'permissive society', are placing great strains on the family as an institution. At the same time it seems clear that the role of the State as a provider of personal social services, a kind of

145

'mother-substitute', has reached a high water-mark and may well decline in future, as governments come under increasing pressure to keep public spending under control and to concentrate on the social priorities. So, to take one concrete example, we may find that it is not only more socially beneficial, but also cheaper, to concentrate on home care allowances as a tax deduction for mothers rather than provide large-scale créches to enable them to go out to work. Nobody can be dogmatic on issues of this kind, but it is my belief that the tide of public opinion will begin to swing back towards placing a greater social value on the maintenance of the family as against other social desiderata than it does today. And this will happen the more quickly, the greater our concern with violence, and urban deprivation, and the greater our disenchantment with the products of the schools.

Such then are some of the elements which in my view should be borne in mind in framing the next social action programme of the European Community. Unfortunately there is no space to describe the precise proposals which would flow from such an approach, nor to relate these to the on-going work within the first social action programme. Some of the new institutions established under this programme—the European Foundation for Improving Living and Working Conditions, the Consultative Committee on Health and Safety, the European Centre for Vocational Training, together with the more informal regular consultations which now take place with the national policy-makers in the fields of employment and social protection policies (and, more tenuously, in public health policy)—clearly have a major potential contribution to make to the development of the next programme. The humanisation of the work-place, which must have a central role in any programme for social reform in an advanced industrial Community, is a complex of measures comprising aspects of labour law, worker participation, health and safety legislation, environmental standards, improvements in training facilities and opportunities, experimentation in work re-structuring and shopfloor democracy, in all of which areas work at Community level is underway; each individual measure may seem small, but the cumulative effect is great.

The Community in short has nothing to be ashamed of in its contribution to social policy in the last few years. But the situation it now faces is a new one, calling for new responses. A somewhat tattered and demoralised Commission needs to recover its nerve, and to remember that the ultimate sanction of the Community it exists to promote and serve lies not in the phrases of the Rome Treaty but in the hearts and minds of the people of Europe. That is the prize which has still to be won.

12 European Agricultural Policy: A Federalist Solution

JOHN MARSH

The pre-occupations of the mid 1970s in relation to Agricultural Policy are different from those which prevailed during the 1960s. Then the emphasis was on the problems of adjustment. Debate focussed on how best to deal with low farm incomes, 'burdensome surpluses' and of the problems posed for domestic markets by depressed world prices for agricultural goods. Today, there is much greater concern for the consumer, the level of food prices, and the adequacy of future food supplies. In part this change in emphasis is a reflection of large price increases in world markets since 1972, but it also derives from more deep-seated anxieties.

There is alarm at the prospect that the rate of growth of world population threatens to outstrip the rate of growth in world food production. Although this adverse balance originates in low income, developing countries, it is believed that the richer countries will be unwilling or unable to resist pressures to channel food towards the needy. These anxieties have been intensified by a loss of confidence in the ability of agricultural technology to continue to maintain recent rates of increase in production. There are some signs of a slackening in the rate of improvement in crop yields; higher energy costs make many modern farming methods more costly; some observers feel that we are likely to encounter less favourable weather conditions in the next decade; and there is concern about the ability of the environment to withstand current agricultural techniques.

This switch of interest from producer to consumer issues may be out of proportion to the underlying change in prospects for agricultural production and consumption but it has some important effects on attitudes to agricultural policy. Ministers have spoken of the need to produce more in Europe in order to reduce dependence on imports. In the UK, for example, such an approach was explicit in the White Paper 'Food from our own Resources'. The decisions taken by governments have not always seemed consistent with this view. For example, in order to keep consumer prices as low as possible prices to farmers have not been raised to offset the whole of the effects of inflation. Concern for farmers' interests has, however, meant that despite this reduction in real prices, governments have failed to take action to lower the nominal prices for some products which are in surplus, defending their inaction on the grounds that in a world of scarcity it must be wrong to cut production.

The Common Agricultural Policy (CAP) provides the mechanisms whereby the European Community responds to these changing aspects of public concern. Outlined in the Treaty of Rome, the CAP has evolved during the life of the Community and now covers more than 80 per cent of agricultural production. Throughout its existence it has attracted strong criticism from various interest groups. Its survival is indicative of the political agility of the Commission and the Council of Ministers. That it survived and enabled other aspects of the common market to reach maturity may prove to be its greatest contribution to the Community. The criticisms it attracted have not weakened with time, although their emphasis has tended to shift. Since it is these alleged defects of present arrangements which make it necessary to seek something better, it is helpful to indicate their nature.

From the outset the protective character of the CAP was resented by agricultural exporters in the rest of the world. Because of the variable import levy system they were denied the opportunity to compete in terms of price with EEC producers. Their distaste for the policy was increased when export subsidies allowed higher cost Community production to be dumped in other world markets.

Within the Community there was also much criticism of the system. Those who were concerned with the plight of small, poor farmers noted that the CAP's emphasis on maintaining higher prices benefited most the large producers who had most to sell. Consumers were usually compelled to pay higher prices for food, although for short periods when world prices have reached peak levels they have benefited from lower prices for some commodities. In general, because prices are normally higher than world prices, agricultural net importing countries have been losers and net exporters of food gainers from the policy. Again this relationship was reversed when, for example, prices of cereals and sugar reached crisis levels on world markets in 1973 and 1974. The policy has also pressed heavily upon the Community's budget. At various stages surpluses of milk, beef, sugar, wheat and wine have had to be bought at the cost of a large share of Community expenditure. The open-ended commitment to intervene on domestic markets and to finance export restitutions make the uncontrolled rise in surplus production a matter of grave concern. Since the introduction of monetary compensatory amounts (MCA's) to bridge the gap between prices in countries whose exchange rates have altered but whose internal support prices remain unchanged, a further open-ended and potentially large drain on the Community's budgetary resources has developed.

Member country governments continue to play a crucial role in determining the economic environment within which agriculture operates. In part this is a matter of different tax rates, different social security arrangements and different standards in the provision of facilities such as water and power supplies. In part, however, it involves direct expenditures from national exchequers in favour of their own farmers. Most of these expenditures avoid direct confrontation with Community policy but they do alter the terms upon which farmers do business.

This disarray in the CAP is the starting point for this paper. The first part explains why existing arrangements prove so unsatisfactory. The second part makes a proposal for dealing with the central problem of the failure to achieve the central objective of the CAP, namely the maintenance of a common price level in all the Member countries.

Why the Existing CAP Fails

In its original conception, the CAP envisages a single market for agricultural goods throughout the Community, shielded from external competition by levies and duties, and stabilised by the operation of intervention buying on the Community market. Price differences correspond only to the costs of moving goods from one area to another. To implement the policy, price levels are fixed annually in units of account by the Council of Ministers. Within each country the prices paid in domestic currency represent the value of the unit of account price. Within such a system goods cross Community frontiers freely, differences in market prices reflecting only variations in local supply and demand conditions. Since any large surplus is purchased by the intervention authorities and any substantial shortage causes prices to rise to the point at which imports may enter, the system appears to offer similar, stable prices to all the Community's farmers. In adition to this regulated market, the CAP envisages further expenditure on structural reform. This it is hoped will aid farmers and member country governments to increase productivity.

This elegant system fails not so much for technical reasons, but because its operation demands a degree of political homogeneity which the Community does not possess. The governments of the member countries have been unwilling or unable to assign to the Community those powers which would be needed to make a single market of this kind work. An examination of some of the problem areas illustrates this point.

Much contention has arisen between member countries about the costs of the CAP. The losses involved were generally obscured from those upon whom they fell. In detail the policy gave different and varying degrees of protection to different products. These products constituted different proportions of the output of individual farmers, of member countries and of consumers, so any calculation of the burdens imposed by the CAP was difficult and likely to change from time to time. Two aspects did however become very clear, transfers between member countries and the budgetary consequences of surpluses. Transfers between member countries were of two sorts, via the trading mechanism and through the budget. When world prices are below CAP prices, the usual situation, net food importers transfer real resources to other members in the form of higher prices for imports of Community origin or by the payment of levies on imports from Third Countries. The CAP has been much the largest expenditure item in the Community budget. Payments occur when surplus production has to be bought at intervention or sold abroad or in support of structural programmes. Such payments tend to be received by the agricultural exporting member countries. Fundamentally they are transfers from consumers to producers. Difficulties arise because they are aggregated in

149

national terms, paid in national currencies and are likely to be defended or attacked by each country's minister at Council meetings. Since the entry of the UK, whose imports of food have traditionally represented a larger proportion of total supplies than in other member countries, the asymmetrical flow of costs and benefits from the CAP has become potentially much more serious.

Another recurrent cause of dissent has been the existence of surpluses. As initially conceived the policy might have eliminated surpluses by progressive reductions in the unit of account price. In fact, although real prices have fallen as a result of inflation, ministers have avoided straightforward cuts in nominal prices. Producers, many of whom are poor, are vulnerable to cuts in their product prices, and are able to exert effective political pressure. Unwillingness to cut prices has encouraged the Community to adopt various expedients in an attempt to limit surpluses. It has paid people to leave milk production and to be given grants for the uprooting of orchards, although this capital may well destabilise other markets, and improved yields rapidly replace the lost production. It has denatured wheat and turned wine into industrial alcohol. Most recently it has required animal feed manufacturers to buy skim milk powder as a condition for access to imported vegetable protein. Since the strength of the political lobbies within countries varies, these tortuous arrangements to cope with surpluses may seem natural and acceptable to one member country but, at the same time, offensive to others.

Exchange Rates and Monetary Compensations

The problems which surround monetary compensatory amounts provide a further example of the incompatability of the CAP with the present state of political development in Europe. When the policy was first conceived it was appreciated that changes in market exchange rates between member countries would create problems. Rather complicated provisions for consultation about exchange rate movements were approved but never operated. Some exponents of the policy suggested that in practice the CAP itself would prevent future changes in exchange rates, in effect bringing about a *de facto* type of monetary union. Such expectations were misconceived. Member governments faced with divergent rates of inflation, of real economic growth and unemployment were compelled to apply policies they thought appropriate to national needs. Some countries continued to earn large surpluses in terms of foreign exchange while others remained in considerable deficit. To have maintained fixed parities in such a situation would have exacerbated unemployment in some countries and would have placed unmanageable strain on the foreign exchange markets. Only if transfers of real resources from countries in surplus to countries in deficit had been possible would exchange rate stability have been tolerable. The reluctance of Members to spend more than modest amounts on the Community's regional programme indicates the impracticability of such transfers.

The CAP implied that internal support prices, measured in member country currencies, should be simultaneously adjusted when exchange rates varied. For devaluing countries this required an increase in local prices; for those countries whose currencies appreciated, market prices should be cut. Governments resisted such automatic adjustments. In countries with weak currencies inflation was already a problem and sharp increases in food prices not only contributed directly to a higher cost of living but also made any negotiations on wage restraint much more difficult. Although lower food prices would have benefited consumers in countries with strong currencies, ministers were left in no doubt of the hostility of farmers to such a move. Particularly for those countries which became the recipients of subsidies paid by FEOGA (the Community's agricultural fund) these political pressures were reinforced by economic gains. The contrast in political and economic interests is demonstrated by the attitudes of Ireland and the UK to raising their farm prices. In Britain, the strength of consumer interests and the receipt of subsidies in the form of MCA's, created reluctance to devalue the 'Green Pound' even when current market rates were 40 per cent lower. In Ireland, the stronger agricultural interest and the fact that MCA's on exports are taxed made it a matter of priority to bring the Irish Green rate nearer to the market rate.

National Agricultural Policies

The CAP has always had to work within the context of substantial expenditures by national governments on their own agriculture. In 1974 71 per cent of total expenditure on agriculture was financed from national sources and in 1975, when CAP expenditure rose by almost half, 66 per cent of expenditure still came from national budgets. It is thus clear that Member governments do not regard the CAP as adequately replacing national policies to safeguard farmer interests.

Direct payments from national budgets fall into three main categories, structural measures, social measures and 'miscellaneous' measures. There is also expenditure in support of markets not regulated by the CAP. In 1975 3 per cent of this national expenditure was for such market support, 37 per cent for structural reform, 43 per cent for social expenditure and 16 per cent for miscellaneous measures. The precise content of these categories is not well defined but it is necessary, in principle, that the aid given should be consistent with the operation of the CAP, and especially that it should avoid any distortion of competition between member states. In practice it seems doubtful that this can have been the case. For example in 1974 and 1975 Germany continued to rebate VAT to farmers in compensation for revaluations of the Deutsche Mark despite the fact that revaluation had reduced production costs compared with other member states. Holland too provided direct aids to farmers to compensate for the revaluation of the Guilder. In 1974 France spent 1.700 million Francs in aid to stock farmers and in 1975 made a grant of 1,700 Francs per farmer to cover part of the increase in production costs not covered by the Community price increase. Belgium gave similar aids to stock farmers, while a number of countries gave assistance to horticulturalists to help them to overcome the increase in costs following the energy crisis of 1973 and 1974.

In addition to budget expenditure, governments aid farmers through tax reliefs and by allowing farmers some marketing monopolies. Tax reliefs cover the whole range of direct and indirect taxation on current and capital expenditures. Their incidence is hard to document not least because the process of accounting for farm income and expenditure is not evenly developed across the Community. Marketing agencies can give considerable power to farmers if the demand for the product is inelastic. In most countries governments have sought to encourage cooperatives or other farming organisations. The UK Marketing Boards require all producers to sell through, or according to the instructions of, the boards. In practice marketing boards have met with varying degrees of success but the most successful, for milk, hops and wool, have become a very durable element in the agricultural scene. Their activities have been closely monitored and to some extent regulated by government and it seems clear that the substantial powers they possess have been used responsibly. However, the purpose of such boards is to achieve for the farmer a better deal than he would be likely to realise in a competitive market. Since they are not evenly distributed throughout the community they must distort competition within the EEC.

The failure to create an effective policy for establishing a common market in agriculture and the expression of discontents at a national level have destroyed the *Community* interest in the policy. Discussions between ministers are principally about trade-offs of gains or losses from a national point of view. The Commission seems principally concerned to get some agreement and to facilitate this bargaining process rather than to identify a Community interest distinct from that of the nation states. Despite immense efforts in negotiating details in Brussels the impression remains that pressure has to be exerted not on the Community but on national governments if any interest is to be safeguarded or any new initiative introduced.

It may be argued that the actual adjustments made within the Community were as fast as was politically tolerable. Between 1958 and 1975 the agricultural population fell from more than 15 to less than 8 million. This transformation involved considerable social dislocation and some hardship. Remote rural villages became depopulated, losing first their younger and more enterprising members, while those who were old had to contend with the decay of facilities, for shops, transport, health etc. which became more costly as the population became more sparse. In the large cities many migrant workers faced the rigours of an unaccustomed factory discipline and the discomforts of the scarcity of urban housing while separated from their families. The social and political implications could not be ignored by responsible politicians.

Nevertheless the Community has been unable to reach a situation of sufficient flexibility in the farming sector to make a system of common, uniform producer prices acceptable.

To sum up then we might say the CAP fails because it has the form but not the reality of a common market. It is unlikely to achieve a real common market, not because of technical difficulties but because the political forces opposed to the rapid adjustment which an agricultural common market would imply are too strong. In present circumstances even the form of a common market is threatened as ministers seek to safeguard national interests and the Commission is unable to resist these fissiparous tendencies in order to safeguard the Community's interest.

Planning and Competition

The misfortunes attending the CAP make clear that the difficulties in the way of *any* common policy are formidable, and may produce more construc-

152

tive thought. First, they prompt the question, what must be common and why? Second, they direct attention to the need for political development and not just to some re-arrangement of price or structual policy. Third, they make clear that advances toward a more common policy depend upon promoting and making less painful the process of adjustment.

The decision to create a Community within which competitive forces would be encouraged was founded in political as well as economic realities. The implications of competition were an overall improvement in the use of resources which would form the basis of higher living standards for the Community as a whole. The process of competition meant that individual enterprises might collapse and that people might have to find new jobs. Within a fully employed expanding economy, however, competition was also creating new opportunities. The benefits of a competitive common market would thus be widely diffused and accessible to all who had the energy, skill and initiative to seize opportunities.

Of course competitive forces did not operate without defect. In some areas private monopolies distorted competition. In others state industry or state purchasing policies favoured domestic producers. Competition has not prevented, and may even produce, acute regional problems where whole areas of a country become non-competitive. Those citizens who lack ability, energy or the willingness to move to seek new jobs might not benefit and could suffer. In general terms the Rome Treaty attempted to remedy such defects either by specific provisions such as those about monopoly, or through programmes of a social or regional character, or through the social security systems of each member country which were to be brought up to a common standard. Fundamentally, policy was a corrective to a market which was essentially competitive. In contrast the CAP does not correct but replaces market forces. Prices are fixed not to allow markets to work better but to prevent their movement causing intolerable hardship to farmers or undermining what are held to be vital national interests.

The difficulties of organising a 'planned' sector within a competitive economy are well illustrated by the CAP. Three rather different categories of problem can be identified; the first associated with the identification, definition and weighting of objectives. Within the Community clashes of national interest, differences in tradition and in institutions, intensify the difficulty of agreeing on objectives.

A second group arises because the existence of 'free' market forces in the rest of the economy may upset or distort policies designed to give effect to agreed objectives. For example, a policy of encouraging labour to move out of agriculture may become unacceptable if there is a general rise in unemployment. Similarly high prices offered for finished goods, agricultural or otherwise, are likely in a market economy to attract into the industry resources whose cost would not be justified at lower price levels. Thus a policy intended to relieve social hardship by raising farm incomes may have the effects of increasing farm costs and making any subsequent reduction in prices politically very difficult.

A third group of problems arise because existing policies gain a momentum which makes any substantial change difficult. Part of this inflexibility is the result of political pride; it is hard to admit that policies were wrong. It is also a reflection of the immense bureaucratic skill which a policy like the CAP demands and ultimately secures. Having evolved 'answers' to each of the crises as they occur, administrators become increasingly sceptical of radical cures and claim that it is only realistic to work from the present basis. A further difficulty is that some people develop personal interests in the continuation of present arrangements to which they have adjusted their activities. Finally, as a policy ages, surviving repeated crises, there tends to develop a public acceptance of its provisions. It becomes increasingly difficult to visualise alternatives and those who propose changes seem to be substituting threatening uncertainties for known arrangements.

Within each member state each of these problems arises in relating a 'planned' agriculture to a market economy. However, over time each society has evolved political processes which allow broad concensus views to be discovered and modified. Thus within each country at any one time there tends to be a working agreement, for example, as to the relative priority to be attached to food prices as opposed to farm incomes. Within each country power exists to regulate, for example by taxation, subsidy or direction, aspects of the working of the competitive market which impinge on the plans made for agriculture. An overall view can be taken about employment policy, regional policy and the role of structural policy in agriculture. Again the momentum of each country's traditional ways of handling policy problems makes it tend to prefer its own sorts of solution.

Within the Community, however, those factors which lead to homogeneity within member countries tend to create divergences which correspond to national frontiers when issues such as agricultural prices have to be determined on a European scale. Especially where the economic structures of countries differ, national interests may run along divergent lines. This makes it almost impossible to formulate a truly European policy unless there is some sense of a European identity which transcends local loyalties in the same way that prosperous regions or rich people within countries accept that it is 'right' for them to support less fortunate citizens in their own country. To undertake a 'planned' agriculture in the absence of such a political awareness is to put the cart before the horse. This danger is well seen in the CAP which manages simultaneously to anger UK consumers by holding prices up and French farmers by preventing them from rising.

Two-tier Prices

The lesson seems plain. If European agriculture is to be part of the Community it is necessary to distinguish those things which can be attempted on a Community level from those which must be left to national governments or to smaller scale organisations. In general terms any genuine common policy must, in present circumstances, have a competitive basis providing opportunities within the Community for resources to be used more effectively and to earn higher rewards. It is plain, however, that no government is prepared to expose its agricultural sector to unfettered competition. Within countries different reasons for 'planning' agriculture operate. For some the emphasis is on external earnings or import saving. For others greater weight may attach to

154

farm income problems. Sometimes the primary concern may be security of food supply and stability of prices; at other times greater weight may attach to economic efficiency and the contribution of agriculture to economic growth. Nevertheless it is possible to devise a system which would allow intra-Community trade to take place on a competitive basis and yet realistically to allow governments considerable control over internal price levels.

Present arrangements point the way in which the CAP might evolve. What has been achieved is a regulated and preferential basis for intra-EEC trade and a modest but significant contribution towards the modernisation of agriculture. The system ensures that trade between Members takes place at prices which are relatively stable compared with prices in world markets. There is no reason why this system of trade should not be retained, although its existence does not justify levels of Community preference for agriculture which normally exceed the degree of preference accorded to industrial goods. Provided the price level for trade between Community members is made to adjust in the direction of movements in world markets, so that the gap between the two does not remain excessive for long periods, the present system of variable import levies and export restitutions seems best adapted to give effect to a Community trading price and to Community preference. Should it become possible to negotiate international commodity agreements fixed charges might even be substituted for varying levies and export subsidies. But at present it would seem irresponsible to expose Community trade to the uncertainties of the world market, distorted as it is by the actions of many governments.

To establish the Community price for trade between Members, and to give effect to preference for goods of EEC origin, the Council of Ministers would meet annually, as at present, to agree a Community trading price denominated in units of account. Each country would undertake to buy and sell at this price both in trade with non-EEC Members and within the Community. Trade with non-EEC countries would be subject to import levies to bring lower world prices up to the EEC trading price, also as at present. Export restitutions could also be continued where appropriate.

However, each Member state would be free to determine the internal price level appropriate for its own situation, on condition that *any deviation from the Community trading price would have to be wholly financed from national sources.* Within that constraint considerable flexibility might be permitted on methods of price support. For example, a country which wished to keep food prices at the EEC level and yet increase returns to its farmers could make direct payments either of a deficiency payment character or in the form of income supplementation, or in terms of subsidies on inputs. A country which wished to have lower than EEC prices for its consumers could do so, by means of food subsidies, welfare payments or the issue of food coupons enabling selected groups, such as pensioners, to buy at lower prices.

Distortions to trade between Member countires would be prevented by compensatory taxes or subsidies equivalent to the gap between domestic and EEC trading prices. Countries keeping producer prices above EEC levels would have to tax their imports from and subsidise their exports to other Members. Countries whose producer prices were below would have to tax their exports to and subsidise imports from other Members. The system would in fact be not dissimilar to the use of border tax adjustments, for example the remission of VAT on exports and its charging on imports.

Trade with non-EEC countries would be subject to similar charges, but there would be some room for discussion about how the responsibility for taxing and subsidising should be distributed between the Community budget and those of the Member states. A completely symmetrical system would imply that all levies on imports required to bring the lower world price up to the Community trading price level would be appropriated to the Community budget (and similarly all subsidies [export restitutions] needed to bring the price of Community exports down to world price levels from the Community trading price would be a charge on the FEOGA) but any taxes or subsidies required to implement a higher or lower level of national price than the EEC trading price would be dealt with in the national budgets. The operation of a system of this kind can be envisaged better by examination of the example shown in the Chart.

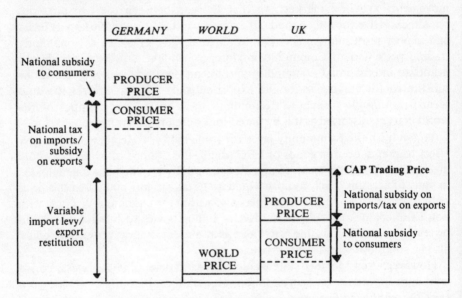

However, if it were desired to bring some pressure to bear on national agricultural policies to bring them into line with the Community's desired level of trading prices, alterations to this symmetrical system could be envisaged. For example, if the EEC Council decided to attempt to dissuade Member governments from keeping their prices much higher than the Community trading price, on the ground that this would tend to keep resources allocated to high cost areas of agricultural production, it would be possible to require that some or all of the national taxes levied on imports, in order to maintain a national price level above the trading price, should become the revenue of the Community. Thus the policy of accepting the separation of national price levels from the Community trading price level is not inconsistent with a continuation of realistic policies to maintain progress towards an eventual common market.

Such a procedure would institutionalise but limit the system of compensatory amounts, and recognise that it may be appropriate for countries to have different internal price levels for reasons unconnected with transitional period or exchange rate changes. Since national governments have to take responsibility for inflation, employment and most regional policy issues, it is realistic to give them the opportunity to plan agriculture and to regulate food prices. At the same time the cost of deviating from Community norms would be borne by the country concerned and would be visible in its domestic accounts. Such visibility might well prove the most effective deterrent to excessive degrees of protection.

Within such a system *monetary* compensatory amounts paid by the Community would cease. If a government wished to maintain lower prices in local currency after a devaluation or higher ones after a revaluation, it could do so at its own cost. Although it is convenient for some countries to benefit from Community subsidies on food imports following a devaluation, there is little justice in such an arrangement. Such merit as may exist would vanish if there were an assurance that Community prices would not normally be greatly in excess of those on world markets.

It cannot be denied that such a system would permit distortions of competition to persist, based on the relative generosity of governments. However, it must be doubted whether these open distortions would be more serious than the current disguised distortions brought about by the complex national policies for agriculture cited earlier. The blunt truth is that in the present political climate some distortion is inevitable.

A change in this direction would, however, make it much easier to negotiate a price at which competition between members worked to the advantage of the Community as a whole. Because the duty to protect vulnerable groups was clearly seen to fall on national administrations, there would be no justification on social grounds for the maintenance of excessive EEC prices. A surplus which was costly to the Community's budget could be removed by a reduction in the price at which goods changed hands between members. Pressure would then fall on national budgets if the surplus goods were taken off the market but it would be in the interest of the countries concerned to promote the eventual adjustment of their own industry and economy to the new pattern of prices

One of the important effects of this proposal would be to reduce expenditure on agriculture from the Community budget, since monetary compensation subsidies would no longer be Community financed. However, any taxes which were imposed on imports by Member countries who wished to increase domestic producer prices above the level of the Community trading prices would be paid to the Community. Indirectly, the greater freedom the Council would possess to manipulate the price at which goods changed hands between Members would make a more important contribution. Because surpluses would be discouraged and their cost to the Community budget reduced by price cuts, a substantial part of current expenditure on intervention and export restitution would be removed. To some extent this might be offset if lower internal prices led to lower levies on imports from third countries and so to a reduction in budget revenues. It seems unlikely, however, in view of Community preference that imports of products which are in surplus in the Community, and for which intervention or export subsidies are needed, could be very large.

This relief to the budget creates important opportunities for the Community. There should be no automatic assumption that the funds saved should be devoted to other aspects of agricultural policy, but initiatives in this direction, might well be possible. Within the Community differences of national interest and divergences in economic performance make common action difficult. These tensions are specially obvious in agriculture and have not been lessened by by the attempt to impose a uniform level of prices. If in place of this largely unsuccessful strategy the Community redirected the emphasis of its agricultural policy towards actions which promote a convergence of interests, a more effective and harmonious common policy seems likely to emerge. Two fields in which the Community is already active, structural policy and regional policy, promise well in this respect.

The development of the Community's structural policy since 1968 suggests that its contribution to agricultural adjustment may be more effective as selective aids than as payments made across the whole area and paid to national governments. The extension of the CAP structural programmes for farmers in less favoured regions provides a good example. By making it possible to aid the development of crafts or tourism the policy aids adjustment by increasing the economic base of the vulnerable household. More generally the coordination of regional policies designed to stimulate new jobs and policies which ease the adaptation of people to a different pattern of employment and agricultural policy must continue to depend on national governments. But the Community can help specific vulnerable sectors of the economy to respond to competitive pressures.

Aid to Depressed Regions

In reality the most acute needs arise at levels more narrowly defined than the larger nation state. For example in western France, in southern Italy and in the hilly areas of the UK, adjustment to competition may be especially difficult. By operating with local organisations to aid such depressed regions the policies of the Community could be seen to be making a positive contribution. The transfer of funds between countries on such a basis would also conform to natural justice in the sense that the rich would assist the poor. By doing so, it would ease rather than exacerbate the balance of payments problems of the poorer countries and so increase their chances of attaining higher sustained levels of income growth. The size of such intra-member transfers is likely to be limited so it is all the more important that they should be used in ways which promote healthy economic adjustment rather than maintain unwanted agricultural production. By freeing the Community from its largely ineffective role as the defender of all farmers through price policy, it would become capable of offering a larger real benefit to those whose need was most acute.

The benefits of such structural and regional initiatives are not limited to those who receive support. Since these changes help to increase the competitiveness of the businesses helped, there is likely to be a long term gain to all citizens as consumers. Because farmers in these regions remain viable the process of adjustment may take the form of a movement of resources from farming to other sectors in those regions of the Community where alternative employment opportunities are more readily available. This seems likely to involve smaller material costs and less painful personal adjustment than taking people from remote rural areas and employing them in distant urban centres. The total gain is not just lower food prices but lower costs of adjustment and the increment to non-farm output made by those who find jobs in other sectors.

The institutional innovations such an approach to agricultural policy would involve should not be exaggerated. The Community trading price would still be fixed by the Council of Ministers. National governments would have responsibility as at present for their own food and agricultural programme. The idea of the Community by-passing national authorities in regional initiatives raises some new possibilities as well as problems. The Community's contribution is likely in the immediate future to be peripheral to national, regional and employment policies. Its concentration on areas of greater need might have some justification in making the benign aspects of EEC presence apparent. It could also help to match the current mood in favour of a greater degree of regional autonomy felt in a number of the larger member countries. But it would be mistaken to exaggerate the scale such initiatives are likely to achieve. The amount available to be spent in this direction from agricultural sources is limited, and great reluctance to finance an ambitious regional policy was expressed when this was canvassed within the Community. The need for action of this nature occurs in other sectors as well as agriculture and may as a result of the recent divergence of member country economies have become more severe, but it seems unlikely that expenditure on current scales could do much to remedy the situation. However, a successful if limited action associated with the Community might help to cultivate the concept of a European identity, to encourage people to look beyond national governments and to foster a greater awareness of the other people within the framework of the Community. If such successes could become common then the possibility of creating a framework of political consensus within which more ambitious common policies could operate would be greatly enhanced.

Conclusion

The suggestions made here may seem to represent the abandonment of the CAP. If by that is meant that the Community ceases to attempt to make uniform centralised decisions about prices inside member countries such a conclusion would be justified. However, the ideas outlined seem likely to lead towards a system of trade which corresponds more nearly to a genuine common market and to a form of Community initiative which can contribute to the development of a deeper sense of European identity. By making the degree of Community preference independent of internal social and regional problems an equitable basis for trade between members can be established, while still encouraging intra-Community movements. By allowing governments to deviate from common trading prices at their own cost, the reality of current economic, social and political differences is acknowledged and the decision taken is made responsible to those who will pay. By permitting more localised initiative through the structural aspects of the CAP, especially where these can ease acute problems of agricultural adjustment, the sense of a Community which is more than the sum of its national states is likely to be awakened.

Ultimately the ability successfully to pursue a more homogenous, interventionist policy at a Community level requires political progress. This is true whether the subject of policy is economic and monetary union, social welfare, transport or agriculture. The ideas outlined in this paper would contribute to this process and so in a sense represent a more truly common approach to agricultural problems than the premature attempt to attain the appearance of conformity which has caused so much difficulty and division within the present Community.

PART C
EUROPE IN THE WORLD

13 How Large a Community?

GEOFFREY EDWARDS

T HE integration of the industrialised economies of France, Germany, Benelux and Italy into a customs union and, potentially, a political union, has proved a sometimes contentious issue for the remaining countries of Western Europe. The history of Britain's relations was, to say the least, chequered, through both domestic factors and the opposition of France to British membership. The acceptance of Britain's application, together with those of Ireland and Denmark (and Norway who subsequently withdrew after a bitter referendum) was eventually achieved only in 1972. The Community's relations with other Western European countries have been determined by a variety of measures. Norway, along with the other remaining members of EFTA signed individual free trade agreements with the Community in 1972. Several of the less-developed countries of Southern Europe signed Association Agreements; those between Greece and Turkey and the Community envisaging eventual membership of the Community; those with Cyprus and Malta the establishment of a customs union. Spain and Yugoslavia signed only preferential trade agreements.

The round of enlargement concluded with the accession of Britain, Ireland and Denmark is now to be followed by a further round, as significant for the development of the Community as that of 1972. The Greek Government submitted a formal application for membership in June 1975 and negotiations opened on 27 July 1976. Portugal applied in March 1977, and Spain in July 1977. Both are therefore watching closely the negotiations on Greek membership. So too will Turkey whose Association Agreement envisages a slow transition to membership in the 1990s. Although not a candidate for membership in the near future, Turkey's relations with Greece and its strategic position on the southern flank of NATO add complications to the debate on Greek membership.

The decision to admit Greece has already been taken in principle by the Council of Ministers. Membership before 1980 has been declared the aim. The decision was taken on political rather than economic grounds, largely in the interests of strengthening the position of the newly revived democratic regime in Greece. It was in marked contrast to the Opinion of the European Commission which was published in January 1976. While that Opinion recognised the political and strategic importance of Greek accession, it emphasised more the economic difficulties, for Greece and the Community, of assimilating a semi-developed economy into the Community and the implications for the future of the Community, including the implications for the Community's relations with Turkey.

The Commission's Opinion reflected a concern that further enlargement should take place at a time when the Community appeared to be stagnating and progress limited. In many ways it reflected past arguments used during the debates over British membership of *profondissement* versus *elargissement*. Further enlargement, that is, should not take place without substantial improvements being introduced into the Community's decision-making processes and the institutions strengthened. Such arguments, however, tend to over-simplify the situation. On the one hand, the present members do not seem able or willing to agree on any substantial measures which might mark a significant step towards European Union (except perhaps direct elections). On the other hand, meanwhile, the Greek application has to be negotiated, and positions drawn up on Portuguese and Spanish membership.

The criteria of membership
Under Article 237 of the Treaty of Rome any European state may apply to become a member of the Community. All the actual or potential candidates are eligible on these grounds. Turkey's membership of the Council of Europe as well as the terms of its Association Agreement would seem to dispose of any doubts which may have been expressed about its geographical qualifications as a European state. Other criteria appear, however, to have emerged: the applicant must be a democracy, and its level of economic development must be relatively close to that of existing Community members.

Political considerations have tended to dominate the Community's reactions to applications for membership. The Council's decision on Greek membership is an example, even if economic factors will play their part in the actual negotiations. Spain actually applied for Associate status, with a view to future membership, as long ago as 1962. It was refused on the grounds that only fully democratic regimes were acceptable. In January 1976 the then British Foreign Secretary, James Callaghan, asserted that Spain must be "well down the road towards a pluralist democracy" before membership could be considered. The precise point at which the Spanish regime becomes acceptable is thus left open. Similarly the economic criteria to be applied are open to highly political interpretation, General de Gaulle's veto of British membership being the most obvious example. Since both Greece and Spain have experienced rapid industrialisation and their economic development as expressed, for example, in terms of GDP, already approach that of Ireland, economic criteria alone would perhaps prove insufficient to withhold membership. They might, however, be more telling in the cases of Portugal and Turkey.

But if in principle there are few grounds for refusing membership, one of the lessons made clear by the debates over British membership is the scope available to existing members to delay the process. The prospect of enlargement also gave member states an important element of leverage to achieve particular Community goals. The French, for example, agreed to British membership only with the implementation of the Financial Regulation from which they expected to benefit. The further enlargement of the Community is likely to provide similar opportunities and, indeed, perhaps increase them in view of the greater disparities between the Mediterranean applicants and the existing member states.

The choice open to the Community is, therefore, difficult. The grounds on which it can refuse membership are limited and are likely to arouse criticisms of exclusiveness. On the other hand, the accession of new members, with differing interests and problems, is likely to have profound consequences for the future development of the Community. Little serious consideration appears as yet to have been given to the possible repercussions of further enlargement, either for the Community itself, or for other possible members from northern Europe. Attention has only slowly begun to focus on some of the difficulties thrown up by the new applications. The impact of nine million Greeks may not be radical. But, although enlargement negotiations are now under way, each application cannot be viewed in isolation given the interest of other Mediterranean countries.

The Political Issues

While each of the Mediterranean countries have differing problems and perspectives they share certain significant common features. Politically, Greece, Spain and Portugal have emerged or are emerging from periods of dictatorial government, and are in the process of establishing pluralist democratic systems comparable to those of members of the Community. Turkey has also been evolving towards such a system, with interruptions since 1950. Their present stability of course varies. Despite the strike-law riots of May 1976, the stability of the Karamanlis Government can be under-estimated—it may indeed have been strengthened by the nationalist fervour aroused by the dispute with Turkey—and the possibility of a coup exaggerated. Nonetheless, it is perhaps significant that in the general enthusiasm of the welcome given to the Greek application little serious consideration appears to have been given to the possibility of dealing with a member state which is no longer democratic.

Such considerations have, however, been present in the attitudes adopted towards other possible members. The Community's reaction to the post-coup Portuguese governments was extremely cautious. Reactions to the new Spanish government have been even more so, except on the part of France. Yet despite the severe economic difficulties facing the government of Dr Soares, and reports of continuing conflicts among, for example, the armed forces, the first democratically elected government of Portugal for some forty years may well be able to overcome the problems it faces and the deep divisions which still persist. The election of General Eanes as President in June 1976 at least reflected the strong desire of the majority of the electorate to return to stability. In Spain the situation is in some ways similar. While much of the political uncertainty has been removed with the June elections, the economic recession may yet create a volatile situation the government finds difficult to control. Considerable optimism has been created by the government's handling of the evolutionary process towards democracy against both a seemingly entrenched right wing controlling many of the levers of power, and parties determined upon a speedier break with the machinery of Franco-ist dictatorship or upon regional autonomy. If Sr Suarez can repeat his political success in the economic sphere it will prove even more difficult for the Community to rationalise any refusal to consider possible membership given its reaction to both Greece and Portugal.

The effect of Community attitudes on the internal development of these possible members is an important factor in considering the issues raised by enlargement. The Greek Government has committed itself heavily to early membership of the Community. That commitment was influential in the Council's decision to override the more cautious conclusions of the Commission. Membership has been seen in Greece as conferring respectability on the government, strengthening the political system, and undermining the position of the opposition forces whether right or left, civil or military. In Portugal, Community aid and assistance, once given, was a contributory factor in restoring morale and support for the socialists and the parties of the centre and centre/right oriented towards Europe against the apparent success of those oriented towards either the Third World or Eastern Europe. In Spain, it has been argued that it is in the Community's own interests to view the present government's policies with more sympathy in order to strengthen its position and reduce the possibilities of Spain disintegrating into chaos. Similarly in Turkey, Community policies which appear as either pro-Greek or pro-Greek-Cypriot tend to alienate supporters of the more Europe-oriented political parties.

But future membership is regarded not simply as conferring an accolade of respectability or even as a reward for democratisation. It is regarded too as a means of achieving national aspirations. In Greece, Spain and Portugal the concept of 'Europe' is important; their heritage, political, economic and cultural, is European. Turkey's identification with Europe is also supported by the vast majority of politically conscious Turks. There is therefore a belief that each has its contribution to make to the evolution of the Community, and that such a contribution should not be denied in pursuit of Community exclusiveness. Moreover, such arguments are reinforced by the existing integration of their economies into the Community. Consequently, and the argument will be familiar to British ears, they should not be ignored in the decision-making processes of the Community. If Association has provided only limited opportunities for influencing Community policies (and Turkey especially has complained that its interests have not been sufficiently taken into account) then membership is necessary, both to offset any decisions which might adversely affect domestic policy decisions, and to avoid the allocation of scarce Community resources elsewhere.

Economic Issues

If the political and emotional arguments have been most influential among

166

the potential members so far, they also have high expectations of economic assistance for the development of industry and agriculture. In many significant ways the economies of the Mediterranean countries are already closely integrated into the Community. Their trade dependency is high, some 40-50 per cent of total trade being conducted with the Community. Their dependency measured in this way is, indeed, not far short of that of France, Germany and Italy, and significantly higher than that of the UK. Together with Yugoslavia, they also provide the main sources of migrant labour for the continental members of the Community, which reinforces their dependence on it.

If the current economic development of Portugal and Turkey remains far below that of the Community, the development of Spain and Greece has been rapid. Spain is ranked eighth in industrial production in the West. The strength of the Greek economy is reflected in the lack of noticeable dislocation of Greek industry after the final removal of tariff barriers on goods subject to the twelve year transitional period in November 1974. During the period of Association, Greece was alone among Associated states in increasing its share of imports into the Community while appearing to suffer little from imports from the Community. Concern nonetheless exists as to the ability of the potential members to cope with Community competition under a customs union and its regulations.

In its Opinion on the Greek application the Commission pointed out that the high rate of sustained growth in GDP was based mainly on the rapid devlopment of key industrial sectors whose capital requirements were, to a considerable extent, met by foreign investment. A similar situation has existed in Spain and in Portugal before the coup. In the Commission's opinion a significant inflow of long-term private capital is required to avoid a critical increase in other forms of foreign indebtedness. Much of the success of the Mediterranean producers has resulted from the supply of cheap labour, and the absence of free trade union bargaining. This competitive advantage may well be undermined with membership of the Community and the introduction of Community regulations coming on top of higher wages. Industrial growth has tended to concentrate in particular areas: in Greece around Athens-Piraeus; in Spain around Madrid and the autonomous-minded regions of the north and north-east (only seven of the fifty provinces of Spain have per capita incomes above the national average). While such regional disparities are familiar enough among present members of the Community, they may well be harder to correct among the potential members.

Agriculture must be considered a further major difficulty for the potential members. Agriculture has tended to lag behind the boom in industrial production and has remained largely backward. Holdings tend to be small and soil conditions often difficult impeding the introduction of modern technological methods. Irrigation remains at a premium. Agriculture provides a limited share of the national product (in Greece, for example some 16%, while in the Community 5%) notwithstanding the still high proportion of the actively employed population remaining in the agricultural sector (36% in Greece and only 9% in the Community). For the potential members problems will include the continuing one of under-employment or unemployment in agriculture and the possible increase in costs of imported cereals and meat. A major problem for both potential members and the Community will be the exacerbation of existing Community difficulties; the major exports of the potential members are in existing problem areas such as wine and citrus fruits.

Such generalisations are of course broad and can be criticised. In Greece, for example, an emphasis on foreign capital can ignore increasing domestic investments; greater industrial opportunities may absorb some of those drifting from the land and reduce the numbers of unemployed or of those seeking work abroad. In many cases cooperative farming methods have been encouraged, and even if capital availability as well as terrain prevents a great deal of mechanisation, modern technology in fertilizers etc may lead to an increase in production. In general, however, the possible costs of member-ship to the potential members have been subordinated to the political benefits seen to accrue to membership.

Economic Implications for the Community

The possible implications of enlargement to include the semi-industrialised countries of the Mediterranean are profoundly important. In many ways, for example, the CAP is already a highly complicated set of off-setting distortions, brought about by shifting agricultural populations, relations with third countries, changes in world prices, fluctuating exchange rates and consumption. Italy, in particular, has considered that the distortions have acted against its interests. Those interests will be further subject to stress with the accession of other Mediterranean producers. On the other hand, Italy would no longer appear so often as the odd man out in the Council of Ministers. The potential members would also seek to increase the at present limited expenditure on the structural element of the CAP, and will demand protection and support similar to that which is afforded to temperate producers. The potential strain of such demands on an unreformed CAP would be immense. The costs could be such that alternatives to support and protection might be considered more acceptable, including more autonomous actions by the member states. In other words, radically new pressures will be felt for the reform of the CAP.

One major problem which will be brought to the fore by enlargement but which is foreshadowed under the various free trade agreements signed by the Community, is that of making room within the Community for the growing industrial exports of the potential members. Specific sectors (the textile industry already) will come under strain, even if the prospect of a wider market for consumer durables or high-technology products may offset some problems. Perhaps the only available instruments to overcome them may be an active labour market policy and investment promotion. Such policies may mitigate unemployment in problem areas, especially within the weaker economies where older low-technology industries persist. Enlargement would certainly point up the limitations of the Community's present regional policy; the Regional Development Fund is, after all, only of marginal assistance. Some members will be concerned over possible reductions in their

168

share of the existing RDF; others will be concerned if enlargement led to the introduction of a Community policy to influence the location of investment.

The accession of new members directly competing for limited Community resources will be difficult to accept by the weaker existing members. Yet if the traditional concept of solidarity is to be maintained the new members should expect to be able to benefit from Community policies in the same way as existing members. But to use the same criteria as at present to allocate resources might increase the Community budget beyond all recognition. It is difficult to imagine an enlarged Community being able, or even attempting, to secure roughly equal benefits for both existing and new members. Such difficulties suggest that more serious consideration should be given to the question of whether a single-tier Community is viable or whether a more complicated structure is necessary.

Institutional Implications for the Community

For many, therefore, further enlargement raises the prospect of the greater dilution of Community coherence. Such a prospect is an anathema to those inspired by the ideals of Jean Monnet and of a United States of Europe, but reinforces the views of others more pragmatic in their approach to the construction of 'Europe'. For both groups, however, enlargement comes at a time of apparent Community stagnation and a re-assessment of the efficacy and appropriateness of not merely the long term goals of the Community but its institutions.

The Commission has already been subject to criticism for lack of efficiency, overstaffing etc. Yet it is difficult to imagine the existing larger member states giving up their two representatives, even perhaps in circumstances in which Spain, with a population of 35 millions, and Turkey, with a potential population of over 40 millions, both demand two Commissioners thus making for a Commission of 19 members. As yet few have focussed on the possibilities of reforming the Commission beyond some rationalisation of portfolios by the new Commission presided over by Mr. Jenkins. But without major reforms the battle over portfolios is likely to get worse, and the Commission itself may become wholly transformed into a more typical bureaucracy. One of the major problems already facing the Commission will also be made more difficult: already delays in translations create one of the biggest bottlenecks in the operation of the Commission. Yet it is difficult to envisage new members foregoing the introduction of their languages as either official or even 'working' languages.

One of the major fears of those wary of enlargement is the complete incapacitation of the Council of Ministers without the introduction of reforms such as majority voting. The search for acceptable package deals among thirteen member states will stretch out marathon sessions even further. Of course, the assertiveness or passiveness of the new members may make a difference to their impact on the Community, but their problems and expectations, as well as their domestic audiences may well lead to a self-assertiveness which would further hamstring the Council. It is possible in such circumstances that, if majority voting remains unacceptable to all existing members, other means of resolving differences might be sought. The Gaullist idea of a

Directorate has already been resurrected by President Giscard d'Estaing. M Tindemans in his report on European Union suggested a two-tier or two-speed Community for progress toward economic and monetary union. If such a two-tier system was accepted it might be possible to extend it further. In view of the differing positions on defence, for example, not least Irish non-membership of NATO, it is possible to envisage an inner core of members cooperating in defence while others did not. Even if such concepts are opposed by several existing member states the strains of enlargement and of economic diversity may lead to the emergence of such a system in practice.

One institution which might to some extent counteract such an evolution is the European Parliament. The impact of enlargement itself on the Parliament may not be particularly radical although it may create additional language problems, especially in committees, and may complicate the emergence of European political groupings. The direct election of the European Parliament could, however, have important repercussions, despite the Parliaments' limited powers. Directly elected members of the Parliament, responsive to their constituencies needs, are increasingly likely to press for Community action and commitment rather than national ones, especially in regional and social policy fields.

Implications for Other Countries

The effect of enlargement upon the Community's relations with other countries cannot be ignored in the present debate. The inclusion of additional Mediterranean producers will obviously affect others producing similar products, especially if enlargement results in increased agricultural protection. The major problem for the Community will be in adjusting the carefully balanced series of agreements, not simply with other Mediterranean countries but also with those who have signed the Lomé Convention.

By extending membership of the Community to countries in the eastern Mediterranean the Community will be very much more closely involved in the future of Yugoslavia as well as the whole complex of Middle East relations. So far Yugoslavia has tended to be treated in economic terms only; the death of Tito and the complications of Graeco-Turkish relations could have important repercussions on the Western balance, which the Community will have to recognise. It is doubtful if in the foreseeable future the Community could play any substantial political or security role in the eastern Mediterranean, but the concept of the Community as a 'Civilian Power', promoting stability through social and economic development has gained some currency, for example, in the United States.

Greater involvement in the Mediterranean would cause some concern in Norway. Despite Norwegian prosperity and the generally satisfactory working of the Norwegian-EEC free trade agreement, there is a sense of exclusion from the policy of the Nine which has caused some anxiety to both industry and government. In the CSCE negotiations, for example, the Norwegians found themselves somewhat isolated from Western decision-making processes because of greater Community rather than NATO solidarity. On the other hand, greater concern is unlikely to be sufficient to lead to a reconsideration of Community membership. Prosperity has tended to allay fears. High level contact in Brussels, the Joint Committee with the Community established under the free trade agreement, and the bridge provided by Danish membership, have proved adequate to inhibit the resurrection of an issue which so divided the country during the 1972 referendum on membership.

A far more radical change than enlargement to the south will also be necessary before the issue is again raised in Sweden. For Sweden the prospect of enlargement in 1972 led to considerable debates within the political parties on whether Sweden could apply for membership without wholly undermining its position of neutrality. The costs of upsetting the Nordic balance provided by Norwegian and Danish membership of NATO, the eastern orientation of Finland, and Swedish non-alignment were then considered too great. Close contact with the EEC has since been maintained similar to that of Norway. Both are also associated with the Community monetary 'snake'. Further integration on supra-national lines would be as unlikely to appeal to the Swedes as to the Norwegians. On the other hand, if conditions were sufficiently altered and a looser form of European union was proposed, then in Sweden's case it is possible that economic factors could outweigh the desire to preserve neutrality.

The Prospects for Community development

Enlargement to the South is likely to be one of the major preoccupations of the Community over the next ten years. The question is, what choice does the Community have in the face of a series of applications? If enlargement is to take place, and in principle it has been agreed, how much of the present Community structure will persist, and what will be altered? Would the changes brought about by enlargement delay or prevent progress towards European Union in the sense of a highly integrated Community with a supra-national structure, or would they, rather, necessitate a reappraisal of such a Union?

The question of membership has differing priorities among the potential Mediterranean members. Common to all, however, is an interest in membership, and a view that membership will confer political respectability, will make an important contribution to the maintenance of political stability, and will provide assistance in overcoming structural difficulties inherent in the process of industrialisation. In other words, they are not applying to join a free trade area or to extend Association. Their reasons for applying also suggest the dangers of rejecting their applications. The possibilities for greater instability in an already unstable area are increased, with all its concomitant political and strategic implications for the Community itself. The onus upon the Community to accept is thus considerable.

But pressure does not come solely from the actual or potential candidates. Several of the existing members strongly support the further enlargement of the Community. France has been well to the fore in promoting Greek membership; ties between the French and Greek governments are close. Greek membership, seen as desirable in its own right, is also seen as opening the way for Spanish membership which was for long an objective of French policy, until the full implications of Spanish competition began to be realised. Although the present French government might not wish to see enlargement resulting in a looser grouping of European states, they view an enlargement southwards as offsetting the influence of 'Northern Europe'. The attitude of the UK is perhaps more in line with past French policy; the difficulties of reconciling further diverse interests appear more acceptable to those who take a more pragmatic view of European integration. While perhaps less enthusiastic, the German government is known to be concerned about the strategic issues involved, and for security reasons would like to see Spain as well as Greece more firmly anchored to the West.

In opposition to such views are those primarily concerned with the dilution of Community coherence and the postponement of further integration. Enlargement has proved in the past a valuable lever for achieving particular policy goals. There will always be a temptation to use the opportunities provided by further enlargement merely for settling relatively minor policy conflicts. The pressures from potential members, combined with a sensitiveness to charges of exclusiveness if membership were to be rejected, would add to such temptations. But the strains imposed by enlargement on existing policies could more positively provide the opportunity for a radical reappraisal of policies and goals and the resolution of basic problems.

Existing Community policies may well need radical change to accommodate new members. Full accession to the CAP and demands for equality of treatment between producers of Mediterranean and temperate produce would impose unacceptable burdens on the Community budget given an unreformed policy. Similarly in regional and social policies the competition for scarce Community resources would be severe, and, without reforms, would place the weaker economies at a further disadvantage. Such competition might increase conflict between northern and southern members, compounded by the growing convergence of economic and social philosophies within the northern tier. An enlarged Community could thus resemble more the free trade area proposed by Mr Maudling in 1957 than the European Union envisaged by the founders of the EEC. An integrated inner core could emerge which might provide the highest tier of a multi-tiered Community, with the Mediterranean countries and possibly the Nordic countries on a less integrated level.

Such a system if it emerged would do so only over a considerable period of time. One question continually facing negotiators in 1957 was the distribution of benefits and burdens within the free trade area. In a multi-tiered Community it would be likely that heavy financial commitments would be demanded of the inner tier, but the question of the returns available to its members remains problematic. The factors making for continuity in the Community are also strong, within the Commission, the European Parliament, and, indeed, within the Court of Justice, whose interpretations have generally favoured integration. Few governments will be willing to contemplate major treaty amendments or even policy reforms with their delicate balance of costs and benefits.

In view of the acceptance in principle of further enlargement, the argument over *profondissement* versus *elargissement* may be counter-productive and even irrelevant. Such a conclusion is reinforced by the absence of any clear indication that the existing members are prepared to work for consolidation. Nonetheless, concern over the development of the Community may create a reluctance to agree to enlargement beyond that of Greece without some significant *quid pro quo* despite the problems likely to arise from such discrimination.

The question therefore arises of the grounds on which further enlargement could be delayed. The Treaty of Rome provides little assistance in the matter, but there are certain doubts about the potential members which could be used to delay their accession. One such doubt is the political stability of their political systems and the absence of any Community mechanism for dealing with a non-democratic system. There must be some doubt also about the willingness and the ability of potential members to carry out the obligations of membership; even if existing members have not always lived up to their commitments, the Community rests upon the assumption of the supremacy of Community law and its acceptance and implementation by its members.

The question of enlargement is of major importance for the Community. Debates over consolidation versus enlargement will doubtless persist, as will those over continuity versus reform. But despite enlargement much of the present Community will persist. Enlargement could, perhaps should, however, provide the incentive for a more thorough-going reappraisal of policies and goals. Inevitably there will be greater difficulties in operating the institutions and in bringing about agreement on sectoral policies, perhaps even postponing still further the prospect of European Union however defined. But the Community has already shown itself to be a resilient organisation despite its periods of apparent stagnation; it has already proved itself a new type of political and economic organisation which subsumes many of the past distinctions between alliances, confederations and federations. The possible Mediterranean members clearly wish to accede to an organisation which has a political as well as economic potential. The costs of rejecting such members in the interests of pursuing a sometimes illusory, certainly elusive, and exclusive goal will be heavy.

14 A Common European Foreign Policy: Mirage or Reality?

WILLIAM WALLACE

From one perspective the member governments of the European Community have already made remarkable strides towards achieving a common foreign policy. The Nine held together through the Conference on Security and Cooperation in Europe, and have continued to hold together since the 'Final Act' at Helsinki in the preparations for the 'follow up' conference in Belgrade in June-July 1977. They have sat in a 'single seat' throughout the Conference on International Economic Cooperation. They have made real progress towards concerting policies on the Middle East, acting as one within the framework of the Euro-Arab Dialogue, and consulting closely and continuously on attitudes to be taken in other international forums. In the United Nations, year by year, they have come to work more and more as a bloc, voting together on 82% of all resolutions in the 1976 General Assembly, and speaking often as a bloc through the mouthpiece of the country holding the Community Presidency.

In matters of external relations within the competence of the Treaties, they have established and maintained a common commercial policy. The Lomé Convention, which links the European Community with nearly fifty African, Caribbean and Pacific states, has set a number of significant precedents in the response of industrialised countries to the developing world. With the development of a common fisheries regime, the Soviet Union has at last accepted the Community as an international actor. Outside the competence of the Treaties, the framework of political cooperation deals more discreetly with most sensitive items on the diplomatic agenda. In third countries as well as in international organisations the permanent missions of the Nine have come to work together on matters inside and outside the competences of the Treaties: holding regular group meetings at different levels, making common representations, even on occasion sending back common reports. At home their

This paper derives from a study currently being carried out at the Royal Institute of International Affairs on the options and constraints on British foreign policy in the 1980s.

foreign offices are directly linked by a special telex network, still less than four years old, but already carrying a substantial load of messages. Within its sphere of competence, the Commission has built up a number of foreign missions of the Communities as a whole: major posts in Washington and Tokyo, missions to the UN in New York and Geneva, and an expanding number of offices in the states associated through the Lomé Convention.

The context with which the member governments of the Community make foreign policy has thus been radically transformed. Most important issues of foreign policy have become multilateral, rather than bilateral, and the Community (or the political cooperation procedure) has become the major focus for concerting policies. Optimists argue that governments have thus locked themselves in to an irrevocable process, which is likely to lead them into a closer and closer convergence of views and actions, and thus eventually to a common policy. Pessimists point out that the degree of integration achieved in the defence field with Nato some ten years ago or more was comparable in extent to what the Nine have now achieved in foreign policy, and yet has not moved on beyond effective consultation to common policy, strictly defined. The purpose of this paper is to assess whether the progress so far made towards cooperation in foreign policy represents the basis for further advance, or rather a plateau from which further progress is unlikely; to assess the pressures for and against greater cooperation in the foreign policy field; and to suggest those areas in which progress towards a common foreign policy is most likely to be made.

What do we mean by a European Foreign Policy?

It is as easy or difficult to define a European Foreign Policy as it is to define the European Union of which it would be a part. Prime Minister Tindemans laid great stress on the importance of presenting 'a united front to the world' in his Report on European Union, presented to the European Council in December 1975. 'We must', he went on, 'tend to act in common in all main fields of our external relations whether in foreign policy, security, economic relations or development aid.' His definition of common foreign policy was that 'within the framework of the European Union our states must be able together to draw up a policy and to enact it.'

This fairly loose definition raises a number of questions about how far and in which direction the member governments need to go to achieve a workable common policy. The most ambitious definition would be in terms of *common institutions:* aiming to set up some sort of 'decision-taking centre' capable of formulating and implementing foreign policy on behalf of the Community as a whole. Progress along the road towards this would be through the creation of a permanent secretariat in Brussels for the political cooperation machinery, or through ending the current (and to some extent artificial) distinction between questions of political cooperation and matters within the competence of the Communities, which would in effect require an amendment to the Treaties. Outside the Communities this would imply the gradual amalgamation of national embassies and missions, with the eventual objective of full common representation on a European basis, with only separate trade and investment promotion offices left outside.

The sweep of this vision must at first sight be breathtaking to those who have witnessed the succession of grandiose institutional plans, for Economic and Monetary Union, for European Union itself, in past years, and their successive failure to translate their objectives into reality. It should however, be noted that the 'single seat' principle of European representation at international conferences is a first small step in this direction, and that the advantages of sharing facilities in third countries and even of setting up a common representation in newly-independent countries has already been discussed among the major foreign offices of the Nine, though so far without result. The Council Secretariat already provides some limited assistance to political cooperation meetings, and the Secretariat-General of the Commission makes a discreet but significant contribution to ensuring coherence between different sets of discussions. While it is highly unlikely that a full-blown institutional superstructure for foreign policy-making will be created within the next ten years, it is therefore well within the realms of possibility that a combination of pressures and the evolution of existing practices may nevertheless carry the member governments some way along the road.

A less ambitious definition would focus on *common actions and common intruments* as the key to a workable European foreign policy. The Community already possesses a number of common instruments in its external relations, which are not only available for use in the pursuit of wider foreign policy objectives but have already been put to use. The common commercial policy has given the Community leverage which it used against Greece in 1967 to express disapproval of the colonels' coup, and used again in the complex bargaining within the Conference on Cooperation and Security in Europe. Loans from the European Investment Bank have similarly been used for wider purposes in the delicate relationship with Portugal during 1975. The network of association agreements with Mediterranean countries, and the wider framework of association under the Lomé Convention, similarly provide economic instruments for political ends. The Community has not so far demonstrated a great capacity for coordinating these instruments, or for exerting its economic strength for political ends; but recent experiences of policy towards, for example, Yugoslavia, suggests that the Community itself and its member governments are learning from past confusions to concert economic and political objectives more effectively.

Political cooperation provides the member governments with a limited capacity for common action of a declaratory kind. Although Dr Kissinger's proposal in April 1973 for a redefined Atlantic Charter led only to the windy generalizations of the Declaration on the European identity, its indirect result was the Ottawa Declaration of July 1974, in which the Nine and the USA redefined the pattern and basis of mutual consultation. In the aftermath of the October 1973 Middle East war the Nine produced two statements on Middle East policy: declaratory in form and defensive in intent, but nevertheless of value to member governments as a common point of reference in resisting pressure from Arab and Israeli sources alike. A similar declaration of policy on Southern Africa, in February 1976, registered the Nine's concern with developments and their commitment to a common approach (though it also reflected their inability to advance beyond declarations to positive common

176

actions, coming as it did in the aftermath of the failure to concert their recognition of the MPLA regime in Angola, and being closely followed by their failure to agree on a proposed common initiative in Southern Africa). Common declarations, jointly sponsored resolutions, and voting solidarity in international conferences and organisations provide another form of common action, a diplomatic instrument with sufficient influence to be valued by all member governments and to increase the respect accorded to the Nine by other states.

The Internal-External conundrum

But this collection of commercial, economic and diplomatic instruments presents at best a limited and lopsided basis for an active foreign policy. With the significant exceptions of the CSCE and Portugal, Community foreign policy cooperation has so far been almost entirely reactive. The Nine have responded to events rather than anticipating or attempting positively to shape them. They have been concerned defensively to limit the damage to European interests which a disunited posture might threaten, to prevent third countries exploiting internal differences to their own advantage, rather than actively to attempt to exploit opportunities themselves or to mediate in disputes among third countries which might adversely affect the interests of the Community. Further progress towards a common foreign policy defined in terms of common instruments and the capacity for common action therefore rests upon the development of a wider and more balanced range of instruments: the capacity to use European industrial and financial strength in international negotiations in support of political objectives, the development of a more clearly defined security role, and perhaps also a common defence capacity. These in turn raise two fundamental questions about the possibilities of achieving a common foreign policy: whether it is possible to move very far towards integrated policies in external relations without parallel progress in developing common policies within the Community, and whether it is enough for Europe to be a 'civilian power' in the world without a parallel defence dimension.

Had the Community successfully pursued the Werner Plan towards Economic and Monetary Union, it would naturally have evolved towards common action in international monetary negotiations. The looseness of the Community's existing cooperation in economic and monetary matters is, conversely, reflected in the looseness of Community cooperation within the International Monetary Fund and the OECD. Had the Community been more successful in its attempts to harmonise industrial policies, it would have found it easier to act in response to the demands posed by the Group of 77 within UNCTAD and within the Conference on International Economic Cooperation, and to maintain a coherent position in negotiations with Japan. Had a common energy policy been evolved, the solidarity of the Nine in relation to the Middle East oil producers would have a firmer foundation. Common internal policies in all of these areas would considerably have strengthened the Community's position in relation to the United States.

It may be objected that all of these are outside the reach of foreign policy, strictly defined, in the shadowy field where domestic policies and external relations overlap. But the whole tendency of multilateral diplomacy in recent years has been towards linking different issues together in wide-ranging negotiations. This was, after all, Dr Kissinger's aim in the 'Year of Europe' in 1973-4. The CSCE was essentially an attempt on both sides to bargain from areas of strength to areas of weakness. The Euro-Arab Dialogue and the CIEC represent similar delicately balanced negotiations, with different 'baskets' simultaneously under discussion, and with each side hoping to achieve advantageous trade-offs in the package that eventually emerges. A Community possessed of only a limited range of instruments, capable of only an incoherent response in significant areas of multilateral diplomacy, cannot therefore hope to be an effective negotiator in a world in which political objectives are more and more often counter-balanced by economic concessions, and economic objectives by political costs.

In assessing the prospects for progress towards a common foreign policy over the next decade, one might however consider the obverse of this relationship between external relations and internal polcies: that is, how far external threats may force the pace of developing internal policies. The oil embargo of 1973 had an immediate impact on discussions of internal energy policy, though the outcome of continuing disunity and divergent short-term interests among the member governments (and of active American intervention) was a higher level of cooperation within an Atlantic rather than a European framework. The threat of Japanese competition in steel and shipbuilding has led already not only to a firmer Community stance in overall negotiations with Japan but also to much more active discussions about internal market management and industrial policy. The complex interaction between internal and external developments might thus quite possibly push the Community towards evolving common policies in areas which would then powerfully reinforce its capacity to act on the international plane. How far and how fast such defensive developments might go will depend upon the pattern of external pressures, which will be discussed in more detail below.

The Security Dimension

After the failure of the proposal for a European Defence Community in 1954 the proponents of European Union long fought shy of raising the issue of an autonomous European entity in defence and in security. Doubts about its impact not only upon relations with the United States but also upon the level of tension in Europe reinforced this reluctance to reopen the issue. In the last two or three years however it has been clearly reopened. Mr Tindemans in his Report roundly declared that 'Security cannot . . . be left outside the scope of the European Union', which 'will not be complete until it has drawn up a common defence policy.' This is not the place for a full discussion of the arguments for and against a common European defence policy; but again, while recognising the unlikelihood of achieving any neat institutional blueprint within the foreseeable future, it is worth noting both the extent of progress already achieved and the incentives for further development.

The CSCE was a landmark in the evolution of a common European security policy. With the United States content to play a passive role, discussions on European security shifted from within the NATO framework to that of political cooperation, in looser consultation with the other member governments of NATO. There is little sign of this unity of action breaking down in the transition from Helsinki to Belgrade. Concern over the future of Yugoslavia has led the Nine into political discussions of their common response to a security threat in that area. Continuing tension in the Eastern Mediterranean, and the prospect of Greek accession to the Community, has stimulated consideration of the Community's security role in that area, and will continue to exert pressure for a more active response. Even while military forces remain a national responsibility, progress towards a European security policy is already impressive; and the incentives for greater solidarity are strong.

In the field of defence, more narrowly defined, there has been little incentive for attempting a degree of interaction which would call into question the delicate military relationship with the USA. One may therefore suggest that Europe is likely to continue to lack the traditional foreign policy instrument of integrated military forces, unless there is a radical change in American policy. It is difficult at present to predict the impact upon the Community of the need to patrol and protect its extended marine limits, in terms of developing common forces or common methods of financing them; but it is unlikely that developments in this area will provide more than a marginal addition to its foreign policy capacity. The awkward problems of military procurement are however more likely to throw up demands for common action, and to pose problems which force a common response. The Eurogroup and the European Programme Group represent successive responses to the parallel problems of the transatlantic imbalance in defence effort and military procurement and of the need to protect European defence industries, by providing them with a market large enough to support long production runs and by sharing the budgetary burden of research and development. The cost, and the opportunity, of further integration of military procurement among Community member governments would be that shared production would eventually force a common policy on sales to third countries: another instrument available for use in pursuing political advantage, though one in which the domestic interests of those employed in the Community's arms industries would be closely intertwined.

A still more modest definition of what is involved in achieving a common foreign policy, leaving aside the evolution of common instruments and institutions, would focus on the emergence of *common attitudes:* the cumulative convergence of assumptions and perspectives among member governments which would lead to concerted action, rather than to common action on the basis of integrated institutions. As the President of the Council delicately put it after the European Council in the Hague in November 1976, member states are already attempting 'progressively to exercise their sovereignty in a convergent manner.' The essence of the political cooperation process, M. Davignon argued in an interview in March 1976, is:

'the habit of working together . . . That in my view is the principal success of political cooperation: to have infused into diplomatic behaviour the reflex that, when confronted with a given policy issue, it is useful to know what your partners are doing before taking up your own position. This reflex is further cultivated by the need to consult, and consultation clearly implies the possibility of reaching a joint position'.

Officials in all the foreign ministries of the Nine remark on the degree to which the development of political cooperation over the past six years has affected their working assumptions and their reaction to international developments: a change in perspectives similar to that which years of close consultation on international financial policy has brought about among members of central banks and finance ministries. Foreign Ministers have repeatedly expressed their appreciation of the close network of consultation which has so rapidly built up; Mr Callaghan, in the aftermath of the British referendum in July 1975, saw this as providing 'wide scope for adopting a common foreign policy'. Continued and satisfactory experience of consultation over a number of years, reinforced as they are already by direct communication links among national capitals and by closer ties among diplomatic services, is likely to lead to a greater convergence of views.

A limiting factor on the convergence of ministerial and official attitudes so far has been the lack of convergence of prevailing attitudes among political parties and domestic publics in different countries. The confidential and unpublicised nature of the political cooperation procedure, in sharp contrast to the processes of Community discussion and policy-making, has militated against such a supportive shift in the wider parameters of opinion within which ministers and officials make policy. It may well be that the impact of a directly elected European Parliament on the political debate within the member states, and the ability of that Parliament to focus greater attention on the Community's foreign relations, may be such as to bring about a gradual shift of predominant attitudes in the different member states towards a degree of consensus. This must, however, of necessity be a long and slow process, in which for several years at least the imperatives of domestic politics and of national political traditions continue to predominate over the European dimension. Above the level of domestic politics, however, it seems likely that the elite network which links together ministers, officials, and international civil servants will grow more tightly-knit, and that this will in itself prove a significant constraint on the pursuit of divergent national policies.

Pressures towards a common foreign policy

The strongest pressures towards greater solidarity among the Nine come, as has already been suggested, from outside the Community. In a world which is moving towards block diplomacy, an effective group offers the prospect of substantially increasing the collective influence of its members. The experience of the CSCE, of the increased stature of the Nine in the UN General Assembly, of the pivotal role of the European Community in the multilateral trade negotiations, has brought home to all member governments the advantages of closer cooperation. Unless the present trend towards a world of blocs, or at least diplomacy between groups of states, is sharply reversed within the next few years, the argument that member governments can achieve more of their national objectives through common action than through bilateral diplomacy will gather more weight. It is an argument which will necessarily appeal more to the smaller member governments than to the larger; though among the larger members only Germany, and to a lesser extent France, can now aspire to an independent stature in international negotiations sufficient to make the support of the Community auxiliary rather than central.

More subtle, perhaps more equivocal, pressures come from external expectations, threats, and crises. The European Community is perceived as an international actor by third countries and by groups of third countries. Their leaders do not understand or care about the delicate distinctions between matters of political cooperation and matters within the competence of the Treaties, or between a 'civilian power' and a power *tout court*. The Arab oil producers, the United States, even the Soviet Union, have on occasion during the last five years made demands of the fragile structure of European foreign policy cooperation which were greater than it was able to handle; but on each occasion the response has been, in part, to attempt to extend the capacities of that structure rather than to risk the disintegration of what had so far been achieved.

The effect of external threats and internal crises on the integration or disintegration of national foreign policies is harder to assess. The experience of the 1973 oil crises was not encouraging: caught unprepared, the Community almost fell apart. Less acute threats, however, such as the perceived commercial and industrial and industrial challenge of Japan, the politically linked threat to oil supplies from the OPEC countries, and the Soviet Union's political and economic domination of Eastern Europe, have aroused more constructive responses. One may predict with some confidence that, unless acute crises intervene of an intensity sufficient to overload the developing capacities of European cooperation, a defensive response to external challenges will push members of the Community not only towards common attitudes but also to common action. A desire to limit the damage to one's national interests from outside challenges may not be the most glorious motivation for a European foreign policy, but it may well prove to move national governments more powerfully than any more idealistic or ideological objectives.

Similarly, the most powerful pressure from within the Community for greater solidarity of action is likely to come from the demand for protection from external threats and challenges, and the recognition of the Community as a resource in warding them off. At present the most apparent threats to particular interests within the Community are economic and industrial, leading businessmen and trade unionists to press to push for an active Community external policy in those fields. But if a more immediately apparent threat to West Europe's security were to emerge, in central Europe, in the Mediterranean, perhaps even around its maritime limits, one would anticipate an upsurge of domestic demands for a Community response. Self-interest, rather than commitment to the European idea, is the key to a rise in internal support for a common foreign policy; but, as has been suggested, the potential for the recognition of shared self-interests within the Community framework is relatively high.

There are, nevertheless, a number of sources of internal support for common action in the foreign policy field. Prestige and attachment to symbols are never entirely absent from foreign policy; and the Community offers some potential for both. Particularly for the smaller member states (but not *only* for them), the rotating Presidency of the Council of Ministers offers a chance to play a more prominent role on the international stage, an opportunity to regain as leader of a group the international status which West European states are no longer able to aspire to individually. It is not entirely irrelevant that one of the successes of cooperation within the UN so far has been successfully to nominate Gaston Thorn to be President of the 1976 General Assembly: an indication that European solidarity may cumulatively help to regain from the Afro-Asian countries some of the dominance of international organisations which they have achieved in recent years. Cumulatively, even the symbolism of a deep lilac common passport will help to shift national perspectives, to create a rather wider sense of European identity among the public at large. It is not impossible that a directly-elected European Parliament may help to focus discussion of common interests in foreign policy, and so generate a convergence of views among parties and publics as well as among governments. These, clearly, are all auxiliary rather than primary forces for progress; but their combination suggests, again, that there will be significant pressure for movement towards a greater integration of foreign policies, rather than an acceptance of the present balance or a move back towards separate national policies.

Relations with the US

Perhaps the largest question-mark hanging over the whole subject is posed by the attitude of the United States. Successively sponsor of European integration, ambivalent senior partner, and direct challenger, the American government now seems happy with the *modus vivendi* on transatlantic consultation agreed at Ottawa in July 1974. This relates however only to political and security matters, narrowly defined; and it is in the network of Atlantic and global international organisations within which the United States and its European partners interact that the relationship between acceptance of American leadership, cooperation on an Atlantic basis, or partnership between a coherent European grouping and the USA still remains open to question. The United States remains Europe's dominant partner and ally, in security, defence, financial, economic and industrial matters. The attraction of the American connection, as against the purely European, is evident in the enthusiasm with which the governments of Germany, Britain, and even of France greet the development of Atlantic economic summits on what may be becoming a regular basis. It was evident, too, in the choice of the International Energy Agency, within the OECD framework, rather than the EEC as a response to the threat to Europe's oil supplies.

American involvement in Western Europe, politically, militarily and economically, is so direct that a determined and well-managed effort to maintain the priority of Atlantic cooperation would do much to inhibit any substantial progress towards a distinctive set of actions and institutions for European foreign policy. Conversely, any substantial withdrawal of American political and military involvement in Western Europe would pose a threat sufficiently direct to force the pace of European integration in the foreign policy sphere. Between these two stark alternatives, the Europeans must hope for a high degree of American forbearance and understanding as they edge slowly towards common policies through slow-moving and untidy procedures, considerably higher for example than that which obtained during most of Mr Nixon's presidency. In an interview shortly after his election in November

1976 President Carter stated that 'we should deal with Brussels . . . to the extent to which the Europeans themselves make Brussels the focus of their decisions', an equivocal commitment which is capable of different interpretations in practice. Political sources of tension within the transatlantic relationship are numerous enough for some experts to argue that it is in any case difficult to see how the present balance can survive another decade. But whether a shift in balance will be successully managed without any serious dissention, or whether a sharper break may threaten, must be very much an open question.

European issues

The second question-mark is of course posed by the prospect of further enlargement. It may well be that the admission of Greece, Portugal and Spain raises larger problems for the Community's internal development than for its foreign policy; but the foreign policy implications need to be weighed in the balance. If Spain is admitted to NATO, and if Turkey declares its intention of following the path towards eventual membership, the Community will come much closer towards embracing the European component of the Atlantic Alliance, thus easing the path towards adding a defence dimension to European foreign policy, except on the sensitive northern flank. On the other hand, the Community will be drawn much more actively into the complex, perhaps intractable, security problems of the Eastern Mediterranean, in particular the continuing rivalry between Greece and Turkey. The Community's largely passive role in the Cyprus conflict since 1974 does not augur well for its capacities for managing such local rivalries. As a significant Mediterranean power, the Community would also be pressed to play a more active role in the complex of political and economic relations with the states of the North African littoral (most particularly Algeria, a leading member of the Group of 77) and in the Arab-Israel conflict, which will again place great strain upon the capacity of the Community to act in common. The problem of relations with the non-member states of Northern Europe, which share close economic, industrial and security interests with the Community, will also require some positive attention in a community which is tilting towards the South.

Two further potential question-marks should be noted in passing: the problem posed by the increasing dominance of West Germany within the Community, and that posed by the ambivalent attitude of the Soviet Union to European integration. Unless current trends are reversed, the Community's capacity to act internationally in the mid-1980s will rest very heavily on the economic and industrial weight of Germany; its defence (and therefore its perspective on security) will also be dominated by the German contribution. Both the Germans and their partner governments may conclude from this that an integrated common policy on a European scale is the best vehicle for containing a preponderant German contribution; but it is not impossible that a future German government might grow weary of the reluctant cooperation of its weaker partners, or that the French government or other members might take fright at the implications of accepting German leadership. Soviet acceptance of the Community as a legitimate negotiating partner would reinforce progress towards a common policy; but determined Soviet attempts at advantageous bilateral relationships, or a shift in the pattern of Soviet control of Eastern Europe within the next decade, might well reopen doubts in some member states about the desirability of a too-rigidly divided Europe.

Internal problems

There are a number of readily apparent obstacles within the Community to further progress. The most immediate is the institutional confusion of the Community's evolving procedures for concerting foreign policies, and the difficulties of carrying through institutional reforms. The non-congruity between political cooperation and the procedures of the Community is an irritating, though not insurmountable, barrier to the achievement of coherent policies. The duplication of work, and the consequent problem of coordination, is evident in parallel discussions within the OECD and the EEC on international economic policy, within the Eurogroup (and now the European Programme Group) and within the Community on the industrial implications of arms procurement policies. The capacities of the Commission and of the Council Secretariat, international secretariats bedevilled by problems of national balance and inflexibility of personnel, leave room for some disquiet. The lesson of political cooperation, evolving without a tight legal framework into an extensive and moderately effective network over the past six years, with it own well-established procedures and its own communications structure (though not yet its own staff) is however instructive. Institutional evolution on an incremental basis *is* possible, and over a ten-year period may well amount to very substantial change. Major changes in central structure, however, such as the creation of a planning capacity or of some sort of 'decision-making centre', would require formal agreement; and it is difficult to see where a positive commitment from national governments sufficient to bring them to yield up a visible part of their sovereignty to a common institution might come from.

For it is the reluctance of national governments to accept more than a limited and incremental approach to cooperation which represents one of the most intractable obstacles to the achievement of common policies, in the foreign policy field as elsewhere. Where immediate common interests are apparent, or where an external demand suggests the advantages of a common response, progress is possible; but 'practical' politicians in almost all the governments of the Nine resist longer-term speculations, and resist also racing ahead of domestic opinion into schemes which involve a visible diminution of their authority in favour of some supra-national body. Politicians win elections by pointing to the actions they have themselves taken on behalf of their voters, not by referring to their interventions in the collective decision-making of international bodies. If the pattern of domestic politics in the different member states converges over the next decade, the importance of this obstacle may be somewhat mitigated by the evolution of a Community-wide consensus. But if, as must be considered quite likely, the pattern of domestic politics diverges, with for example more left-inclined governments in France and Italy and more right-inclined governments in Britain and Germany, the strains which the divergent perspectives of different governments and the different domestic pressures under which they operate will impose even on the existing level of Community cooperation might well be considerable.

Two further internal obstacles should briefly be noted: the need for some parallel development of common internal policies to provide the foundation for common policies abroad, already discussed above, and the problem of cost. Part of the success of European political cooperation has been due to its concern with those aspects of foreign policy which least often involve direct costs; thus enabling member governments to concert policies without being forced to consider the budgetary consequences and the distribution of costs and benefits among different governments. Once foreign policy moves out of the strictly diplomatic field into using economic instruments for political ends, into linking technical assistance, debt relief or the provision of credits to the supply of oil or to attitudes to the Arab-Israeli dispute, or into considerations of common policies in arms procurement, arms sales, and defence, the problem of differential distribution of costs and benefits immediately arises. During the Nine's long discussions of the developing situation in Portugal in 1975, for example, British ministers felt inhibited from putting forward proposals for too ambitious a use of economic levers of influence, since they recognised that it was the German Government which would be called upon to put up the cash. An effective common foreign policy, with a range of common instruments to support concerted action, will therefore require some considerable development in the budgetary powers and procedures of the Communities: an internal development which would raise some fundamental questions about the future shape of the Communities as such.

Conclusions

Looking ahead to the mid-1980s, we are unlikely to have witnessed the establishment of a tidy institutional structure for a common European foreign policy. In a disillusioned Community governed by 'practical' men, no such deliberately planned progression towards a clearly defined goal is to be expected. In the loosest sense of common policy, however, considerable progress has already been made towards the creation of common attitudes on a range of issues, through gradual convergence of views. The Community already has a number of common instruments at its disposal for use in foreign policy, and there are some signs that during the next decade these may be complemented by others, possibly even extending into the field of defence.

On the always very risky assumption of the continuation of current trends and the absence of major discontinuities (such as a radical change in American or Soviet policies towards the Community, or sharply divergent political developments within member states), one may say with some confidence that the substantial degree of collaboration already achieved will have become both more intense and more broad in scope. In the event of major discontinuities, of acute international crisis or a sharp change in the Community's international environment, it is arguable that under particular circumstances the Community might *either* move forward much faster and more positively towards integrating foreign policies, or might buckle under the strain and lose much of what has already been achieved. The least likely outcome is that the Community's capacities in foreign policy in ten years' time will closely resemble the peculiar collection of instruments and institutions which we have now. Without at any point deliberately deciding to commit themselves to a distinctively European policy, member governments may find that the gradual evolution of attitudes, procedures and institutions has carried them towards a position in which very few issues remain primarily bilateral in content. Little by little, they may have become sufficiently constrained by accumulated agreements on policy, by requirements to consult and commitments to joint action, that they will be no longer in effect pursuing separate national foreign policies but rather taking part in a cumbersome and untidy process which will nevertheless produce recognisable common foreign policy.

Governments may well be content to drift slowly towards such a common policy without grasping the institutional nettle or pressing more positively for coherence. If one hopes for a revival of commitment to positive integration among the leaders of the Community, then institutional progress must again become a priority. The procedures of political cooperation would be much strengthened by the establishment of a central secretariat, staffed by senior officials on secondment from national foreign offices, and by the creation within that of some capability for planning and joint assessment. Proposals, already under discussion, for greater cooperation among diplomatic services in third countries should be pushed ahead, with the intention eventually of creating a common service. The remaining barriers between political cooperation and Community external relations should be dismantled. The interdependence of progress on internal policies and unity in external relations should be explicitly recognised. The European Parliament should be encouraged to debate the wider choices at stake in Community external policies. Only with such a deliberate approach will the Community achieve a common foreign policy in the strict sense; a capacity for action based not only on common attitudes and instruments, but also on common institutions.

15 European Defence

SIR BERNARD BURROWS

In the fragmented history of the European Community's gropings towards federalism defence has played a brief but notable part. The proposal for a European Defence Community (EDC) was put forward by France in 1950, as a centralised and explicit 'supra-national' element in a union comprising 'common institutions, common armed forces and a common budget'. The point was emphasized when Britain refused to join because it was 'part of the intention of the EDC plan as a whole that it should lead to federation' and Britain 'would not feel willing to join in a federation of that kind'.[1] Partly because of this refusal the proposal failed in 1954. With it disappeared a proposal for an equally supra-national political community. Instead of the Defence Community France, Germany, Italy, Britain and the Benelux countries formed Western European Union, which contained a strongly worded mutual defence commitment but no supra-national organization. The defence interests of WEU were almost immediately handed over to the Atlantic Alliance, whose mutual commitment was rather less sharply worded, but to which was later added a defence organisation (NATO) providing for integrated planning in peacetime and integrated command in war. France withdrew from this integrated organization in 1966, but not from the Atlantic Alliance.

It would be wrong to see these events as representing solely the rise and fall of the federalist idea. They were greatly influenced by external circumstances. The EDC proposal was largely due to a combination of American pressure for a German contribution to the defence of Western Europe against Russia and French reluctance to see a reborn German army. German contingents dispersed in a common armed force were thought to avoid this risk while allowing German manpower to be effectively used. At the same time the EDC proposal clearly owed much to the integrationist philosophy which had already given birth to the European Coal and Steel Community.

The EDC failed in 1954 mainly because of two strong currents in French politics, which were both to be found repeating themselves at a later stage. The

---

[1] *Mr. Eden in the House of Commons 14 April 1954.*

right objected to the fragmentation of the greater part of the French army which the EDC would have imposed on all its members and not only on Germany. The left were afraid of adverse Russian reactions. Without British participation, the French Government, at that time desperately embroiled in Indo-China, made no serious attempt to force it through against a largely hostile parliament. Twelve years later De Gaulle repudiated the integrated organization of NATO, largely on grounds of national sovereignty—i.e. the rejection of federalism—but also at least in part because he did not want Europe to be dragged into war through America's involvement in Vietnam and because he wanted to play the leading role in a policy of detente with Russia.

Since then a partial European presence in the defence field has been re-created through the Eurogroup and the European Programme Group (EPG). The former consists of most of the European members of NATO, but not including France, and deals with a variety of mainly logistical subjects. The latter is a more recent creation, technically separate from NATO, and including France in its membership. Its function is to plan the joint production and procurement of military equipment and to promote a 'two-way street' through which European equipment may be sold to America as well as bought by European states from America.

With this background the objects of this paper are to examine the pressures for and the limitations of further European defence integration, how action, or inaction, in this field may be related to the evolution of the European Community and to the relationship between the Community or European states individually and the USA. The questions most relevant to the general discussion of the new federalism are whether some form of unified defence effort is an essential part of a Community evolving towards a more federal constitution; where in the scale of priorities such unification should be put; whether in fact it is a subject which should impel the Community forward along this road or whether, owing to the sensitivity of opinion on a matter which has been held to be so vital an aspect of national sovereignty, it will be left until last and may even be seen as an obstacle to other aspects of integration; will defence, in other words, provide a last rampart for the nation state facing the transfer and distribution of its powers, by devolution down to regions and, through European Union, up to a European centre?

The Need for European Defence

The threat which led to the creation of Western European Union and of NATO still exists. Russian military capabilities are formidable and increasing in comparison with those of NATO. It was fashionable for a time to argue that Russian intentions could no longer envisage a march across Europe to the Channel Ports, but were rather to use military preponderance as a political weapon, to secure finlandization by consent and by degrees. It is also possible that the two methods might be combined, and that actual seizure of territory—preferably small and remote territory—might be used as another means of political persuasion. It may be urged that the issues between East and West, and the threat to western influence in general, are now global rather than European. Even so, Europe remains the greatest prize.

Detente has produced two great results: the establishment on a quasi-permanent basis of the SALT dialogue between the US and Russia—and the continuance of the dialogue is at least as important as the numerical limitations which have been partially achieved—and the Ostopolitik agreements, implying the renunciation by West Germany of the objective of German re-unification, at least for the lifetime of present politicians. The latter, while in itself removing one of Russia's obsessions, at the same time made possible a more whole-hearted dedication of West Germany to the construction of the European Community and has therefore left open the possibility that a unified Community would also have a defence function. Recent indications suggest that Germany is in fact in no mood to proceed in this direction at present and is on the contrary rather frustrated with the Community. Russia, however, remains sensitive to the concept of a European defence system as in 1954, and has claimed that such a development would be contrary to at least the spirit of the Ostopolitik agreements. It is in fact open to argument whether Russia's first objective is the withdrawal of American forces from Europe, which might be the one thing needed to precipitate a new European Defence Community, or rather to prevent German participation in such a structure, particularly if this implied the common possession or control of nuclear weapons. The Russians may feel that continued American military presence is the lesser evil, particularly if they regard bilateral Russian-American relations as more stable and predictable than those with a reinforced Community having a greater measure of defence autonomy.

In spite of detente, Russian capabilities remain very great and are increasing; Russian intentions are to use military preponderance for ideological gains whenever possible, ideology and nationalism being in this case hardly separable. Opportunities for tension or conflict exist in many parts of the world, including some potential opportunities in and around Europe, such as the Middle East, a possibly fissiparous Yugoslavia post-Tito, and possible defections from the Soviet sphere of influence which might present the West with agonizing choices. To guard against these risks the countries at present in the Atlantic Alliance will want to remain in a defence system which seems to meet their needs for national security, even if in some cases they would like to vary the terms of their participation. But at the same time they will have quite contrary inclinations to believe the risk is less and to save money on defence so that they can spend it on industrial investment or social benefit.

Europe in the Atlantic Alliance

The Alliance at present rests, in the minds of most of its members, on the combination of American commitment, including the involvement of the American strategic nuclear forces, and of sufficient European effort, in common with American forces, to make the American commitment credible not only to their adversaries in Eastern Europe, but to the Americans and to the Europeans themselves. No foreseeable European evolution can replace the ultimate protection afforded by the American strategic nuclear forces, provided that these remain a credible part of the system. The problems of European nuclear forces are well known. They cannot be 'European' until there is a unified political entity to exercise control. Germany has renounced the possession of nuclear weapons and a change in this respect is generally regarded as the one thing which might drive Russia into a European adventure. The British and French nuclear forces are therefore likely to remain under national control for the foreseeable future. It will be increasingly difficult and costly to maintain them in viable condition. They can be regarded either as a useless extravagance, a dubious guarantee of national sovereignty if all else fails, or as 'held in trusteeship for Europe as a whole',[2] until, presumably, there is a European state or federation to inherit the nuclear capability of its component parts. Meanwhile, the important and urgent need is to have a consistent policy for the use of tactical nuclear weapons, including those of France, since these form an essential element in establishing the credibility, and therefore the effectiveness, of the western defence system as a whole. Possible methods to achieve this coordination are discussed below.

It is not only the nuclear weapons which differentiate the US from the European defence effort. There is also the whole scale of research and development, the application of new technology to arms production, bolstered both by a vast domestic market and by massive exports.

The disparity between the two sides of the Atlantic resulting from the nuclear situation and the technological gap is increased by the greater strength of the US as a single government dealing in the Alliance with 13 separate and often discordant European governments. Attempts to redress this imbalance have been made by speaking of an 'Atlantic Community', or alternatively, of the 'two pillars' of Atlantic defence, namely the US and a more united Europe. The Atlantic Community has never been more than a rhetorical aspiration. On the other hand there is little doubt that progress towards realization of the European pillar would strengthen the American interest in the security of western Europe and therefore the American commitment to its defence. The key to the future of the Alliance is thus largely in European hands. Pressure in the US for deliberate American withdrawal from Europe is almost wholly absent; pressure for the reduction of US forces in Europe, the erstwhile hobby-horse of Senator Mansfield, has died away. European distaste for being associated with a US engaged in a misconceived and unsuccessful war in Vietnam has rapidly declined with the ending of that war, even though this amounted to a defeat for America's allies. The US refusal to be involved in Angola suggests that new military adventures are for the present most unlikely. The most serious risk of decoupling the US strategic deterrent from the defence of Europe would occur if the European allies reduced their forces to such an extent as to make conventional defence unrealistic. In the longer term there have been European suspicions of a tendency towards greater bilateralism in US-Russian relations, or towards a condominium of super-Powers dictating to the rest of the world, Europe included. Some of the bilateral agreements, even a multilateral one like non-proliferation, have seemed capable of this interpretation. A variant risk, no more palatable to other Europeans, is the still highly speculative idea of 'bigemony' between the US and Germany, if the other European allies chose to suggest that they were no longer capable of or interested in continuing to share the burdens of alliance.

These dangers are far off, and to a large extent it is within the power of the European countries to ensure that they do not come any nearer. The more

[2] *Mr. Edward Heath: Godkin lecture 1967, published in Old World, New Horizons, OUP 1970.*

these countries organize their defence efforts so as to be more unified and more effective the more likely is the system to continue. This is not to say that it could not be modified. The common action of two pillars (US and Europe) might well have results in organization and responsibility which differed from the present arrangements between a super-Power and 13 small to medium independent providers of a mixed collection of military hardware and manpower. Within such a system the role of European defence organization would be twofold, to seek practical commonality between the European member-states, and to prepare common views and positions on strategy, tactics, and anything else which arose, for use in the continuing Alliance-wide debate, including the US and Canada, on how the Alliance should be run. There may on occasion be significant divergences between European views and those of the US, deriving perhaps from the concentration of the Europeans on the defence of their part of a single continent, contrasted with the more global view of the US. Some of these are at present glossed over because they are inadequately formulated and because the right fora do not exist.

There have in the past been objections to European defence unification on the grounds that it was either dangerous because it could only come about as a result of American withdrawal, and to talk about it prematurely might hasten such withdrawal, or useless because even a unified Europe could never match American strength. The first argument is refuted by repeated American expressions of support for European unity, even if some manifestations of it are not always favourable to American commercial interests. As to the second, it is true that Europe by itself can never aspire to all the military attributes of a super-Power, but this has never been and never could be a condition of the Alliance. America is in the alliance because it believes that its own interest requires that western Europe should remain part of the free world, and because it has proved possible to achieve this by combining American and European defence efforts, even if these are in some senses disparate. But there must be limits to what is a tolerable disparity. It is in the nature of a super-Power, as of God, to help only those who will in some measure help themselves. More rapid progress towards unity would help the European allies to ensure that the acceptable limits of disparity shall not be exceeded.

What can Europe do?

The public distaste for military expenditure has become a major constraint in Western European defence policy, and could become a major reason why defence has to be done on a more common basis. While the European Community was progressing in the direction of political union it was also possible to see this as a motive for a united defence effort.[3] Even the less utopian objective of a common foreign policy pushes in the same direction since foreign policy and defence policy are almost inextricably intertwined. But the impulse in these directions is now feebler than it was, and the rising cost of defence may be a more potent driving force.

At the same time there are two considerations which somewhat differentiate

---

[3] *E.g. Edward Heath, op. cit. 'Can one conceive of a Europe growing together in an increasing number of ways and yet not trying to provide coherently for its own defence?', and Tindemans Report on European Union, Brussels, December 1975, Chapter II, C. 3, 'European Union will not be complete until it has drawn up a common defence policy'.*

defence cooperation from other functions, actual or potential, of the Community. The nation state was largely formed for purposes of war, or, to put it less bluntly, its size and composition were largely determined by the power of a government to control it and to defend it successfully against attack. Sometimes this meant a narrowing down after extension which proved too great for a system of a population to maintain, as England after decolonisation, France after Napoleon, Spain after Charles V; sometimes the accretion of formerly separate units which were too small to have a satisfactory existence in independence, as in the 19th century formation of Germany and Italy. Although the two World Wars have proved that the European nation-state is no longer capable of carrying out its original function of independent defence of its territory, the mythology lingers on and modern nations are still sensitive about pooling their defence resources in peace-time.

Secondly, common defence demands a decision-making and executive apparatus which are different in kind to those required for a common foreign policy. The decisions have often to be taken quicker, and they have to be carried out in more complex, detailed and practical ways. A decision on common action in a foreign policy situation can often be executed by sending telegrams to Ambassadors or sending a Minister to the UN. In defence policy a decision is quite likely to require translating into movement orders, tactical handbooks, industrial production or research. The decision is either very urgent in a moment of emergency or it has a long lead time and therefore requires much staff-work to follow it up, monitor progress and report back. None of this sounds very like the present meetings of national Ministers and officials in the forum of 'political cooperation', with no permanent secretariat and a rotating presidency. Defence would introduce an institutional imperative into Community affairs which nationalist sentiment would at first sight find repugnant.

Resistance to defence unification should not be underestimated. After 25 years of NATO the progress towards standardization of equipment and procedures is pathetic. The military establishments and industrial protectionism are as much to blame as political chauvinism. If these hesitations could be overcome there might be a two-way approach to the question of institutions for European defence within the Atlantic Alliance. The Ministers of the European Community countries meeting in Political Cooperation or as the European Council, could decide to deal with major aspects of defence policy. As Françoise de Rose says[4] they could consider together questions like the level of conventional forces, the nuclear threshold, the possibility of bringing their defence expenditure into an agreed and proportional equivalence. Secondly, so as not to involve them in too much detail, the European Programme Group could act as staff and clearing-house for a wider range of tasks than its present responsibility for advising on joint production and procurement of equipment. The fact that the EPG and the Community do not consist of exactly the same countries is one of those untidinesses which will have to be tolerated on the long march towards a more effective European defence system. At least they both contain the major European members of the Atlantic Alliance so far as the central front is concerned, including the French. With Community enlarge-

<hr>

[4] *La France et la Défense de l'Europe, Seuil, Paris 1976.*

ment they could become more nearly coterminous—except for the northern flank. All progress in this field is so slow and difficult that it is wrong to await perfection before making a move.

Joint Arms Production

The EPG's first mandate is to explore European arms production with a view to selling more to the US, with the possible arrière-pensée that, unless the Europeans first rationalize and standardize between themelves, their arms industry may be swamped by American competition.[5] It has to be accepted that joint production between two or more countries may often be more expensive in unit cost than production by a single country. It may nevertheless be worthwhile because the share of each participating country will be less, and because a single country would very likely not be willing or able to bear the whole cost alone, with the result that the equipment would not be built at all. Various items are being or have been built jointly in this way between European states, Jaguar and MRCA for example, but there are many other cases where common production and standardization have not occurred and a bewildering variety of types are in use, often requiring different fuel, ammunition, servicing arrangements etc. To overcome this wasteful and inefficient multiplicity three things are necessary: greater integration in the planning and programming of equipment needs, including the basic operational doctrines from which such needs are derived; encouragement of international industrial consortia not only for individual equipment projects but as a more lasting and initiatory factor in the European industrial scene; (rival consortia could even reintroduce an element of competitiveness which the weakness of individual firms or the nationalization of all such firms has tended to suppress); and the acceptance in principle by governments that the advantages of standardization and interoperability should weigh heavily against the advantages of independent national production or independent external purchase. Industrial compensation by component sub-contracts or otherwise can be helpful in this context, but insistence on juste retour within each individual project would probably frustrate the whole policy.

Levels of Technology

But there are two more radical matters on which the effectiveness of a European defence effort will more crucially depend. One is the question posed, in an Atlantic context, by Richard Burt,[6] whether we have sufficiently considered the underlying implications of technological development on the conduct of warfare in Europe, or whether we tend more to introduce a new weapon system just because it is there, and then bend our ideas on operational doctrine to fit its introduction. Since many of the technological advances come from America there is a particular interest for Europe to make up its collective mind about their application to European conditions before taking part in an Alliance-wide debate. The simplest example is perhaps the long standing argument between the anti-tank weapon and the tank. Is the best way to stop a

---

[5] *See e.g. page 23 of Towards Rationalizing Allied Weapons Production, by Gardiner Tucker, The Atlantic Institute for International Affairs, Paper No. 1 of 1976.*

[6] *New Weapon Technologies, Adelphi Press No. 126, IISS, London 1976.*

tank attack to have more or better tanks in defence, or to have a far greater quantity of relatively cheap anti-tank weapons widely distributed to small defence units? Is there a place, as Burt asks, for intermediate technology on the battlefield? These questions are at present not discussed in sufficient depth either in an Alliance or a European framework. So far as Europe is concerned it would require an extension of the EPG's current role to include the study of them in its mandate, but there seems no other suitable forum which contains the French, and after all it should in principle be desirable to agree on what sort of weapons are required for what sort of battle before starting to discuss how and where they should be produced.

Specialization of role

It has long seemed absurd that each European member of the Alliance should think in terms of possessing a balanced force of all arms (except Iceland, which has only its redoubtable coastguards, and Luxembourg, which has no navy or air force), when most if not all of them are incapable of fighting a battle on their own. If they were each prepared to give up certain roles and specialize in others the costs of administration, training, supply and maintenance could be significantly reduced because they would be concentrated on fewer types of activity and equipment. Standardization within each role would be easier because there would be fewer small national units involved. Training in more limited numbers of roles could be more intensive and more suited to the short conscription periods now current.

As a perhaps extreme example of the present disarray four small countries in a more or less coherent geographical area (Belgian, Denmark, Netherlands, Norway) have between them no more than 6 squadrons of transport aircraft comprising no less than 7 types of aircraft.[7] It must make sense for all of these to be procured and operated as a single force by a single country, or at least by a single agency with powers delegated from each country.

There are many other examples of what could be done in all branches of the armed forces. It seems likely that only by a rigorous programme of specialization between countries could really significant savings of unnecessary expenditure be made.

Two important conditions must however be observed. At the present low level of western conventional capability money saved by a country by this means must not be diverted away from defence altogether but used to expand or intensify the more specialized contribution which that country is to make. Secondly, the fitting together of the specialized pieces of the overall defence effort will require not only skilful staff work but absolute trust on the part of each that the others will play their part. This already exists to a large extent, and is in fact the basic principle of the Alliance. It exists more than most politicians, perhaps more than public opinion would explicitly allow. The fiction of balanced national forces of all arms persists long after the time when it has in reality become clear that it is no good one of the allies going to war unless all the others do so at the same time. The acceptance of specialization and the consequent abandonment of some roles by each country would only make plain what has for long been a fact. Nevertheless, the step is usually

---

[7] Details may be found in The Military Balance 1976-77, IISS, London, 1976.

thought to be fraught with political difficulty and has been avoided for that reason. More positively the adoption of this principle by the European allies would be a major step towards the realization of Union. It may however be unwise at present to advocate it on these grounds, but rather as the only way to promote cost-effectiveness in the face of the continued public pressure to cut the cost of defence.

France and European Defence

It has to be admitted that the outright adoption of specialization of role would cause a problem in the growing rapprochement of France with multi-lateral defence. However closely France cooperates in the EPG on the production of arms, however much coordinated plans are made on how the French forces would be employed if France decided to join in a common defence action, there is likely to be stern insistence that the independence of this decision must remain inviolate. If therefore there remains even the theoretical possibility of France going it alone, or refusing to go it in common, then it would be illogical for France to agree that certain functions need not be undertaken by French forces because they would be supplied by allies. Perhaps there is room for specialization by 'benign neglect', as in fact happened for many years in the relative weight given by France to nuclear and conventional arms. The latter were to considerable extent starved of equipment needs owing to the high cost of the force de frappe. But this particular example of specialization poses problems of its own. The greatest difficulty is perhaps that nuclear weapons are generally held to be qualitatively different, superior in decisiveness, and therefore conferring more prestige (as well as 'a seat at the top table' in more global affairs) than conventional ones. The possession of nuclear weapons by Britain and France alone is therefore commonly regarded as more divisive than integrative. The remedy to this criticism should be to seek a more logical and more acceptable linkage between the conventional and the nuclear deterrent by raising the nuclear threshold and thereby limiting the possibility of nuclear use either to defence against first use by the enemy, or to more extreme and more unlikely states of conventional emergency than the almost casual and inevitable requests for nuclear release foreseen by current scenarios. The other allies might be happier with the existence of the Bristish and French nuclear weapons if they thought it less likely that they would be used.

This line of reasoning emphasizes amongst other things the need to have agreement on nuclear policy and tactics. A large measure of agreement, particularly with regard to tactical nuclear weapons, has been achieved in the NATO Nuclear Planning Group. France however is not a member of this group, yet possesses both tactical and strategic nuclear weapons. Given the controversial history of Franco-American nuclear relations and the intensity of Gaullist political feeling it would probably be vain to hope for effective consultation on the strategic weapons. But the potential use of the Pluton tactical weapon by French forces either in Germany or firing it into Germany from France is a vital part of any contingency plan for the common defence of the central front, and must in all logic form part of at least intra-European discussions. Again it would be a pity to make more difficult an obviously desirable consultation by worrying overmuch about where and how it should take place. Alternatives are either directly between Commands, but this is perhaps hardly adequate to give due weight to the political considerations which are inseparable from the question of the release of nuclear weapons, or in a newly invented European Nuclear Planning Group, or by extending still further, perhaps to an intolerable extent, the functions of the European Programme Group.

It is a difficult issue to add to the specialization agenda, but its intrinsic importance is increased by the approaching dilemma of apportioning British and French financial resources between the nuclear and conventional arms. This aspect will be more acute when the moment is no longer escapable for considering the modernization of the two nuclear armouries to match the ever increasing sophistication of the weapons and counter-measures of the super-Powers. When the choice has to be made whether to give priority to updating the British and French nuclear forces or to maintaining more effective conventional forces, the arguments ought to run like this: Either: nuclear forces in Europe, separate in one degree or another from the American forces, are not only a small deterrent in themselves but provide continuity on the scale of escalation with American nuclear forces and thus guard against decoupling the latter from the defence of Europe; moreover they are but one example of specialization of role among European allies, which, is probably the only way in which European defence can be made more effective. Or: the great weakness in defence plans for Europe is that Western forces are becoming weaker than those of the Warsaw Pact, therefore it is becoming more likely that a major conventional threat from the East will have to be met sooner rather than later by the threat or use of at least tactical nuclear weapons, with all that this entails. If, owing to British and French concentration on their nuclear arms, western conventional defence capability falls away still further we shall not be far from the old and discredited trip-wire theory of nuclear response to almost any threat. This is repugnant to western feelings and therefore largely incredible. The right course on the contrary would be to improve conventional forces and so raise the threshold where nuclear action becomes necessary, with the added advantage that conventional forces can be in a much more real sense under European control than nuclear ones.

It is hard to say which argument will win the day. Pessimists would say there will be no clear-cut decision. The nuclear forces will be retained because they are there, but not kept to even a qualitatively high standard, and conventional equipment will continue to be inadequate for lack of funds. It is to be hoped that the arguments may be adequately considered both in a European and an alliance framework before decisions are reached.

Conclusion

The potential independence of western European countries, as of the European Community as a whole, continues to depend on the maintenance of an adequate defence effort in organic relationship with that of the US, that is say for the foreseeable future in the Atlantic Alliance. The present contributions of the European states to this defence system are less effective than they need be because they are still planned on the basis of national self-sufficiency; because their equipment is in many cases not even inter-operable; and because there is no comprehensive discussion or planning of European defence needs and potential capabilities, as a contribution to the planning and capability of the Alliance as a whole. A more unified European Community would need to have a defence policy and an agency for carrying it out. Pending greater unification there would be advantage in making use of the mechanisms which exist, even if this involves some administrative untidiness. For example the European Council, or the Ministers meeting in political cooperation for the harmonization of foreign policy, could take general decisions in the defence field, such as a decision to bring the defence expenditure of the member countries into greater equivalence. The European Programme Group could develop its functions to include not only the more effective European production of military equipment but any others tasks, derived from such Community decisions, or from other appropriate organs, which were relevant to the objective of a more efficient and homogeneous European defence effort. Among such tasks should be the urgent study of

(a) the basic doctrines governing the employment of military forces in the geographical and political conditions prevailing in Europe and the level of technology appropriate to these conditions;
(b) as an important sub-heading of (a), the compatibility of policies for the employment of tactical nuclear weapons;
(c) specialization of military roles between participating countries as a means of reducing overhead costs and equipment costs and as a demonstration of interdependence, including the review of nuclear and conventional priorities.

The results of these studies would be for application by the European allies so far as appropriate and agreed, and for discussion in the wider Atlantic forum as part of the process of the formation of the general policy and doctrine of the Alliance.

History suggests that these tasks are difficult owing to national tradition and short-term interests. On the other hand they have long been accepted as logical and may now be urgent in order to maintain the European defence effort at a level high enough to preserve the credibility of the Alliance.

If such courses were followed, using the existing Alliance framework and existing European mechanisms, but with a new content inspired by a more realistic understanding of practical needs it might be possible to avoid the more philosophic questions which would be posed by any attempt to renew the European Defence Community as such or to inject new functions, not yet prescribed in the Treaties, into strictly Community institutions before general progress towards European Union makes this more widely acceptable.

16 Buying Europe's Raw Materials

TIM JOSLING

If there is a tide in the affairs of men, which, taken at the flood, leads on to fortune, then to many that flood tide for the EEC was the events in the world energy market during 1973 and 1974. Here was the chance for the Community to show that integration meant a common reaction to an external economic threat. The lack of any convincing Community action demonstrated both the inability of European institutions to convince member countries of the benefits of common action, and the lack of confidence of the member governments in those institutions to solve common problems. Europe had failed to live up to the expectations of its citizens; those who hoped that the economic integration of Europe had developed past the point of a common industrial market encumbered by a set of unwieldy measures to support the prices of farm products, had a right to be disappointed.

This discussion is not about specific problems of raw materials; the number of years it will take for the world to run out of molybdenum, or the projected degree of Community self-sufficiency in crude oil in 1985; but about the attitudes towards commodity problems and the choice of a policy to secure future supplies. Where lies the potential benefit of common action? And how can this benefit be squared with the centrifugal forces of economic and political nationalism which appear to be as strong as ever in Europe even after twenty years of integration? For any 'new European federalism' of the 1980s must blend national individuality and private responsibility with shared Community services. The nature of the raw material problem, the variety of solutions to that problem, the role of integration and joint action in those solutions, and the agenda for a Community committed to taking pragmatic steps towards such co-ordination of policies, will be examined.

The raw-material problem

Manufactured goods and refined and processed products can be produced 'to order' in a time-scale largely determined by man. A car, a television set, and a pot of paint are the output of continuous production processes which can be speeded up or slowed down, expanded or contracted, subject to various

198

constraints of investment, the training of workers and the distribution systems. At the other extreme, minerals and other resources taken from the earth's crust are constrained by a geological time-path in general so slow relative to the human life-cycle that they are classified as 'non-renewable'. The extraction of such resources is not a production process as such but a decision on the rate of exhaustion of those reserves that can be conveniently exploited. Between these two extremes, commodities harvested from biological processes, whether animals, fish, plants or trees, have constraints less severe than minerals but less flexible than manufactured goods.

What is the optimal rate of exhaustion of non-renewable resources? What conservation measures are needed for processes which rely on biological populations and ecological systems? How can one share and regulate the uncertain output from plant populations, both those that are renewed annually and those that are harvested over a number of years? These are the major preoccupations of raw material suppliers. For example, whatever other political and economic motives lay behind the increase in oil prices in late 1973, the question of the rate of extraction of the world's oil reserves was in itself entirely legitimate and its consideration long overdue. Similarly, however nationalistic recent moves to restrict fishing rights may have been, the problem of conservation of fish populations is also of considerable importance. And the stabilisation of the prices of agricultural commodities, from grains and beef to coffee, cocoa, and sugar is a genuine problem requiring serious economic and political consideration quite apart from the rhetoric of north against south or the affluent versus the poor nations. The ability of the present world trading system to provide the correct answers to these problems remains seriously in doubt. And the scope for political conflict in such matters is endless.

Commodities and raw materials are valued not in their own right but in their usefulness in the production of processed and manufactured products. At the most fundamental level, human energy can be and is substituted for fossil fuels and other forms of energy harnessed into mechanical power. Similarly, solar and nuclear energy, along with wind, tide and water power can be substituted for energy released by combustion of parts of the earth's crust. Animal and vegetable sources of protein are often close substitutes, and can in turn be replaced by protein synthesised from other organic material. Plastics can do the work of metals and of natural fibres. The 'consumer' problem is thus different from that of the producer. What is the cheapest source of energy, or protein? How can one gratify the wants of modern civilisation by adjusting the use of raw materials to reduce the cost and to improve the quality of both the consumer goods and the capital equipment needed for their production? Can one economise in the 'destruction' of raw materials in the process of providing consumer goods, through re-cycling and reduction of waste? As a broad generalisation, it is probably true to say that the modern economy is rather better at solving these consumer problems than those of resource extraction and the conservation of biological populations. Both the commercial ethic and the political and legal framework of the advanced economy lead to ingenious and inventive adaptation in the face of changes in the availability and costs of raw materials. And the biggest political problem may arise simply from the fact that the consumer in modern societies tends to hold the government responsible for the need to make such changes, an inevitable counterpart to the assumption of greater control by governments over economic life. Economic adjustment is consequently associated with political instability, or at least with undertainty for the politicians who happen to be in power at the time. For the nations, which produce raw materials the questions of depletion of reserves and orderly management of biological processes runs deeper than the popularity of governments; it influences the whole process of growth and development and the social and political adjustments that accompany economic change.

Few countries have an unambiguous interest only in one of these raw material problems. For the Community, as for the US, the USSR, and the other major industrial areas, both the production and the consumption problems arise. The Community has significant reserves of oil, natural gas, coal and minerals; the seas support a high fish population; the temperate climate coupled with advanced farming technology provides most of our staple foods. One part of a raw-materials policy is therefore the husbanding of these resources. But for the Community the more significant issue is the use in industry of these primary products. As indicated in Table I, the EEC devotes about 50 per cent of its export earnings to importing raw materials for industry and the food manufacturing sector. Only Japan, of the major industrial powers, is more dependent on imported supplies.

Table I

Net imports of primary products of the EEC, 1973-1975, and importance of primary products in total trade[a]

	1973	1974	1975
Food	13.3	13.7	14.1
Raw Materials [b]	8.9	10.1	8.2
Ores and Minerals	4.2	6.7	6.1
Fuels	16.7	43.7	41.7
Total Primary Products	43.1	74.2	70.1
Total Imports	104.1	152.6	151.1

(a) $billions: excludes intra-EEC trade flows.
(b) Mainly timber and fibres; in the text 'raw materials' covers all primary products.
Source: GATT, *International Trade 1975/76*, Geneva 1976.

Alternative policies

The need for a policy in an importing region derives from two separate types of concern. First, the short-run instability of commodity prices makes it more difficult to control inflation and to maintain full employment in a mixed economy. Countering this threat requires action at a variety of levels. Within the individual market, there is often scope for ameliorating the effects of

200

shortages. Private firms anticipate market movements and contract forward for supplies; in many cases they protect such forward commitments further by using futures markets to hedge against unexpected price developments; they build inventories when prices move favourably and run them down as the costs of raw materials rise: they make vertical links with supplying firms on a more or less formal basis. Countries have similar options. They too can establish bilateral trading agreements and hold stocks. In addition, they can intervene financially by various forms of taxes and subsidies both at the border and on the internal market. Moreover, they can initiate or support international action to shift or share the burden of instability. Such action on the part of governments has become almost universal in the case of agricultural raw materials and foodstuffs. Domestic farm policies, for long intended as a means of stabilising farm incomes at a politically acceptable level, have become instruments for countering international price movements and stabilising the wholesale costs of domestic food. The relative 'success' of the Common Agricultural Policy of the EEC in preventing the full impact of high world prices for basic foodstuffs being reflected in internal price levels has been evident in the last few years.

At the macro-economic level, stabilisation against external shocks from raw material prices takes on different forms. Foreign exchange reserves cushion the impact on the domestic economy by offsetting the real impact on incomes which would follow adjustments through exchange rates or domestic money supply. Employment policies soften the impact on individual sectors, and instruments of general economic management attempt to control the spread of inflation arising from cost increases. Multi-lateral co-ordination of such macro-economic response is still in its infancy: the tendency at present is for all developed countries to respond in unison to external shocks, and hence to exacerbate their impact on the domestic stability of each individual economy.

Importing countries are also concerned about the longer term impact of changing terms of trade. If the price level of raw materials moves up over time relative to the price of manufactured goods exported to pay for primary imports then real income levels are threatened. Productivity improvements in the manufacturing sector might keep pace with increased raw material costs, thereby effectively transferring the fruits of such technical progress back to the primary product exporter. Or, as many primary producers fear, market control by large corporations or by powerful trade unions could negate this transfer by capturing productivity benefits in higher profits or wages: the terms of trade effect of higher raw material prices would simply be offset by higher price levels for exported manufactured goods. These concerns have, at least temporarily, taken over from the orthodoxy of the period from 1955-1970 when raw material prices were chronically weak and were thought to contribute to the relatively poor economic performance of countries dependent on raw material exports.

It may be worth considering the room for manoeuvre in primary product prices. In contrast to a competitive market for an industrial product, where costs of production at the margin are generally assumed to be roughly comparable to market prices, for some raw materials the difference between extraction cost and final selling price can be substantial. The difference is a mixture of 'rent' (the economist's term for a payment for scarcity, both natural and contrived) and the taxes taken by governments in both producing and consuming countries. The price of a 'scarce' raw material can thus vary within a band bounded at the lower end by the cost of extraction and at the upper end by the price of substitutes acceptable to the users of the product in question. Over time, extraction costs will change, as will the price of substitutes: at any particular moment, this band will define the approximate limits of the international price. But the price itself, within those limits, is determined by a number of forces both political and economic. The struggle for the 'rent' and tax portion of the value-in-use of the raw materials has intensified in recent years, not least because producer governments have expanded their own direct involvement in the extraction process.

A somewhat different type of price 'band' is observable in agricultural markets, in particular in those for temperate zone foodstuffs. The international price in such markets can often be below the marginal cost of production, with governments giving subsidies rather than levying taxes. The 'value' of such surplus production is often very low, as is the case at the moment for skimmed milk powder. The band is determined in this case by the activities of governments attempting to determine prices in domestic markets on the basis of local costs without reference to international values. Again, long-run price movements are constrained by developments in technology and in other factors influencing costs, but the trend in such prices is often hidden by the impact of government policies on the markets themselves.

This raises perhaps the most difficult problem facing a country trying to devise a raw material policy: the separation of erratic movements of prices in the short run from long term trends. The recent 'world food crisis' is an example of such a dilemma. For two years, 1972 and 1974, per capita food production in the world as a whole declined. The advice from 'experts' was inconclusive: some climatologists warned us that the world's weather patterns could shift not gradually over a thousand years but dramatically within a generation: technologists said that productivity increases could no longer be taken for granted and that biological 'ceilings' were being approached: ecologists told of irreversible imbalances in natural populations of plants and animals: demographers added that even with no further increases in birth rates the global 'bulge' would have to be fed for several decades. Others in the same disciplines cautioned against extrapolations based on a few years' data, and gave the comfortable reminder that the world had always adapted to changes in the past. In retrospect, it is apparent that the temporary food shortage did awaken governments to the vulnerability of their basic supplies. Consideration of investment levels in agriculture, reserves held against sudden price rises, nutritional programmes for the poor, and the adequacy of the trading system came to the fore, first in the World Food Conference in 1974 and then in the subsequent deliberations of its offspring the World Food Council. The easiest prescription to give is the most difficult to follow: maintain a flexible response which does not commit the economy on the basis of current conditions to a future posture which might turn out to be inappropriate. To give an example, the dramatic rise in sugar prices in 1974 could have been matched in the Community not by the removal of quantity restrictions and a

202

17 per cent price increase, but by a 'scarcity premium' which would automatically have been removed if, as proved to be the case, sugar prices reverted to much lower levels. Clearly where long-run investments are involved, it is more difficult to retain flexibility. In economic terms, if the investment decisions have taken into account the appropriate risk of adverse price movements then the decisions themselves could still be deemed to have been 'correct' even if the investments eventually prove unprofitable: there should be gains on other projects to offset any particular losses. The flexibility in such cases may be in terms of delaying new investment rather than attempting to justify decisions already made by artificial pricing. To continue with the example of sugar, investment in beet factories should be assessed with respect to the long-term expected world value of sugar: too often they are justified by the expansion of sugar beet output resulting from price support, and the investment in turn provides excess capacity which appears to indicate yet further market manipulation to increase sugar beet output. The concept that a processing sector has to be internationally competitive, as opposed to following slavishly the needs of the domestic and traditionally imported raw material flows is one that is becoming more significant as the producers of primary commodities become more interested in performing these functions for themselves.

Towards a Community Policy

All the preceding remarks apply to any industrial region relying on imports of primary products. The Community faces an additional set of constraints and opportunities. The constraints are inherent in the institutional framework of the EEC. Basically, these have to do with the extent to which individual governments feel that a raw materials policy is consistent with national interests. If all Community members had identical interests then no serious problem would exist. A Community policy would be a national policy writ large. But the balance of trade in primary products differs among countries within the EEC. Dutch natural gas, British oil, Irish fishing grounds, and Greenland's minerals all give a nationalistic flavour to raw material policy discussions, just as Danish, Dutch, Irish and French agricultural interests have influenced the CAP. The best conditions for a compromise would seem to exist when all countries feel that there is sufficient uncertainty to make attractive the 'hedging' of investment decisions. North Sea oil offers such an example. It is clearly expensive relative to established sources, and a guaranteed European market would be of considerable value as a precaution against future price declines. In turn, the economies of Germany, Holland and France would be less vulnerable to future oil embargoes if access to such oil reserves were assured. With comparable degrees of uncertainty as to the future market position, the UK might consider the loss of some control over its national supplies acceptable in return for market guarantees, and the other nations might find a degree of subsidy worth the price for greater security of supplies.

The Community can in turn forge a compromise across commodities. Access to energy sources in one part of the EEC might have as their counterpart access to foodstuffs from another. The CAP, it is often said, was built on the compromise of German industrial goods penetrating the French market in return for French agricultural sales to Germany. Even though experience does not show clearly any such development in trade patterns (French industry and German agriculture have shown little sign of retreat in the face of competition) the concept of such a trade-off was clearly important in early discussions of the agricultural policy. The notion that British oil production could be supported in exchange for a more relaxed British attitude towards over-capacity in continental agriculture has occasionally been aired. Once again, in a situation of 'perfect uncertainty' an implicit agreement of this kind might be forged. But such an arrangement should be carefully examined. The least satisfactory Community policy is one that seeks the 'lowest common denominator' of national aspirations and panders to weaknesses in economic decision-making. To avoid embarrassing decisions on agriculture by devising policies which serve to hide injudicious investment in energy would be folly. The Community needs both a sound energy policy and a defensible food policy.

If a common policy on raw materials is constrained by the need to acknowledge national differences, its greatest opportunities lie in the exploitation of the similarities. All the Community countries face the same basic dilemma. As net importers of primary products, interruptions in supply, sudden price rises, and long-run terms-of-trade movements in favour of raw materials all have their impacts on domestic employment, growth and price stability. The Community, by Article 113 of the Treaty of Rome, is responsible for foreign commercial relationships. It follows that the heart of a Community policy is more likely to be in developing a common external approach to questions of primary product trade, leaving free internal trade and liberalised capital movements to handle the problem of intra-EEC distribution. The Community has of course progressed some way in this direction. At the political level, the dialogue with the Arab countries, though complicating broader approaches to the oil problem through the International Energy Authority and the North-South talks, has at least indicated a possible line of approach. A firm commitment not to facilitate any trade embargoes which discriminate among member states would go some way towards restoring confidence in the ability of the Community to use its collective international influence in a manner consistent with the aims of integration.

The discussions with Canada and, though less advanced, with Australia indicate the possibilities of trade agreements covering a range of commodities of interest to each party. The common identification of raw material supplies with the developing world is far from accurate. Though many low income countries do indeed depend upon such exports, they dominate world supply only in tropical products and in a few minerals. And if one were to exclude the supply of oil from the OPEC countries, the value of primary product imports from LDCs into the Community is significantly less than those from other industrial nations. Table II indicates the source of imports by value in recent years of four categories of primary product. Oil imports, and the increase in the cost of such imports in the period 1973 to 1975 overshadow the other figures. But the value of temperate-zone food imports exceeds that of purchases of (mainly) tropical products from LDCs; industrial raw materials such as rubber, timber, and fibres appear to come largely from other advanced economies; and trade in ores and minerals from LDCs is less than one half of total EEC imports of these products. This lends perspective to the orientation of a raw material supply policy. Naturally, the relations with developing countries in general and with the Lomé signatories in particular are important to the Community. But commercial ties with other advanced countries appear on the face of it to be of equal significance.

Table II

Sources of imports into EEC of Primary Products, 1973-1975[a]

	1973	1974	1975
Food			
Industrial	10.6	11.6	12.0
CPE[b]	1.6	1.6	1.6
LDC	9.1	10.5	11.1
Total	21.3	23.6	24.6
Raw Materials[c]			
Industrial	6.4	7.8	6.3
CPE	1.2	1.4	1.2
LDC	3.2	3.4	2.7
Total	10.8	12.5	10.3
Ores and Minerals			
Industrial	2.7	3.7	3.7
CPE	0.3	0.4	0.4
LDC	1.7	3.1	2.7
Total	4.7	7.3	6.8
Fuel			
Industrial	1.0	⋅1.9	2.8
CPE	1.3	2.6	3.5
LDC	17.5	45.2	41.1
Total	19.8	49.6	47.5

(a) $ billions; intra-EEC trade and EEC exports excluded.
(b) Eastern block trading area.
(c) Mainly timber and fibres.
Source: GATT, *International Trade 1975/76*, Geneva, 1976.

The Lomé Convention itself can only partly be categorised as an element in a supply policy for raw materials. Most primary products enter the Community without significant trade barriers, though protection of processing through tariff escalation is still evident. The African, Pacific and Caribbean countries (ACP) stand to gain more from potential access to European markets for manufactured goods. But the STABEX scheme for guaranteeing export earnings from a group of primary products emanating from the ACP could be considered as a way of encouraging such trade. To the extent that participating countries are penalised (in the sense of forfeiting part of the guarantee) for switching exports away from the Community, some element of supply guarantee for Europe is inherent in the scheme. But as a whole it is the (entirely laudible) objective of assisting developing countries in their economic management that is the justification for STABEX: security of supply for Europe is a possible bonus under certain market conditions. The arrangements for sugar negotiated with the ACP appear to have a more direct bearing on security of supply. Certainly, employment in the port refineries is still dependent on imports of cane sugar from the tropics. But whenever a trade deal involves a commitment to import a fixed quantity, the likelihood is that stable supply is not a paramount objective. In this case the aim, desirable in itself, is to assist economic planning in the ACP sugar-producing countries by providing a stable and remunerative outlet for a part of their exports. To the extent that such quota allocations are jeopardised by non-fulfilment there is pressure, as with STABEX, for the exporter to remain true to the European market, even when prices are more attractive elsehwere. But this again is a side-effect of the sugar pact: it is not the outcome of a considered view as to the appropriate supply policy for a key raw material.

The attitude of the Community towards the UNCTAD talks on commodities again reveals the difficulties faced in pursuing convincing and coherent supply policies. At first sight, the UNCTAD 'integrated programme' offers a reasonable deal for raw material importers. A series of commodity agreements, commonly financed, with provision for buffer stocks and quantity commitments, would seem to be along the lines of mainstream European predilections for managing international markets. But any commodity scheme which requires finance to set up and to operate will tend to be in the nature of a price support programme for producers (witness the intervention system within the CAP) and to act to the disadvantage of importers and consumers. This can be seen by considering an alternative type of buffer-stock programme where producers hold in reserve (not sell to an international agency) products which are in temporary over-supply in order to off-load them onto the market when prices rise. No money is required to set up such a programme. The Community may of course be willing in the interest of equitable transfer of purchasing power to low income countries to support the UNCTAD proposals, though it is not clear that many of the developed countries do not stand to gain as much or more than the poorest nations of the world who tend not to be rich in endowment of natural resources. But as a policy for raw materials it is unconvincing.

This argument leads almost inexorably to a rather unpalatable fact of economic life. It is not at all clear that the altruism and general concern for the plight of low income nations is sufficiently coincident with the desire of the Community to secure low cost raw materials to support domestic industrial growth and to add to economic stability of prices and employment. Indeed the two objectives can conflict. A raw materials policy may be more directly linked with trade relations and policy co-ordination with other industrial countries. In terms of trade relationships, the 'old' economic order of liberal flows of goods and of capital in international markets, coupled with the new flexibility of exchange rates among the major currencies, may have more to offer than the 'new' order of commodity agreements, common funds, indexation, indigenous resource development, nationalisation, producer groupings, and the like. If Europe has a weakness in its approach to the 'old' order it has been its failure to appreciate the link between agricultural trade policy, in which it has been able to attract almost universal opprobrium, though probably with only minimal impact on net trade flows, and policies in industrial and raw material trade, in which it has been a relatively unconvincing *demandeur*. Hence the Community's position in the current GATT negotiations, which attempts once again to separate these issues, may in itself be contributing more to the strains in the trading system than almost any other issue in commodity policy outside the oil price question.

An Agenda For Community Action

If one follows the proposition that the Community should play on its strengths and avoid actions which are likely to be ineffectual or even counter-productive, then there seem to be two areas where a common approach holds out most promise. The first of these is related to the conditions of intra-EEC trade and investment flows and the second to multilateral negotiations on raw materials questions. An additional function, which must accompany any such policy is to inform and stimulate public opinion and debate on raw material issues. These three aspects will be taken in turn, with an illustration as to what elements might be included in such an approach.

The first internal priority is to reaffirm and reinforce the commitment of member states to the principles of non-discrimination within the EEC in trade and access to supplies. This does not threaten sovereign rights to the ownership of resources within defined territorial limits; it does however restrict the ability of countries to reserve supplies for their own industrial use. Without such commitment to non-discrimination, it is difficult to see the relevance of Community membership. It might be thought that twenty years of European integration based on free internal trade would have removed the possibility of such discrimination. But discussion of energy and food supplies still continues within member states on the basis of the security afforded by national self-sufficiency. There is little indication that governments have made the transition from national to Community planning in such areas. In this respect, private sector integration is clearly ahead of that in the public sector. Private investment in North Sea oil extraction is based on likely European demand and on the future balance in the world energy market: government investment seems still to be based on national considerations. The development of a Community view of energy needs will be facilitated by any reduction in the pressure on governments to create and preserve jobs at almost any price, but the establishment of the principle need not await the conditions for its full implementation.

With respect to agricultural supplies, the momentum engendered by the scare of high world prices, in 1973 and 1974 has been lost. Currency movements , together with the *ad hoc* 'monetary compensatory amounts' (MCAs) for relieving the agricultural sectors from their immediate effect, have given countries considerable scope for determining their own agricultural price levels. The concept of a free market for farm products has been the casualty. Different farm prices in member states does not in itself invalidate the idea of enhancing food security by ensuring free access to EEC supplies: the idea that one can allow the agricultural sectors to develop independently in the various countries does however lead logically to the use of further trade impediments. There is a real danger that these might be used not just to maintain national farm prices at politically convenient levels but to defend those levels at times of market disturbance. Unless the Community can find a way of relating the overall levels of farm prices to the world situation for temperate zone products, the divergence of national prices threatens to destroy the advantage of a common approach to agricultural development. Or, to put it more directly, unless those countries at present maintaining indefensibly high price levels for their own farmers modify their attitudes, security of supply will be sought in other member states either by costly expansion of domestic production or by recourse to external trade agreements which offer security without the burden of supporting high cost European agricultural sectors.

The other aspect of internal market measures which is clearly in accord with Community responsibility is the stimulus to investment in raw materials, in particular in energy. Indeed, two of the three Communities, Coal and Steel (ECSC) and Euratom (EAEC), have already developed such investment policies on a Europe-wide basis in accord with their constitutional obligations. There seems no reason why the Economic Community should not also join the act. But the appropriate action should not stretch to include the underwriting at a Community level of dubious national investment plans. Direct EEC budgetary involvement is unlikely to be constructive so long as disbursements from it are seen largely as either inescapable financial commitments arising from policies cobbled together on the basis of intra-member compromise, such as in agriculture, or as sweeteners to individual members to preserve a *juste retour*. Liberalisation of capital movements, harmonisation of company law and tax treatment, and encouragement of Europe-wide consortia for resource development may for some time be more realistic than direct Community budgetary involvement in investment.

External policy

With respect to external policy, the role of the Community institutions can only grow with the development of the degree of political cohesion with which outsiders have credited the EEC for many years. It is inevitable that the major European powers will act as individual countries for some time to come, in the OECD, the GATT, the IMF, the UNCTAD, and other similar institutions. Co-ordination of a 'Community' view is often a shallow pretence; it leads to a weak position in international circles at variance with the promise of more political influence from a united Europe. At the recent meeting in London of heads of government of seven 'western' democracies, the Commission attended part of the discussions ostensibly to represent the smaller EEC members. But the more important issue, since there seems no reason why the Dutch, the Irish, the Danes and the Belgians should be represented to the exclusion of Sweden or Australia, is why there were *four* Community countries present participating on behalf of their own individual interests. A 'new federalism' cannot subsume national individuality, but in discussing matters of world politics the Community will only be able to develop its potential if it is seen to be representing the complex of national and regional interests with a single voice.

Despite this major constraint, the responsibility for external commercial policy gives to the Community institutions the same strength in external affairs as the commitment to a common market gives in intra-European matters. In the raw materials field the attitude towards the improvement of the trading system is the most important way in which Europe's influence as a major importer can be exercised. This basically involves a decision on what aspects of the present trading system require modification, and how far one can reconcile legitimate aspirations of the low-income countries for equity and preference with the fundamental responsibility to safeguard and promote the interests of European citizens. The major decisions on such matters have to be taken within such international organisations as the GATT, the UNCTAD, and the World Food Council. It is no secret that negotiating partners find that the lack of imagination in Community positions, arising from the need to stay within a brief agreed in the Council of Ministers, makes discussion with the Commission somewhat frustrating. Since the essence of successful negotiations in such institutions is the 'give-and-take' of concessions, there seems to be no other alternative but to allow more initiative to the Community-level representatives. The power to take *ad referendum* decisions would allow national governments in turn to assess the outcome of such talks in a wider perspective than is possible at present. Only by increasing the flexibility of Community positions can the collective influence of the member states be constructively employed.

Information and debate

The Community also has a further task, to co-ordinate information and stimulate public awareness on raw material issues. In the specific field of agricultural supplies, the Commission, and indeed the Council of Ministers, have been remarkably reticent about educating opinion on longer term issues. Short-term political expediency and the over elaborate justification of past actions has obscured any broader appreciation of the issues which might help to convince the public that European policy-making was in safe hands. On energy supplies, the contrast between the public debate in the US and the coyness of statements from European institutions is remarkable. The public is left either in ignorance or in confusion, and certainly with the impression that there is little that the Community can offer in the way of solutions. In one sense, this educational function would appear to be the least crucial. Governments themselves do not need to be told of the problems of raw material trade. But there are two reasons to think that this element of EEC activity is vital. First, it seems to be essential that the Community institutions themselves develop the respect of national administrations in terms of their expertise on matters of longer-term economic trends. Until the national governments come to look upon the analysis undertaken by the Commission as an indispensable adjunct to their own appreciation of problems, any Community solution will be at a disadvantage. In many areas of economic intelligence, the information generated by the OECD seems to provide a model; the combination of up-to-date national data and professionally acceptable interpretation gives such work an authority which cannot easily be ignored by governments. But more than this, the sophisticated analysis of policy options, and even of individual country actions, would give the Commission a sound basis on which to suggest alternative strategies.

The development of such an analytical capacity is equally important in the second aspect of the dissemination of information: that of providing a basis for public debate. As the European Parliament develops its confidence as a parliamentary influence independent of national governments, so the Commission could use this body more explicitly as a place to discuss common policy initiatives. The full and public discussion of such policies could provide the Community with the impetus need to overcome the reluctance of the Council of Ministers to involve their governments on longer-term economic issues. Energy, food, and raw material supplies all warrant a broad view liberated from immediate national pressures; a self-confident Commission, armed with ideas and information and backed by a strengthened European Parliament, could have a convincing appeal to the citizens of Europe.

17 A Federal Community in an Ungoverned World Economy

JOHN PINDER

The modern economy was born in Western Europe, of two diverse but complementary strains. Industry was created by individual innovators, their energies first released into the economy by the English liberals; and it was brought under social control mainly by the growing working class movements, but also by conservatives such as Bismarck. These two strains, of liberal individualism and social control, have been blended in Western Europe into a new type of economy.

The new European economy: mixed, efficient, humane

This economy combines efficiency with humanity. It has a labour market, with free choice for workers and employers; but it also has a labour market policy, providing massive public support for training, placement and job creation. Its firms choose their production and investment plans independently, but supported and guided by an industrial policy. Freedom for those with market power to fix prices and incomes is moderated by price and income policies. Commodities are traded in markets, but those produced in these European economies are stabilised so as to rule out the kind of disruption that ignited the great world inflation after 1973, when the international prices not only of oil but also of wheat and sugar had been multiplied about five times. Thus markets and plans are both used as means to enhance the people's welfare, not elevated into competing idols which the people must serve, whatever the cost.

Of course the economies of Western Europe are very imperfect. Too often their markets work badly and their plans go awry. Elements of the new economic management are unevenly distributed among them, and often still in an experimental phase. But if one compares the countries of the European Community, together with some of their West European associates such as Sweden and Austria, with most other parts of the world, the contrast is striking.

The economies of our European neighbours to the East are set in the Russian mould. Here, industry was transplanted into a political system steeped in autocracy, which was taken over by revolutionaries with a doctrine that was read as demanding the tightest central command over the economy. Autocratic social control was in the saddle and liberalism violently thrown. Although countries such as Hungary and Poland have introduced a measure of economic flexibility, the unhappy Czechs have learnt what happens to East Europeans who try to step too far from the narrow Soviet path.

The United States is, economically as well as socially and politically, much closer to Western Europe. Yet the distinction is still quite sharp. Whereas in Russia social control has proliferated while liberalism has been stifled; the American tradition has been much kinder to individualism than to social control. The Puritans, the frontier, and behind it the atomised mass of immigrants, composed a fertile soil for aggressive freedom of enterprise and repudiation of control; and despite populism, the New Deal and the Great Society, the fruits remain, in a powerful ideological resistance to state intervention and a social security expenditure of some 10 per cent of GNP compared to 16-20 per cent in all the members of the Community.

Most of the countries of the third world are at an economic level so low that freedom and pluralism are hard to maintain, even where, as in India, politically conscious people are predisposed in favour. A few, such as Brazil and Mexico, are large and dynamic enough to offer an early prospect of becoming substantial partners with economies of the West European type. Japan has amazed the world by vaulting up to Western Europe's economic level; and perhaps the Japanese will again surprise us by blending liberty and control as West Europeans try to do. But socially and politically Japan remains, for Europeans, an enigma; and it is only a few small and medium economies such as Australia, New Zealand, Canada and Israel, that are at least as close as the United States to the West European type.

Western Europe's type of economy is, then, distinct from almost all others. The United States and a few other countries are more or less similar, and that is all. Just as about half the world's pluralist parliamentary democracies are to be found in the European Community, so the Community is the greatest concentration of this new economic type. Yet we lack a good name for it. 'Mixed economy' seems to be the common usage: the mixture being not so much between private and public ownership as between independent initiative and public control, personal responsibility and social provision, economic liberty and state authority. But how uninspiring a name for what, in the perspective of this paper, represents the highest point of economic civilisation yet attained by mankind. Concepts can lag behind reality, and language behind concepts. Words like liberalism and socialism, that convey economic types with power and conviction, stem from the great intellectual and political battles of the nineteenth century. But in becoming identified with individualism and collectivism, each now represents only one half of the whole of a civilised modern economy. Each half, taken on its own, is damaging. Yet the whole is only dimly perceived. Perhaps this is not surprising, for this complete economic type has been growing to maturity only in the past two or three decades. But a clearer perception and a better word for it are urgently needed.

One aim of this paper will be to suggest a better word. But first, we must examine more closely this mixed economy of ours in its relationship with the rest of the world.

A laisser faire Community wide open to international disruption

The world economy comprises countries with the most diverse economic types, levels and rates of growth. Even a powerful world authority would find it hard to stabilise the anarchic relations between them. Without such an authority, we should not be surprised that instability is the hallmark of the international commodity and money markets, and disruption one of the most-used words in discussions on industrial trade.

The countries of the European Community are deeply involved in this world economy. One tenth of their gross domestic product, a quarter of their output of manufactures, is exported into it. The bulk of their energy and raw materials, and an important part of their food, are imported from it. The money they use for trade, and much of their technology, have come from the leading element in the world economy, the United States.

The Community could not turn its back on the world economy, even if it would. But the experience of the 1970s has shown how damaging the turbulence of the international economy can be. The great inflation, the millions of unemployed, the near-destruction of major industries have all been induced from outside. Without the shock from soaring commodity prices in 1972-73, and the final impetus from the quintupling of the price of oil, inflation and unemployment would never have reached such alarming heights. Nor has the Community itself generated any such violent disturbances as the prolonged dollar deficit, with its impact on monetary stability and the commodity boom, or the devastating growth of Japanese exports in shipbuilding, steel and a number of other industries. We must have some defence against the import of such wild instability.

Such a defence is provided, in one sector, by the common agricultural policy. The founder members of the Community, to whom the policy fully applied, suffered neither shortages of food nor intolerable price rises after 1973; Britain, still partly outside the policy, went short of sugar and was hit directly by the rocketing world prices of food. Unfortunately, the CAP has a bad name in Britain because some of its prices and its financing method bear heavily against the British, who failed to join the Community before certain crucial decisions were taken. Perhaps the CAP goes too far in controls that insulate the Community; but better too far than not at all.

For the rest of its external relations, with this single exception of agriculture, the Community does precious little to ward off the hammer blows of instability. The Treaty of Rome and the common commercial policy have been based largely on the principle of laisser faire. After the establishment of the moderate external tariff, the common commercial policy was to contribute, according to the Treaty, to 'the progressive abolition of restrictions on international trade'. In successive rounds of tariff cutting in the GATT, the Community has indeed halved its general external tariff; and with the generalised scheme of preferences, the Lomé Convention and the agreements with Mediterranean countries, it has abolished the tariff on a good proportion of its imports.

213

A general tariff is a blunt instrument of protection, and perhaps the Community does not need it. But the Community has not replaced the declining tariff by other means of defence against the turbulence of the international economy, nor has it done much to bring the instability under control by common action with its economic partners. Tariff-cutting can be one element in a constructive policy for steady expansion of the Community's external trade and payments. But it must be supplemented by other measures in order to make the Community an island of stability in this turbulent world. Alone, without the other elements, the tariff-cutting represents a sterile laisser faire, exposing us to the dangers of international disruption while doing nothing to master them. The Community's passivity has, in the 1970s, not only exposed the member countries to the inflation and consequent unemployment but also caused them to lose cumulatively, through the recession, perhaps as much as a third of a year's gross domestic product; and this sort of disruption and waste is likely to continue until the Community adopts a more positive posture.

Sources of turbulence: oil, materials, low-wage manufactures

Oil already seems an old story. It is over four years since the Community faced the disasters of industrial breakdown and economic collapse that would result if supplies were cut off. The suppliers chose instead to raise the price in a way that provoked the inflation and unemployment which have been endemic ever since. They are only too likely to do it again once the industrial countries expand their economies and hence their demand for oil; and disaster still awaits us should OPEC choose to cut off supplies. Yet the Community has done little or nothing to promote its own energy production or reduce consumption, and not nearly enough to place its relations with suppliers on a more stable footing.

For industrial raw materials, the situation is more like that of oil than of Community agriculture. The threat is less extreme: there are few materials that seem apt to be subjected to an exporters' cartel, and they are less central to the Community economy. But, with inflation persisting even through the recession, another ferocious commodity boom is not unlikely when the industrial countries expand their economies. Here again, the Community has done virtually nothing to guard against it. The Community attitude has been far from positive towards proposals for international buffer stocks; and it does not seem even to have begun to consider the alternative of the Community piling its own stocks, against the day of wild fluctuations or interruptions of supplies.

Primary products are notorious for their instability. Their behaviour was central to the great depression in the 1930s and the great inflation in the 1970s. But surely, it may be argued, they are a special case, and the unregulated markets in manufactures work better. Less badly, perhaps; but not well enough.

Textiles are widely seen as another exception. It is not acceptable, in the modern European economy, to throw textile workers onto the scrapheap, like the handloom weavers in the nineteenth century. Unregulated, imports of cloth and clothing from low-wage countries would pour into the Community and disrupt whole sectors of its industry. In order to give time to provide training and new work for the threatened workers, the multifibre agreements limit the rate of growth of imports to an agreed percentage. The Community has negotiated many such agreements; but two vital facts are not yet properly recognised.

The first is that the necessary manpower and job creation programmes will be costly if textile workers in the importing countries are to be treated well; and the cost should be borne by the authority responsible for the import policy. The Community's Social Fund should therefore be expanded, and it should be supplemented by a Community industrial policy that is capable of creating enough jobs. Secondly, textiles are only the most mature of the industries in which low-wage countries have an overwhelming advantage. Footwear and many branches of electronics and light engineering are fast reaching the same stage; and if workers are not to be ruthlessly discarded, the pattern of the multifibre agreements will have to be repeated many times. There will have to be a control on the rate of growth of imports, accompanied by powerful manpower and industrial policies to ensure a comfortable redeployment.

Where imports from less-developed countries can be disruptive because their economic levels are different from that of the Community, the East Europeans can also create problems because of their different type of economy. Costs can as yet hardly be measured comparably, so dumping is hard to define. Until recently, the problem was concealed by western quotas and the East Europeans' practice of aligning their export prices on prevailing western levels. Now, however, many of the West European quotas have been removed, and the East Europeans, in their race to earn western currencies, have been cutting their prices. The Community needs an efficient mechanism, either levies or quotas, to defend itself against growing disruption from such imports. Beyond this, it needs the instruments to ensure a long-term expansion of trade with Eastern Europe, through cooperation and specialisation agreements. At present the Community is responsible only for trade policy; it should have responsibilities for industrial cooperation as well.

Ships, steel, cars: the Japanese, and others on their heels

Commodities, less-developed countries and the East Europeans are already major exceptions from the area of 'normal' unregulated trade. But there is more to come. Already in the prosperous 1960s, when the depth of Japanese penetration in the American market for half a dozen major products was turning the AFL/CIO unions from a pillar of free trade into a pillar of protection, it was becoming apparent that the rate of growth of exports from such a dynamic economy could be incompatible with the welfare of workers in a normal western country. The Community paid scant attention. But now, with 90 per cent of the world's orders for ships being captured by the Japanese, and with capital-intensive industries like steel, cars and ball-bearings also under violent pressure, the Community is belatedly trying to improvise its defence.

This is hard to do, because although nobody likes the idea of thousands more workers swelling the ranks of the structurally unemployed, or whole towns losing their main industry for perhaps a generation, the Community lacks the instruments to do something about it and the member governments fail to agree on what should be done. The first essential is to recognise that these capital-intensive industries can work only on the basis of oligopolistic strategies (or, to put it more plainly, cartels) which maintain minimum prices and, if necessary, market shares, so that the capital equipment can be serviced and eventually renewed. In the modern European economy the public authorities need to participate in such cartels in order to ensure that they work in the public interest (much as the government works with the enterprises in the French planning system); and if firms from outside the Community undermine these industries by destructive pricing, then the Community needs the instruments (tariffs, levies, quotas) to keep them at bay while it negotiates with them about minimum prices and market shares.

These capital-intensive industries lie at the heart of the modern economy; and the case of Japanese competition shows they cannot survive a policy of laisser faire. Nor, amazing though Japan may be, is there any reason to suppose that such cases will not multiply. Already the shipbuilders of South Korea, Taiwan and Brazil are hard on the Japanese heels. Soon a dozen such countries will be major producers of capital-intensive manufactures; and the example of textiles, also epitomised only twenty years ago by Japan, will be followed by many capital-intensive as well as labour-intensive industries. Europe's dominance, with America, as the workshops of the world is coming to an end. The Community will lead less in industrial production than in its social provision and the humanity with which it manages economic change. But this humanity will be threatened by the impact of swift, disruptive changes in the international economy, unless we devise effective means to stabilise the growth of trade.

The United States: an easier relationship

It is a relief, after observing past turbulence and signalling storms ahead in the rest of the world economy, to consider the relatively smooth relationship with the United States. In the 1950s, America seemed irrevocably dominant, with twice Western Europe's living standards, with giant firms and technology, and the dollar hard as nails. Now the economic levels in North America and most of North-Western Europe are broadly similar. The Americans dominate only in their currency, in a few technologies (computers, aerospace) and in the strength of some of their largest firms. Across the Atlantic, between economies of similar levels and types, trade has flowed remarkably trouble-free, even through these recent tumultuous years.

In the remaining fields of American technological dominance, a major cause is the public purchasing and support for research and development from a powerful federal government. The Community, by contrast, has been at its most supine in the development of computers and has left the support of aircraft production to twos and threes of the member governments, no match for Boeing's triumphant progress. For countervailing American multinationals with European ones, we still lack a European company statute; nor is there an effective Community policy to keep the multinationals under control. There is plenty for the Community to do if it is to compete in these ways with the Americans. But the bulk of the transatlantic trade seems likely to continue to grow, without causing disruption and with a fair wind for the reduction or abolition of tariffs. The same applies to the Community's trade with other West European countries, which have already for the most part a free trade relationship with the Community, and to Australia, Canada and New Zealand.

With money, the case is different. The dollar is dominant and the Europeans have failed to devise a counterweight, such as the Community's external tariff provides in the field of trade. The Community will remain grossly over-influenced by American decisions on interest rates, exchange rates and the supply of international money until it creates some powerful financial instruments of its own such as a reserve fund, Community exchange control, a parallel currency and eventually a single common currency. Until then, the Community will remain unable to master the monetary storms that have upset our economies so much in recent years. This is the real issue with respect to America. For transatlantic trade, the Community's liberal policies should continue. It is not so much in relation to this area that a radical reform of trade policy is required.

The mixed internal economy needs a mixed external policy

There is an untenable contradiction between the Community's external policy and the domestic policies of the member states. Domestically, the member states use subsidies, taxes, credits and a battery of controls to promote industrial development and to shield workers from the roughest side of economic change. Externally, the Community's policy is much nearer to laisser faire. It has its multifibre agreements, quotas on imports from Eastern Europe and tariff preferences for a variety of developing countries; but it reacts indecisively and ineffectively to external threats, such as oil embargoes, commodity instability or destructive competition, because it possesses no long-term perspective apart from the withering away of the tariff. We have seen how this passivity in its external posture allows international forces to disrupt the domestic economy; and this disruption will continue until laisser faire is complemented by active policies in the Community's external relations, as it is in the domestic economies of the member states.

Ideally, the active policies would be common policies with the Community's economic partners, designed to bring stability as well as expansion to the mutual flows of trade and payments. But often the economic partners do not see the need for such policies, and international agreements or institutions are too weak to administer them. The Community therefore needs its own defences first. Given these, it can work to introduce the necessary element of social control at the international level.

The most obvious defence is the control of imports by instruments such as quotas, levies and tariffs, to prevent their growth at a pace that undermines the welfare of workers in the Community. Because it is the sharpness of the change that is detrimental, and not the change itself, which can benefit the domestic consumer as well as the external producer, these controls need to be accompanied by measures of industrial, regional and employment policy to promote the conversion of industries and transfer of workers into activities in which the Community is more competitive.

For capital-intensive industries such as steel, it may be necessary to prevent the Community's prices from falling below a level which covers capital as well as running costs. This can be done by import levies; and, beyond that, by minimum prices or market-sharing agreements with external competitors. With foresight, investment in excess capacity could be avoided by specialisation agreements which prevent the installation of too many identical investments across the world.

For the more crucial primary products, the Community needs to finance its own buffer stocks, which can be merged into international stocks when there is agreement on quantities and prices; and failing truly reliable security of supply, underpinned by unbreakable interdependence, the Community must move towards self-sufficiency in any vital commodity for which this is possible.

For money, the Community needs its own instruments such as parallel currency and external exchange control, with which to defend itself until a stable international monetary order can be created.

In sum, the Community needs a much more active external policy than it has had up to now. One reaction may be that this is the mixture as before, but a bit stronger. The strength, however, is all-important. Another reaction may be shock at a betrayal of the principles of free trade.

The alternative is autarkic member states

Those who are shocked by the mixed domestic economy as well as by an active external policy are logical, but divorced from reality. The mixed economy and welfare state and the new economic management they imply are not chance or transient phenomena. These things are deeply rooted in people's need for stability as as well as prosperity, and in their ability to secure this for themselves in a political and economic democracy. If external policy is laisser faire while domestic policy is mixed, it is in favour of domestic policy that the contradiction will be resolved, because this new economic management reflects the prevailing social forces and moral values of this age, whereas laisser faire reflected the powerful social forces and ethos of a previous period.

Those who adhere to the conventional wisdom of free trade externally and the mixed economy domestically, on the other hand, are just plain inconsistent; and their inconsistency is liable to produce the worst possible result. For the failure to introduce a mixed external policy for the Community is likely to lead, not to a continuance of a liberal Community mildly at odds with its working people, but to the replacement of a liberal Community by autarkic member states.

The citizens of the member countries insist on a public policy that provides some security of jobs and incomes. If that security is threatened by external forces, they will insist that these forces be controlled or excluded. If the Community does not control or exclude them, it will be done by the member states.

The sharpness of the issue stems not just from higher demands by the citizens, but also from change in the character of markets. The belief that an unregulated market would maximise welfare was at least partly justified when there was something like perfect competition. But the modern economy is pervaded with imperfect markets and market power. Workers and equipment are specialised for particular tasks, and their transfer to other tasks is costly or even impossible. Demand and supply in many markets are rigid and inelastic. Specialisation and interlocking production give producers positions of market power, so that prices and production result from bargaining strength rather than perfect competition. A measure of regulated stability would be needed on grounds of economic efficiency alone, even if it was not demanded on grounds of social welfare. Together, the economic and social requirements cannot be resisted without unacceptable political and economic costs.

218

These costs the member states of the Community will not agree to pay. They will unilaterally protect their workers and industries from violent change, if they fail to do it together as a Community; and in reacting separately to disruption from oil restriction, Japanese ships, South Korean shoes, Romanian suits and scores of other products, they will break up the Community's common market as well as insulate themselves from the world outside.

The resulting siege economies would be disastrous for our people. The East Europeans, having sealed their national economies off from each other as well as from the West, have been struggling ever since to loosen this straitjacket that constricts their welfare and economic progress. For small and medium-sized economies such as those of the Community, at a more advanced technological level, a retreat into national economic redoubts would be even more damaging than in Eastern Europe. Only a Community that provides enough protection for its citizens can forestall this dismal prospect.

The liberal half of a mixed external policy

The need for Community protection has been stressed because the Community's prevailing policy and ideology are laisser faire, and this is increasingly detrimental for our people. Those brought up on adversary politics or marxist dialectics will doubtless assume there is no alternative but to abandon every vestige of liberal principles and to control every last detail of our external trade. But this would be as misguided as to throw the mixed economy overboard and embrace an undiluted laisser faire or directive system for the domestic economy. The valid alternative to laisser faire is not total control but a mixture of freedom with the degree of control that is needed for stability and security.

The instability and bad performance of the Community economy since it was hit by the world economic crisis of the 1970s show that the element of control in its external policy is not enough. We need a shift in this direction. But once the shift has taken place, we should ensure that the Community's policy remains as liberal as is compatible with economic security.

The key to a liberal external policy is a dynamic domestic policy facilitating industrial change. First and foremost, this means an active and massive manpower policy, of the kind that is farthest developed in Sweden. Secondly, an industrial policy is needed that will promote the replacement of out-dated plant in old industries by modern plant in new industries, located where the jobs will be required. The more effective these domestic policies, the faster imports can grow without damaging workers in the Community.

On the basis of this flexible and dynamic domestic economy, the Community can negotiate with its trading partners for a rapid growth of trade, without fear of a backlash from redundant workers which would induce a flight into autarky. Armed with adequate funds and powers, such a Community could pull its full, enormous weight in creating the conditions for a stable and expanding international economy.

A federal Community, both political and economic

If the world's politics had caught up with the world economy, there would be functions of economic government dealt with at five or six levels, from the

219

local authority, through the province, nation-state, regional group (European Community), wider economic system (Atlantic or Soviet groups), to the world as a whole. Much of the present international disorder stems from the lack of economic government over the wider areas.

Ideally, those higher ranks of government should be quickly installed. In reality, the world remains too politically and economically diverse for this, and progress beyond the absolute sovereignty of the nation-state can best be made in a regional group such as the European Community. The welfare of our people will best be served by a powerful Community government which can defend its economy against external shocks that are inevitable in an un-governed world, while at the same time encouraging any feasible progress towards international government. This implies a federal government for the Community, because looser forms of association will be too weak for the heavy tasks of external as well as domestic economic management.

This political conclusion is not independent of the type of economic man-agement envisaged. Laisser faire requires but little action by the government, and if the Community were essentially a customs union with a disappearing tariff, its present institutions would be strong enough. But the argument of this paper is that laisser faire is not enough, we must have social control as well. The Community must reflect the character of its member countries by walking on two legs, which may roughly be called liberalism and socialism.

This mixed economy is the economic analogue of a political federation. The essence of political federalism is the distribution of the functions of govern-ment among different levels of government, with each function carried out at the lowest level compatible with justice and efficiency, that is at the level which covers most of the people who will be affected by the decisions and to which they can have the best access. The economic equivalent is an economy in which matters of public concern, such as fairness among the social groups and stability of the system, are dealt with by the appropriate level of public auth-ority, while other matters are decided within the enterprise. What is usually called a mixed economy can, then, properly be called a federal economy.

Economic and political federalism, with an external policy strong enough to defend it in a rough and uncertain world and to advance the cause of federal-ism in the world economy and polity: that is the pattern for a Community that should reflect the best in European civilisation.

Postscript
The Value of Federalism

GEOFFREY DENTON

To compile a book consisting of many papers by separate authors on a subject as nebulous as federalism may be considered a foolhardy undertaking. With a remarkable degree of cooperation from the eminent and therefore busy authors of this collection of papers, the Federal Trust succeeded in eliciting papers from seventeen contributors. Some gaps in the original list of papers were inevitable but the editors were able to fill these to some extent by asking other contributors to cover some of the ground. The overall result is that the subject area defined in the opening paper on 'The New Federalism' has been discussed in a reasonably comprehensive way.

To succeed in putting together a set of papers, however, does not in itself justify the endeavour. It is also necessary to achieve an outcome that suggests that the exercise was intellectually worthwhile in the first place. The purpose of this valedictory postscript is to argue that there are indeed benefits to be obtained from investigating a number of important social, political, institutional, economic and industrial issues from the viewpoint of federalism; and moreover, that it makes sense to investigate them together, so as to achieve a 'new federalist' appreciation of current trends in national and international affairs.

The authors of these papers, of course, were aware of the overall purpose of the series, and presumably in accord with its intentions. But they were by no means all convinced federalists, nor were they put under pressure by the editorial committee to cast their papers in a federalist mould. In these circumstances it is remarkable how often their final titles, which differ from those originally proposed in the invitations to contribute, contain the word 'federal'; that is, how often they felt that this adjective was a useful way of describing the general nature of their policy proposals. This was perhaps most striking in one of the more technical papers: that by John Marsh on the European Community's agricultural policy. Given the original broad title: Agricultural Policy, it nevertheless appeared appropriate to describe the final paper, with its original but realistic proposals for providing more freedom for the national governments to operate their own policies, while keeping the essential parts of the common policy, as a proposal for a 'federalist solution': that is, a policy which assigned to the Community institutions functions they could best perform, while recognising that, given the diversity of economic and monetary conditions

221

persisting within the various parts of the Community, governments must be given the right also to operate their own policies, together with the financial responsibility for them.

A major purpose of these papers has been to bring together areas of thought that are frequently kept separate: the development of the European Community; political and administrative structures within the nation states; and the structure and functioning of firms and their relations with governments. Some of the contributors are well known for their work on the European Community, others for their work on aspects of social, political and economic development within the nation states. What frequently emerges in these papers is that there is no conceptual separation between integration 'upwards' in the EEC, devolution 'downwards' within the nation states, and 'functional' federalism in relations within industry and between government and industry. This does not mean only that these are different elements in a continuum of allocation of responsibilities to appropriate levels of government. More important, they are interwoven in such a complex way that it is only by studying them together that they can be fully understood and appreciated.

For example, the impact of European monetary integration on the various regions, and the new regional policies that would be needed in a monetary union, are closely related to the degree of political and economic devolution that is accorded to the regions. Federalism upwards is intimately connected with federalism downwards. Or to give another example, economic integration encourages the interdependence of industry across the frontiers (through trade, investment, mergers, etc.) so that it becomes essential for the EEC to develop a policy for the structure of European enterprises. Each country cannot continue indefinitely to operate its own separate legal framework for company structures, worker representation in industry, access to capital markets, etc., given the increasing unification of the market environment within which industry operates.

The study of federations indicates that generalisations about their structures and development are difficult, if not impossible. But at one time or another many countries have operated or have attempted federal structures, and the persistence at least of some of the federations suggests that there was and is a real need for them. If federal structures have enabled countries as diverse as the United States, Switzerland, and Australia, to combine central policies on matters of common interest with continuing diversity of policies in areas where interests do not coincide, it is not inconceivable that they could also help to structure the relations between England and Scotland, Flanders and Wallonia, France and Germany. The fact that federations have failed in Central Africa and the Caribbean is not conclusive against attempting them in Western Europe; they have also succeeded, in recent years, both in Malaysia and in the German Federal Republic.

Some of the papers in this collection also serve as an antidote to the poisonous suggestion that federalism is to be condemned as a revolutionary ideology. There are indeed 'revolutionary' federalists, and inevitably there are those, not so revolutionary, who support federalist proposals not only for their own intrinsic merits, but because in the process of achieving them other objectives might be served. Thus, some supporters of devolution to Scotland and Wales within the UK have considered that an important bonus would be the shake-up of existing power structures and institutions. The Parliament at Westminster might be reformed and proportional representation might be introduced, in the process of creating new assemblies for Scotland and Wales. The direct elections to the European Parliament are similarly being used as a wedge to push open the door to wider acceptance of the case for new electoral systems. In this sense federalism could be considered revolutionary. However, it is equally plausible to accuse federalism of being a conservative force. For example, to the 'anti-marketeers' of the Left the EEC is objectionable because they regard it as a means to perpetuate the existing market economy and class structure of the UK and the rest of the Community.

In so far as federations permit diversity of the parts to be combined with common policies for the whole, they obviously, and deliberately, envisage that the political complexion of the governments at the lower levels may vary. As to the political stance of the federal government, it will be determined by the political balance of the whole federation, as indeed that of the central government in a unitary state is determined by the political balance of all its provinces.

The most sensible conclusion on this question, whether federations may be revolutionary or conservative, is to recognise that federalism, like other bandwagons, will be supported by many who have not much interest in it for itself, but see it as a means to pushing through some particular reform to which they are attached, or as a means of preventing a change they abhor. This is neither surprising nor unusual, and certainly is not a condemnation of federalism. One should not jump to facile conclusions about the nature of an animal from a mere glimpse at its tail!

If there are valid reasons for transferring some of the functions of the nation-state to the level of the European Community, and devolving others to regional governments, while not increasing the role of government as a whole, the powers remaining to the nation-states will certainly be diminished. In this sense it is true that much of what is proposed in this book has negative implications for the nation-state. But there is in these papers no hostility to the nation-state, no attempt to saddle it with the blame for all our problems. It is perfectly consistent to accept that the nation-state confers many benefits on its citizens, while recognising also that it may be found to stand in the way of achieving certain purposes that have now assumed importance. To say that its powers should be reduced is not to show hostility, but merely an appreciation that changing circumstances may require different institutional and political structures from those of the past. The role of the national governments would remain immensely important in a Europe where some powers had been handed up to the Community level and others down to regional level. Exactly how important is a question that could not, and should not, be answered. The role of the nation-states would evolve continuously as structures of government were gradually adapted to meet the varying needs that create the pressures for a more federalist system.

Nationalist anti-federalists are at least consistent in their opposition to federalism both upwards and downwards, regarding both as an attack on the sovereignty of the nation-state. Defenders of existing systems are dismayed by the diffusion of power which is already taking place, to smaller regional units and to interest groups as well as to international entities. These, of course, can wield power without making any claim to supra-national sovereignty. The IMF and the British trade unions have had much more influence on British economic policy decisions since 1973 than has the European Community, and probably more than the British electorate. But opponents of federalism in the UK have included many whose approach has been unbalanced and even inconsistent. They oppose the loss of national sovereignty upwards, through transfers of powers to the institutions of the European Community; at the same time they support devolution within the UK, or handing over greater powers to trade unions and other sectoral interest groups. They do this in response to short-term pressures, often for electoral reasons, and without any plan for the future polity these changes would create. A comprehensive study of the various aspects of federalism would allow such developments to be examined in an interrelated way, such that each could find its place in a logically structured system. The rights and obligations of component parts of the system could be balanced with each other and with the rights and obligations of the central authority, each being controlled by prior agreement and with provision for adjustment of disputed areas by negotiation and arbitration.

Federalism claims to provide a framework for this process which safeguards authority at existing levels, especially the nation-state where this is appropriate, but puts the other centres of power in an ordered and intelligible relationship with it, in contrast to the disorderly power struggle which is now experienced. National parliaments won their position by acting as the channels for popular interests and grievances against authority. Now local and functional interests seek ways of putting their case against the authority of parliament, while parliaments complain that they are losing sovereignty to other areas of collective decision. The creation of assemblies or other means of popular consultation to match every level and type of decision-making is an inherent part of modern federalism. If this general principle is accepted, the most urgent task would be to find the correct division of responsibilities between the different levels and their associated assemblies, that is, to find the appropriate federal structure.

Much of the antagonism towards discussion of federalism comes from those who have established positions within existing institutions and fear that their positions may be challenged as new federal structures are developed. This kind of resistance to change on the part of vested interests is normal, and not necessarily reprehensible. However, it is no argument against federalism. A more serious suggestion is that federalism would mean adding yet more to the excessively frequent institutional reorganisations that have already taken place in recent years, thus adding to confusion and uncertainty, and delaying the time when the bureaucracies can settle down and restore their normal efficiency. This is indeed a serious problem for any who propose changing existing structures of government. But the answer cannot be to condemn, on this ground, all proposals for change. Rather, this difficulty is an argument in favour of the wide-ranging, comprehensive approach taken in this collection of papers. If the full scope of changes that are on the agenda can be grasped, a programme of feasible reforms can be gradually introduced in assimilable stages. With some concept of what the overall objective should be, and where the parts fit into the whole, it is more probable that reforms can be made consistently and purposefully, avoiding reversals of policy and minimising uncertainty. Without insight into the overall prospectus, individual reforms are likely to be inconsistent, divisive and untenable.

One criticism of reform proposals is the uncertainty they create, especially for bureaucrats. Another is that they create more bureaucrats, which is a problem for the rest of us. Many of the reforms proposed in recent years have appeared to take the form of creating new institutions, requiring more officials to run them, while failing always to abolish redundant organisations and re-deploy their staffs. Federalist proposals are particularly vulnerable to attack from this direction, because they ostensibly seek to create more levels of government. It is not enough to counter that the bureaucracy which runs the European Community institutions is tiny in comparison with national government departments, or that the assemblies and departments needed to control and administer a devolved system of regional governments in Scotland, Wales and the English regions, for example, would also be small. If they developed as many of their proponents anticipate, they would require more officials. There are two responses to this criticism. First, it may indeed be the case that more officials would be needed to run a federal system, but this could be a cost worth paying in return for the benefits of greater participation in, and acceptance of, government. If national governments are performing functions for which they are inappropriate, some additional expenditure on representation and admin-istration may be justified in order to have policies decided at and administered from the right levels. Secondly, it is not necessarily the case that more officials would in fact be required. Smaller authorities, running more manageable areas, in closer touch with problems and people, might find it possible to function with fewer officials than the centralised administrations they replaced.

An important report published since these papers were written has confirmed the correctness of the approach taken by the authors. Douglas Dosser was writing before the publication in April 1977 of an EEC Study Group Report on *The Role of Public Finance in European Integration*. This report, completed under the chairmanship of Sir Donald MacDougall (now Chief Economic Adviser to the CBI and formerly Head of the Government's Economic Service), consists in a detailed and dispassionate study of the fiscal arrangements in five federations (Australia, Canada, Germany, Switzerland and the United States) and in three unitary states (France, Italy and the United Kingdom). It is not surprising that the study of the first five systems should show an allocation of fiscal powers and responsibilities to different levels of government, together with a degree of equalisation by transfers, either from the federal to the regional governments, or among the regional governments. The report also reveals remarkably similar structures of equalisation between regions in the unitary states, though in these cases the transfers are restricted to those between the central and the regional level.

So-called centralised systems are in this sense far more 'federal' in their fiscal structures than is usually recognised. This suggests that, far from being a revolutionary concept, federalism is in fact almost synonymous with realism: with recognising that all systems of government for large and complex industrial societies have to be, and are, organised on several levels. And there is no great advantage in perpetuating a myth that this is not so. If this book has helped to de-mystify the subject of federalism, it will have served its purpose.